Other Books by Jeff Greenfield

A POPULIST MANIFESTO: The Making of a New
Majority (with Jack Newfield)

THE ADVANCE MAN: An Offbeat Look at What
Really Happens in Political Campaigns
(with Jerry Bruno)

NO PEACE, NO PLACE

Excavations Along the Generational Fault

Jeff Greenfield

NO PEACE, NO PLACE

Excavations Along the Generational Fault

1973
DOUBLEDAY & COMPANY, INC., GARDEN CITY, NEW YORK

Grateful acknowledgment is given for permission to reprint lines from "The Second Coming" from *Collected Poems of William Butler Yeats* (Copyright 1924 by The Macmillan Company, renewed 1952 by Bertha Georgie Yeats).

"The First Days of Television: Eavesdropping on the Elders" was first published in The New York *Times Magazine*, July 4, 1971, under the title "A Member of the First TV Generation Looks Back" © 1971 by The New York Times Company. Reprinted by permission.

ACKNOWLEDGMENTS

The idea for this book is five years old; at the time, it was supposed to be a history of the early days of rock and roll. Hard as it is to believe, there was no such work in print at the time. It was my confident feeling that I could finish such a book by 1968. Thanks to some detours into the world of politics, the book progressed not at all. I was convinced by 1969 it would never be written.

Only the infinite patience of Sam Vaughan of Doubleday gave me the fortitude to reshape the concept of the book into an attempt to probe more generally into the postwar years. Through countless free lunches and occasional short, encouraging notes, Sam Vaughan assured me that he would *not* bring suit or send armed thugs to persuade me to finish this book. His belief that I had something to say was the real motive power behind me.

In its final stages, the work of Betty Prashker and Diane Matthews of Doubleday was indispensable. I owe them deep thanks.

Finally, to my wife, Harriet Carmichael, I offer the gratitude that she knows she has for making my life far more joyous than it had ever been before.

For my mother and father; not simply because they created and raised me, but for their patience and love, and their capacity to withstand the sorrows and appreciate the joys.

CONTENTS

WHERE HAVE YOU GONE . . .

AN INTRODUCTION

The crowd is growing impatient, restless. For twenty minutes on a stifling, sticky Saturday afternoon they have sat watching the old men trot onto the field, some white-haired, skin mottled with stigmata of age, barely able to turn a halting walk into a shuffling gait, others still lean, bronzed, old only by the ruthless standard which discards bodies no longer honed to the highest pitch.

There are good ballplayers on the field now, all of them with special skills that took them into prominence a decade, a half century ago: Earl Coombs and Buck Leonard, Hank Bauer and Bill Dickey, Carl Erskine and Clem Labine, Tommy Henrich and Joe Collins, but the crowd on this Old

Timers' Day in July of 1972 has not come for them; they have come, instead, for two men not yet introduced.

Now. He waits, one leg up on a dugout step, and before his name is called Yankee Stadium is engulfed in cheers, thunderclaps, whistles, a pounding of noise rising, rising like the home run on Memorial Day, 1956, rising until it slammed against the roof, eighteen inches short of being the only fair ball ever hit out of Yankee Stadium, and he trots out to join the line of Yankees between first and second base, his face impassive, bowed, his body shuffling slowly from foot to foot, and for Mickey Mantle the cheering goes on and on and on. Three minutes. Four minutes, falling back, then rising again, driven by a crowd unwilling to let go of the moment. Mantle, center fielder of the Yankees in their last glory days, from the midst of their five straight world championships in 1951 through the last pennant victory of 1964. Mantle, booed throughout his career by fans who found him arrogant or a quitter (he played his career on crippled legs, ending his major league days taped like some parody of a mummy), now crushed by the power of sheer sound.

Five minutes. And now Mantle tips his cap, grinning, motioning down with outstretched arms, *okay, enough, thanks, all right,* and the gesture of acknowledgment sends the crowd off again. And now, barely audible above the roar, the public address system introduces the man voted "the greatest living baseball player," and Joe DiMaggio, silver-haired and with a face chiseled out of Roman stone, trots out next to Mantle, and the cheers that have gone before are only a prelude to the madness exploding now. After a handshake and a mumbled word or two, DiMaggio and Mantle respond: their arms around each other, standing like candidates for national office, Mantle's right arm up, DiMaggio's left, they stand for minute after minute, while the fans cheer not simply two superb athletes, but their own lost selves as well.

To a cynic, this outpouring of emotion may sound more like the ring of the cash register than the ring of affection. Each year the promise of Mantle and DiMaggio brings sports fans into Yankee Stadium; a feat the current Yankees seem less and less capable of managing themselves (Yankee attendance in 1972 was the lowest it has been since World War II, while the New York Mets exceeded two million home attendance, a charmed circle for stockholders of major league baseball clubs). Three years earlier, the Yankees had unveiled plaques mounted on the center-field bleacher wall honoring DiMaggio and Mantle, and a similar roar of approval from a large house was heard.

And yet the fans were honoring something no management, however cynical or manipulative, could taint; a sense of tradition and glory which neither baseball nor much of our lives now seems able to offer. DiMaggio and Mantle were for the Yankees a classic equivalent of the Moses-Joshua myth which Erik Erikson claims lies at the heart of healthy Western Society: the old leader, wise with insight but frail of body, leads the younger Joshua to the mountaintop, points the way, and ends his life's journey there while his heirs take the new promised land. For the Yankees, DiMaggio had come to them in the first year of their four straight world championships from 1936 to 1939; he had remained their star center fielder until 1951, when the team was one year short of tying that incredible mark of four straight championships. At the start of that year, he had announced it would be his last; his legs could no longer take those long, loping strides, bringing Di-Maggio from nowhere under the deep fly, not with a flash of energy, or a sudden, desperate leap, but rather with the calm certainty of an aristocrat who knows what his duty is, and executes it with ordered dignity.

As DiMaggio faltered, a new face; a nineteen-year-old crew-cut Oklahoman, fresh from the class C minors, of uncertain poise and polish but with neck muscles wrought of iron, shoulders and arms humming with tensile strength. Midway through the season he is sent to the minors, to Kansas City, for three days to discipline his desire; there he hits four home runs, and on his first day back with the Yankees he drives a home run dead into the left-center-field bleachers, a distance reached by fewer than a dozen men in the thirty-year history of the Stadium.

With Mantle taking up from DiMaggio, the Yanks complete the journey from the mountaintop into the promised land, winning five straight world championships; by the time the dream ends with the pennant of 1964, the Mantle-Di-Maggio reign has brought the team twenty-two pennants and sixteen World Series titles in twenty-eight years. Then it stopped. Not slowly, but stopped. Dead. From a pennant-winning team fighting to the seventh game of the Series against the St. Louis Cardinals, the Yankees dropped to sixth place in 1965. Then ninth. A second-division ball club year after year. And when Mantle turned to pass the torch, no one was there. As with so many other parts of our lives, the sense of nobility had gone, leaving us with the bitter weapons of scorn and ridicule. We could mock the paralytic hitting of the Yankees, a team that hit fewer home runs now than Mickey Mantle and Roger Maris hit by themselves in 1961; we could groan at the desperate lunges for respectability by the broadcasting team, pumping a quick fix of verbal methadrine into the dreary season ("Say, Phil, if the Yanks can just string six or seven victories, they'll be real close to playing .500 ball by Labor Day." "Holy Cow!") but we did not want to laugh; it was just that there was nothing else left. And so when Mantle and DiMaggio returned, when the bearers of authentic greatness stood before us, arms outstretched, we cheered what we remembered of their youth and strength and skill because they were *real;* they had been permitted to act as Heroes and as Heroes we would remember them. We had to. More than an indulgence, our passion was close to a necessity, born out of all we had gone through between the time DiMaggio had yielded to Mantle at the start of the second half of the twentieth century, and the time, twenty years and centuries later, when they stood together as living artifacts, some scrap of proof that things had once been better. Those two intervening decades had been a time when Heroes had gotten very hard to come by, when pleasant myths were denied existence, when reality became a succession of horrors or embittering, sullen revelations.

Consider, as a metaphor for a thesis, the Eisenhower Experience. To the Americans of World War II, Dwight Eisenhower was a Certified Hero, Supreme Commander, Allied Forces in Europe, five-star general, architect of D-Day, the ultimate leader who commanded a united country past the deadly shoals of Fascist Conquest. To the War Babies, Eisenhower was as President a Dumb Grownup. I mean by this no disrespect; to the first generation of the television age, as you will discover, the Dumb Grownup was a well-established symbol, a necessary foil for the frolicsome spirit of Youth, creating a clash which presaged by a decade the Yippie-counterculture-Sheepskin Left attack on Age as a necessarily contemptible attribute. For us, Dwight Eisenhower was simply a flesh-and-blood equal of Howdy Doody's Phineas T. Bluster, a Very Old Man with a great deal of power, and an air of befuddlement. Poor Ike couldn't seem to get the words to come out right.

The Presidential Press Conference was Eisenhower's Theatre of the Absurd. Here was all the solemnity of State Authority: the newsmen rising to their feet, the Great Seal of the Presidency, lecterns, men in coats and ties and women in flowered print dresses and pillbox hats, and there was the President of the United States, the leader of the Free World, a man whose finger perpetually rested on the button that could vaporize us all, and yet for this poor Dumb Grownup the journey between the beginning and the end of a sentence was more treacherous and difficult than the beaches of Normandy. Murray Kempton, a writer with that rare combination of brilliance and wisdom, has written that Eisenhower was not what he seemed; that in fact he was a shrewd politician and a clever practitioner of statecraft. I see no reason to doubt Kempton's conclusions, but in the perceptions of a generation coming into its first stirrings of Awareness, Eisenhower was a joke, a symbol of every piece of Grownup Authority stripped of any sense of legitimacy, as if he had been fashioned by extracting the purest elements of Assistant Principals, Ushers at Movie Theaters and Ballparks, and Grandfathers who could not stay awake through Thanksgiving Dinner. Our Elders had taken the most admired, successful hero of their times and given us a cobwebbed, tongue-tied surrogate grandfather. *Hey folks,* the murmurs might be faintly heard, *is this the best you can do? Is this it?*

It was not, however, the fault of Eisenhower nor the fault of our Elders that an artifact of World War II should have presided over the decade of the '50s as a tarnished idol, his remarks laughed at rather than studied worshipfully in the pages of the press. It was, rather, that the tone, the sensibility of World War II itself could not survive outside the hothouse atmosphere of a worldwide conflict for survival, could not withstand the reassertion of reality once the war was over. And it was when we began trying to test out the hopes and impulses of Wartime that we began to understand just how far we had misled ourselves, or been misled; just how little things were working out as we had told ourselves they would, once the scourge of totalitarian Fascism had been defeated by a united people; just how unconvincing the assertion of heroism seems when the stridency and exaggeration is not muffled by the sound of gunfire around the world.

Correspondents in combat cleave to the phrase "war-torn nation" to describe a conflict. America in the Second World War was a war-healed nation; our most pressing domestic upheavals and divisions excised by the imperative of conflict. The Depression was still a fact of life by 1940; after Pearl Harbor, there was a job for everyone. Throughout the '30s, there was suspicion and distrust of politicians, and countless movies, from Frank Capra's political films like *Mr. Smith*

Goes to Washington and *Meet John Doe* to B-flicks with clever detectives outwitting stupid cops, insisted that Those Who Ruled were up to no good. With the War we were brought together for a higher purpose, and while criticism did not cease by any means, some of the hot-bloodedness went out of our political life; it was hard to really hate the Chairman of a congressional committee when Tojo and Hitler were across the oceans.

Perhaps most remarkably—and, as it turned out, most destructively—the spirit of the War suggested a purposeful conflict with personal serenity as its goal, rather than a conflict with a negative imperative of preventing the eradication of democracy. In speeches, in endless advertisements in the mass media, our Elders were told that a victory in this conflict would bring a lasting sense of satisfaction, personal comfort, and serenity: the restoration of old values, wrapped in a package of wondrous technology:

• A Family stands proudly by its gleaming new car, parked by a comfortable house in a sparkling neighborhood. "Sure you'll be proud of it. There's a Ford in your future . . . When your new Ford car arrives—some day, not far away—you'll want the world to know it's yours!"

• A gleaming boat, anchored in a blue sea. "Ready after victory. See your Chris-Craft dealer . . . Buy U.S. war bonds today—Tomorrow, command your own Chris-Craft."

• A ribbon of highway cutting through mountains. "Don't look now! . . . But one day soon this will be a safe, new U.S. highway . . . part of one of the greatest plans for American security and prosperity in the post-war years to come. You'll

soon ride down new roads in a peaceful and prosperous
USA."

• "Eyes on tomorrow," promises the Pennsylvania Railroad, summoning us to a vision of "new, modern trains, daring
designs, exciting and novel innovations, new speed, new
power . . . new comforts and luxuries . . ."

We were, as a people, promised something beyond the defeat of evil; we were promised, rather, that the agony of death,
privation, and separation would win for us a Utopia of comfort and ease. Work now, fight now, the unspoken message
hammered at our Elders, and soon the struggle will be over,
and with it all struggles. You will return to your way of life,
to a way of life serene, peaceful, undisturbed, and rich in the
luxuries of a new technology. In the minds of millions of
Americans, the fight was not for the right to boo the Dodgers,
but rather for the right to watch the Dodgers on the new
marvel of television on a plot of land that was ours and our
families', yet somehow connected with comfortably familiar
surroundings. In the 1950s, that dream was to be put to the
test; and swiftly it would come apart.

There was, first of all, the hidden fact that the War itself
was shredding apart the structure of small-town, pluralistic
America. The demand was for materiel, as swiftly and continuously as it could be turned out. This meant, in overwhelming force, that it was the giants of industry who got
the goods, the contracts, the manpower, not out of any conspiracy, but out of the simple proposition that General Motors
could produce more jeeps and trucks and tanks than Harry's
bicycle shop in Shady Bend. Shipyards; auto plants; airplane

manufacturers; it was these giants that were hooked up into a huge, nationwide transfusion of supply and demand. For those in the small plants and on the retail level, there was nothing to do; a war was on. More than three hundred thousand retailers shut down in 1942; two hundred thousand small businesses went under in the first two months of the War. We would come out of the Second World War with a concentration of power, in government and industry, undreamed of in our history, even as our public and corporate propaganda painted a future replete with small-town drug stores, shops, and shady trees.

With these newly strengthened sources of power came families looking for jobs, and houses to shelter them; and huge-scale housing tracts sprung up in new population centers: Mobile and Charleston; San Diego and Los Angeles; Seattle and Detroit and Muskegon. The American universe was splitting apart and re-forming; we were remaking ourselves each day we fought to preserve Our Way of Life. Once the euphoria of Unified Purpose was gone, we could begin to look around and see what we were creating. But there was no turning back. There was no way to even ask the question, "Is this where we want to be going?" because by the time we understood that such a question existed, we were already There, swept along by forces, each of them separate, yet combining to hammer the landscape of our country beyond recognition. Once we understood the question, there was no possibility of any answer save a shrug at the passing of another symbol of stability.

What we seemed to be creating was a society dedicated to atomization: separating ourselves as much as possible from each other. Perhaps the years of war, throwing men into barracks and women into factories, crowding us up against each other, had been simply too exasperating. What we wanted now were suburban tracts, not apartments; cars and highways, not trains and buses where we once again were crowding each other; comforts, luxuries and entertainments we could enjoy in our own homes, in a small, tightly knit group. Of two postwar promises from the magazines of World War II, one was kept beyond its writer's wildest dreams: a forty-thousand-mile Interstate Highway System, whose cost would ultimately exceed sixty billion dollars, knocking down stable city neighborhoods for off-ramps between downtown and suburb, and making another promise—those new, comfortable trains—irrelevant. There was indeed a Ford, a Chrysler, a General Motors car, in our future. Technology had delivered its promise of indulgence.

All through the 1950s, General Motors would sponsor a "GM Motorama" to promote its new cars; crowds would line up, often for hours, to enter the Waldorf-Astoria and pick up the free catalogues, walk around the new model autos flanked by baton-twirler beauties, open and close doors. The magnet of the "Motorama," however, was not the present, but the future—the "dream cars," pedestaled throughout the Grand Ballroom, with hundreds of horsepower, chrome and ducts and scoops in shapes out of a Buzz Corey or Tom Corbett adventure; lush Astrodome interiors with TV sets and hi-fis in the back seats. Then the ballroom would go dark; on would come a movie painting a glorious future on wheels; cars driven on highways automatically; gas turbine cars; elevated highways ringing the tops of hundred-story buildings; finally, the movie actors would emerge from the wings and, in song and dance, hail the wonders of science from General Motors. No one talked about carbon monoxide. No one talked of safety. No one asked for movies of high-speed subways, or questioned whether we would be sitting in our futuristic autos, moving at three miles per hour on the Long Island Expressway. General Motors' dream was ours.

And even as we would travel from home to work and back, without the intrusion of other human souls, so we would spend our leisure time apart from each other, in the bosom of our family, gathered round the television set, watching other people move and listening to them talk. Television would finish the job begun by radio; segregate audiences, render them into small units, unable to rely on other people to stand against an affront to logic or taste, unwilling to rely on themselves. As with radio, only with far more impact, television would divide and conquer; its owners and masters understood fully that you sell far more effectively when you sell to an audience of one or two than to a crowd of several hundred or thousand. Crowds always boo politicians at baseball games; very few people stand up and challenge authority on their own.

This, then, is what the 1950s contained: a new American landscape, unfamiliar and coldly impersonal, thrust into existence by the upheaval of World War II; a series of promises to our Elders that took the shape of material comfort and private indulgence; the keeping of the material; promises without any spiritual satisfaction; and the slow settling-in of a loneliness that seemed to grow steadily into a kind of national despair. For what no one understood in the midst of

World War II was that it felt good to be together; it felt good to be working for the same thing; to be part of a great enterprise whose worth was understood and accepted. Not always, no; privacy had its points. But if we were too closely pushed together in the War, then in the '50s we were pulled apart, violently and completely. Older generations could gather at a corner bar, an ice cream parlor, a newsstand, a busy intersection, to pass the time and greet friends; in the new landscape, there were no corner bars. There were no corners. There were huge new shopping tracts, built to inhuman scale, as if automobiles rather than people were the real constituents of such an emporium. But there were no social clubs, within a few blocks, or a bus ride, from home, no centers for unstructured meetings and comings and goings, no place where a person could simply drop in for a game of cards or a glass of beer. And you could not talk back to a television set.

Something seemed not quite right, somehow, as though the Prospectus we had been given had a sentence or two missing. But no, it just *seemed* as if it would be different back during the War; it seemed as if a home and family and car and TV were all we could want; nobody told us that the connection between ourselves and friends would be severed as thoroughly as it was during the 1950s. And was it that we forgot—or rather that we never knew—that a single family by itself could not sustain an entire life? Two adults, one of each sex, and two or three children, might make a good family; but as a totally enclosed unit, it would not work. Where were the other people, friends, acquaintances, strangers, to leaven the experience? Marriage and family somehow seemed different

in the 1950s from what we had been promised such a short
time ago.

Some of us understood this, vaguely, uncertainly. I remember that some friends and I, who used to meet every
summer at a cooperative community, began to spin a crazy
kind of fantasy. Why, we wondered, did we have to each
go our own way, in our own home, in some huge suburban wasteland? Why could we not all live in an enormous
home somewhere outside of metropolitan centers, somewhere where the land was cheap, the trees and grass sweet,
the water clean, and pressures small. We had varying hopes
of what we wished to be: two doctors, a lawyer, a writer,
an architect, a gardener. Why not pool our skills, and a
share of our incomes, let our architect design our home, our
gardener raise our food, our lawyer protect us from legal
problems, our doctors serve the surrounding towns and our
own families. No one understood that such a lifestyle could
exist; no one used the word "commune" to describe it. In
the late 1950s, the Rules of the World were only beginning
to be attacked root and branch as smelling of rigidity, joy-
lessness, death. Our community was a fantasy, understood
and talked of as such; had anyone proposed a trip upstate
to look at some property, we would have turned indifferent,
and dropped the fantasy at once. It is this crucial distinction,
this unwillingness to act on our impulses and unformed un-
derstandings, that mark us as standing, however reluctantly,
with our Elders on the far side of what would become a
Generational Fault—not a "gap" but a wide and lethal shredding of the American terrain, a product of underground
forces so powerful and sudden that they send a scar along

miles and miles of one peaceful, seamless territory, leaving it cleaved through with a crevice almost impossible to bridge.

It began with the Music. Nothing we see in the Counter-culture—not the clothes, the hair, the sexuality, the drugs, the rejection of reason, the resort to symbols and magic—none of it is separable from the coming to power in the 1950s of rock and roll music. Brewed in the hidden corners of black America's cities, its rhythms infected white Americans, seducing them out of the kind of temperate bobby-sox passions out of which Andy Hardy films are spun. Rock and roll was elemental, savage, dripping with sex; it was just as our parents feared. Not in the conspiracy theories of moral guardians, not that we dropped our books and molested children, but in the more subtle sense of what the music did, unleashing with its power knowledge that our bodies were our own Joy Machines. It would take years for successive generations of young Americans to work the equation out fully; it would take a disillusioning that included a wretched War, a wave of violence, and a brace of public murders of great men to spur on the rejection of reason as a tool of death, and the embrace of rock and roll not as pleasure but as salvation. But in rock and roll it began; the first tremors along the Generational Fault.

It grew with our exposure to television, an instrument ultimately so subversive of good order as to raise doubts about its origin (Two Bolsheviks in a cellar? A maniacal Anarchist? A disappointed office-seeker . . . ?). Part of what television did was to expose a younger generation to the stupidities and excesses of their Elders, thus producing a massive, sped-up loss of innocence among the young. What television did, further, was to fracture the power of authority by increasing our propensity to be bored. In the schools of America, the first television generation began to stage a revolt so pervasive and deadly as to prevent any counterattack: *we began to stop listening.* Once we realized the trap of school—the program went on all day, and you couldn't change the channel!— we simply did not listen because we could not. A generation living with thirty-second entertainments and seductions, and the power to change reality with the flick of a wrist, could no more indulge the dronings of teachers for minutes on end than a literate group of Americans could listen to a ten-hour chant of a primitive Elder. In how we listened, how we learned, the generation born to television is separated by a Fault that is utterly uncrossable by a generation raised on print.

Finally, the 1950s seemed to have a quality of absurdity, a quality darker and more foreboding than a President untutored in third-grade English, or quiz show heroes who got by with a little help from their friends. For another promise of World War II, that of a future serene and troubled, did not seem to be coming true. With Nazism and Fascism dead, the Soviet menace was now our mortal foe—and this time the foe was armed with nuclear weapons.

One of the clearest memories of a 1950s childhood is the "take-cover" drill, practiced weekly, it seemed, in elementary school. At a sudden signal, we would drop from our chairs, pull ourselves into a fetal position, and crouch under our desks, and wait until the A-bomb had fallen. The A-bomb, we were taught in an assembly film strip, was identifiable

WHERE HAVE YOU GONE . . .

by a sudden flash of light, the signal to "take cover." What
made this so unreal, even to nine- and ten-year-olds, was
that newspapers and magazines often ran diagrams of what
would happen if an atomic bomb fell on New York City.
Concentric circles displayed the consequences: if the bomb
exploded at the Empire State Building, everything up to
110th Street would be vaporized; above 110th Street, total
destruction would result. I remember, as a resident of 106th
Street, feeling jealous of my friends from 111th Street who
would simply be totally destroyed, rather than vaporized.
(Once in a while it would occur to us to ask our teachers
why we were crouched under our desks when the newspapers clearly suggested that we would not exist if the
A-bomb fell; on the other hand, we attended a school built
by an architect working out of the Maximum Security school
of Architecture; our school was brick and stone, its yard
surrounded by a six-foot-high fence. No A-bomb could melt
its impregnable fortress.)

Such absurdity was tolerated, or laughed at, or cursed,
but it was accepted. The dissidence was within, or contained
in jokes and sallies. To act on our sense of absurdity, to
refuse to play out the rituals of the Elders, seemed impossible. Where was the support for such conduct? Suppose they
put black marks on our Permanent Record Cards, those passports to college and life after school? We had no sense that
behind the absurdity were paper tigers, unable to resist a
simple, clear-cut "No!" We laughed at the Rules, but played
the Game. The seeds of discontent were elsewhere: in the
music we danced to, in the televised glimpses of America

we watched each night. The fruits of those seeds—the over-turning of the Icons of the Postwar World—were forming slowly, but with certain, inexorable patterns. In the 1950s, they would grow; in the 1960s, they would explode.

Book 1

ARTIFACTS

ROCK

Terror.

Perhaps you think you can define it. It is sitting in the cockpit of a jet fighter, plummeting to a crash landing in a hostile terrain. It is losing your footing on a mountain ledge in the midst of a blizzard. It is walking down a deserted city street in the dead of night, with the sudden, certain sound of footsteps behind you.

No, that is not terror. I will tell you what terror is. Terror is waiting on line at six-thirty in the morning on a school holiday in 1957, waiting for the Brooklyn Paramount to open for Alan Freed's Rock and Roll Revue.

You have been up since five-thirty on your first day of vacation, Christmas or Easter (Hanukah or Passover in my set). You have staggered into the predawn darkness, found your friend Alan (another normal, neurotic Jewish kid) and

weaved your way into the subway. There you pass interminable time, speeding past unfamiliar stops, emerging into the
sullen dawn in downtown Brooklyn (downtown *Brooklyn?*).
There, about a block away, is the Brooklyn Paramount, a
huge movie palace built to hold the thousands who do not
go out to movies anymore. On the marquee are big red
letters: "Ten Days Only! Alan Freed's All-Star Rock 'n' Roll
Revue!"

You walk to the theater, past the shuttered luncheonettes
and cheap clothing stores. There is already a knot of kids
waiting on line, even though the doors will not open for
two hours and forty-five minutes. And there you will begin
to learn the meaning of terror.

These people are different. They do not look the way I
do. They do not talk the way I do. I do not think they
were born the same way I was. All of the males are six
feet, seven inches tall. The last six inches is their hair, carefully combed into a pompadour. They are lean, rangy, even
scrawny (except for one who is very, very fat). They have
the hard faces of the children of the working poor. They
read auto specs at night, not college catalogues. They wear
St. Christopher medals, white T-shirts with their cigarette
packs held in the left sleeve, which is rolled up to the muscles. They have muscles.

The girls are all named Fran. They have curlers in their
hair and scarves tied around their heads. They chew gum.
They wear jeans and sweaters, and their crucifixes bounce
on their breasts, some of which are remarkable examples of
stress under pressure.

Their conversation is guttural, half-sentences and grunts, with innuendoes and veiled hints of lubricity.

"Eh, that party, eh, Fran? Remember, heh heh? Nah, she don' remember nuthin'." Fran is giggling, blushing. There is about these people an overwhelming sense of physical force, the same sense exuded by the students of Ascension High who chased the Jews home from school every afternoon: they hit other people a lot. Every joke, every question, every insult is followed by open-handed jabs to the face, punches on the arm, slaps which barely miss being punches. It is like watching Leo Gorcey and Huntz Hall in the Bowery Boys movies.

At this point, there is only one stark thought in my mind: what in God's name am I doing here? These people are going to kill me and steal my five-dollar bill and I will not be found for days. Consequently, the strategy of waiting on line at the Paramount is clear. You do not talk with your friend about your grades on the Social Studies test. You do not talk about where you want to go to college. You do not engage in precocious arguments about socialism. You keep your big mouth shut.

The vow of silence makes time go slowly, so you look at the posters over the Paramount entrance: the pictures of the stars blown up on cardboard, the names spelled out in letters glittering from gold and silver dust. There is Buddy Holly and the Crickets—he will die a year later in an airplane crash, one of our first martyrs; the Cleftones, from Jamaica High, in white satin dinner jackets and red slacks; Jo-Ann Campbell, "the blonde bombshell" who wears high-heeled shoes and very tight skirts, and whose biggest hand comes when she turns her back to the audience.

If you talk at all, it is in grunts to the others.

"Yeah, Frankie Lyman. I saw—seen him last year. You heard the new Fats Domino?" You clutch for this common ground, waiting for the doors to open, for the sanctuary of the dark theater, for the Terror to go away.

What were we waiting for, those dark mornings? For the singers and their songs, yes; but there were shows that were clinkers. Alan Freed often paid mediocre fees to his talent, splitting the net with his partners and himself. Sometimes the big names in rock and roll did not come; sometimes he was left with acts that had recorded a single hit that we knew would not be repeated. No, it was something else. We waited for Alan Freed and what he was for the children of the 1950s. And we waited because of something in each of us: an unspoken, undetected yearning for a sense of unity; an urge to join and celebrate this music that was ours as a community; an impulse that a decade later swept our younger brothers and sisters out of mainstream America.

We were children of the war to end wars. Our parents had left Depression and isolation behind, swarming onto beaches and into defense plants, cherishing the promise of a thousand magazine advertisements that the life to come would offer ease. Win the war, and the Cornucopia would open.

So our parents had fought, or waited to fight, they had left their homes and the communities where their fathers had found roots and friends and lovers and mates, where homes had been built and pride too. They had fled to the

Levittowns of the future, stripping away grass and water, knocking down a thousand city blocks, sinking concrete pillars for the four-lane expressways, mortgaging their lives for the fifty-foot plot of grass that separated them from their neighbors. They had stuck metal into the sky and brought another kind of world into their living rooms, abandoning the local bars and meeting halls, leaving the streets of the city deserted and dangerous; they had built schools for the flood of children they had conceived for the better world to come.

And by midcentury, they knew—and we sensed—that it was not working. It was not what they had been promised. There were enemies, they were told, within their own government, and things cost more, much more, and there was a weapon that could vaporize them, leaving them not simply dead but vanished, turned into atoms, without the fact of death around them, and They had that weapon. We went to schools and crouched under desks when the bells rang, we learned about the flash of light and fire storms, Conelrad triangles on our radios; in all our magazines there were concentric circles laid over our cities; here there would be nothing, here devastation, here a chance to live, charred and crippled. We saw pinpoints on the Empire State Building, and we knew that if we moved to Westchester, we might live for weeks when the Bomb fell.

And we learned, too, that there was no peace; that a place on the other side of the world, Korea, could put our fathers back into uniform and summon our brothers to be killed and maimed. There were no bands, no sense of a national struggle, no victory gardens or paper drives or scrap metal drives, or patriotic posters pinned to the bulletin boards. There was just dying and suffering and anger, that they had worked so hard for this.

By 1950 a Cleveland newspaper editor could sit down and write the most famous editorial of the decade:

"What is wrong with us . . .

"It is in the air we breathe. The things we do. The things we say. Our books. Our papers. Our theatre. Our movies. Our radio and television. The way we behave. The interests we have. The values we fix.

"We have everything. We abound with all of the things that make us comfortable. We are, on the average, rich beyond the dreams of kings of old . . . Yet . . . something is not there that should be—something we once had . . .

"No one seems to know what to do to meet it. But everybody worries about it."

Yes, said dozens of newspapers and thousands of Americans, that was it. Something we once had. A general, hero of the country, said let us press on to victory, and a bespectacled, bookkeeper of a President fired him. We didn't want to win our wars anymore, and it was a lot longer to the home than we had realized, and things weren't really working, either, and our kids seemed to be getting into more and more trouble. We were coming down off a national high and the morning was cold and gray.

Our music, like our other national products, had been frozen by the War. By midcentury, the tastes of young Americans were in kind the same as their parents in the 1930s. *Billboard,* the music industry's paper of record, had polled America's kids in 1951: they liked the Mills Brothers, the

Ink Spots, the Ames Brothers, Bing Crosby and Perry Como, Stan Kenton and Ray Anthony and Les Brown. Television was pulling people away from their phonographs and radios, and the record business was losing 10 percent of its business every year. Music did not seem to matter.

It was an exquisite agony. The men of the Brill Building, that Broadway Art Deco center of music publishing for a generation, had a powerful ally. Radio, its dramatic, entertainment, and news centrality stolen by television, was turning to music as its principal product; it was cheaper to put on the air, and could sustain a profit even though advertising dollars were flowing into the new medium of TV. But they did not know what kind of music would reach its listeners.

A new sound, of course: not swing, not the dying big bands, not bebop or jazz, but something new was needed. Yet, it seemed, the only product they could move was the Novelty Record; a sound which, by definition, was unique and could not be turned into a trend. They made "Rudolph the Red-Nosed Reindeer" as sung by Gene Autry, one of the biggest records in history, but they could not create animal heroes forever. They made Les Paul and Mary Ford a hot item, with Mary Ford singing to her own electrically recorded harmonies; but there was no industry-wide trend in that. They gave Rosemary Clooney a gold record with "Come on-a My House" in 1951—the strange, Armenian accents and effects written by William Saroyan and his nephew Ross Bagdasarian (who would later write "Witch Doctor" and create "Alvin and the Chipmunks"). But there were not enough Armenians to go around.

Inspiration, God and country, got a run for the money.

When General MacArthur addressed a worshipful joint session of Congress after Truman relieved him of his Korean command, he concluded his address by saying: ". . . one of the most popular barracks ballads [of West Point days] proclaimed most proudly that soldiers never die, they just fade away. And, like the old soldier of that ballad, I now close my military career and just fade away . . ."

A dozen versions of the record were in the stores within a fortnight—from Vaughn Monroe to Bing Crosby they sold. And so desperate was the record industry for some hook to hang a trend on that Spike Jones cut a song called "My Daddy Is a General to Me." It sank without a trace.

A year earlier, a forty-two-year-old Cincinnati housewife wrote a song of religious devotion, "Our Lady of Fatima," which offered a rosary for peace. It caught the sensibility of stark fear that Korea had generated, and was a smash hit. But God stopped at this song: child singer Tommy Tucker recorded "I'm Praying to St. Christopher" to no one's applause, and in the black record world, hidden from mainstream eyes, the Swan Silvertone singers declared that "Jesus Is God's Atomic Bomb."

For a time around midcentury, it seemed that popular music would reach into one of the two segregated fields of music and make the country sound the key to the new popular music. For a generation, country records had enriched the men of Nashville, Tennessee. Unheard on pop music shows, unsold in big-city record stores outside the South, country music had its own vaudeville circuit, its own record chart, and its sound of wronged men and women and the life of the country. When it was brought into the Brill Building world, it seemed to work. Frankie Lane's "Mule Train" and

"My Heart Goes Where the Wild Goose Goes" were hits; so was Red Foley's "Chattanooga Shoe Shine Boy" and the folk songs of the Weavers: "Good Night, Irene" and "Tzena, Tzena, Tzena." And Patti Page's "Tennessee Waltz" became one of the biggest records of the decade, selling more than five million copies.

But country records were not reaching the key to record success—the teenager. Country music was too parochial, even when sifted through pop singers, to become the basis for a new kind of music. For a time, it seemed the crooners might come back; the pretty boys who could turn the adolescent girls into weeping, screaming children. Johnnie Ray, who wept and wailed his way through "Cry" and "The Little White Cloud That Cried" was a prime candidate. So was Eddie Fisher, twenty-year-old discovery of comedian Eddie Cantor, who went from organist at the New York Paramount to TV star and hit singer of "Any Time," "Wish You Were Here," "Lady of Spain," and "Oh! My Pa-pa."

But there was a flaw: these were *personalities*, not styles. It took promotion, television exposure, and luck to penetrate the record-buying audience. Something more fundamental was needed, something that could turn an unknown into a hit record artist without this limited access. And, to the shock of the entire record business, and, ultimately, to the horror of white America, the sound was found in the hidden other world of the country: in the heart of black America.

The record industry had a name for it; they called it "race music." It was played in every big city, sold in record stores, and performed in theaters, and white America never heard it. As certainly as the black American had been herded into his own neighborhoods, shut off from the comfortable white world, so his music had been funneled carefully into mainstream America. Benny Goodman could play Fletcher Henderson's swing arrangements, muted through the clarinet; Paul Whiteman could crown himself "King of Jazz" by playing black people's music; Louis Armstrong could cavort and nigger-grin his way to fame. But the music of black America was as hidden from our parents as the world of the black American was kept out of our movies and magazines.

For thirty years it had been recorded. In 1920 Mamie Smith's "Crazy Blues" had sold two million records on the small Okeh record label, rarely found outside ghetto music stores. Paramount signed up Ma Rainey and Columbia signed up Bessie Smith, but their music—"race music" for the "sepia market"—was shielded by customs as strong as a Mississippi school system from the white world. Into the late 1940s the music was aimed at and sold to the urban black adults: with a heavy beat, blunt, often sexual lyrics, and a sense of raw energy considered too shocking for the tender sensibilities of whites.

Record companies, independent of the giant conglomerates of Columbia, RCA, and others, flourished by selling to this market. Although usually owned by whites, these companies—Imperial and Specialty in Los Angeles, Chess in Chicago, Atlantic in New York—took "sepia talent" and gave them a home. Often, these artists covered a popular hit, such as "Tennessee Waltz" or "Old Soldiers Never Die," using black artists to bring these songs into this segregated market.

It was a strange world, totally alien to the listening habits of white youth. For the New York adolescent, his music stations were also the stations of his parents: WINS and "Listen to Lacy" (the guy with the smile) which came on right after the Yankee ball game, Martin Block's "Make Believe Ballroom," WNEW's Jerry Marshall. It never occurred to us to wander above 1130 on the radio dial, where the foreign tongues of ethnic stations, and the strange sounds of the Negro stations, played to their hidden audiences. Had we ventured into the upper reaches of the band, we would have heard undiluted shouts of joy and pain, folk wisdom and celebration: "Chicken Shack Boogie," "Drinkin' Wine, Spo-de-o," "Saturday Night Fish Fry," "Don't Want No Skinny Woman," "Gotta Give Me What-cha Got," "Come On In," all songs of blatant sexuality, protected not by the first amendment so much as by white America's own habit of tuning out the black world.

And we would have heard, too, the sexuality of specific terms: "My Baby Rocks Me with a Steady Roll," "Rockin' at Midnight," and "All She Wants to Do Is Rock." Just as, a generation earlier, the slang for sex—"jazz"—had been turned into the accepted word for music, so "rock and roll" —again, black argot for balling—had become a term embraced by their music.

As with country music, "race music" had its own loyal audience, centered in urban ghettoes and in the southern black belt. Fats Domino, a New Orleans pianist, sold millions of records of such songs as "Boll Weevil" and "The Fat Man" without once finding himself on a list of top-selling pop records: a fact explained by the habit of gathering "pop" listings only from mainstream record stores which sold to white buyers. And, in the first years of the 1950s, an occasional black-oriented song had found a mainstream audience. The Five Keys, doing a "black" version of "Glory of Love," had reached into some popular music markets. The same thing happened to the Clovers, a group recording on the Atlantic record label, with a song called "Don't You Know I Love You?"

The latent sense of race as an American dilemma had even begun to reach the music industry. In 1949 *Billboard* magazine changed its black music listing from "race" music to "rhythm and blues," noting that there were indications of wider acceptance for this kind of music than the strictly Negro market. It was left, however, to a man who died facing criminal charges and poverty in 1965 to bring this music—full-throated and undiluted—into the homes of young white Americans. By this act, he did more than any other single individual to alter the life style of this country. His name was Alan Freed.

In the 1940s Alan Freed was working in the obscurity of Middle America, beginning his career as a forty-five-dollar-a-week disc jockey in New Castle, Pennsylvania. In 1945 he moved to Akron, Ohio, to station WAKR at sixty dollars a week. After a legal hassle with his employers—he wanted to take a better offer with a rival Akron station—he moved to WUW in Cleveland. It was in Cleveland that Freed discovered an intriguing fact: white teenagers were attracted to rhythm and blues records recorded for black adults. It was an accidental discovery, but one Freed seized on. He changed the format of his radio show, dubbed himself "Moondog" —until the blind Viking-costumed New York street poet enjoined him from using the name—and began pumping rhythm and blues music into white homes.

But Freed didn't call the music rhythm and blues. Perhaps he picked up the title of a 1951 Little Son Jackson record: "Rockin' and Rollin'." Perhaps he read the 1952 *Billboard* ad for Paul Williams' Savoy recording "Rockin' Chair Blues" which proclaimed "It jumps! It hops! It rocks! It rolls!" Or Johnny Otis' "Rockin' Blues," or Piano Red's "Rockin' With Red." Whatever the source, Freed took the term and slapped it onto the songs he was playing. He called them "rock and roll."

In an industry where historically trends are controlled from New York, and manipulated by record executives, Freed's success seemed authentically grass roots. He took his music into the most moribund field of all—the live concert. And the kids followed. In March 1952 Alan "Moondog" Freed staged a "Coronation Ball" at the Cleveland Arena. An all-black rhythm and blues lineup was on hand to celebrate Freed's self-proclamation of himself as "the ole king of rock and roll." More than twenty-five thousand teenagers poured into the Arena—the largest dance crowd in Cleveland since the end of the Second World War. That July, Freed returned to Akron; his dance at the Summit Beach ballroom drew three thousand customers at two dollars a head. In 1953 his "Rhythm and Blues" show in Cleveland pulled in ten thousand teenagers, paying three dollars each—and, to the amazement of the press, more than one third of the audience was white—to hear artists unknown to their parents.

By 1954 Freed was ready for bigger game. His Cleveland radio show was heard on tape as far east as Newark, New Jersey. On the heels of heavy plugging on the show, Freed arrived in Newark in May for a "Moondog" concert. The Akron and Cleveland turnouts were duplicated; ten thousand people came, and thousands more were turned away, to hear once strictly ghetto acts such as the Clovers, Charles Brown, Sam Butera, Muddy Waters, the Harptones, and the Buddy Johnson orchestra. It was a scene out of one of Freed's later movies: the horde of teenagers rushing the stage, grabbing mikes, the singers dancing with the kids, and a general mass of hell-raising.

"Not since the heyday of the swing band has a dance in the East created such excitement or pulled as strongly," *Billboard* wrote of the event. "The size of the crowd indicated the tremendous feeling that 'cat' music now has, and the intense interest of many youngsters in rhythm and blues . . . the kids want their music with a beat to dance to . . . Alan Freed has found out what they want, and this is why the Newark date grossed so much more than the average pop dance and show date."

A week later, Donald Clem, disc jockey at KMMO, Marshall, Missouri, indignantly wrote the trade paper what must be the first prediction of the death of rock, since it precedes its rise. He wrote:

"I disagree wholeheartedly . . . It will never approach pop plays and sales. Teenagers like Ray Anthony, Buddy Morrow, and other orchestras."

It was the most common theme of the mainstream music world over the next few years—this couldn't be the music of the future, not this jungle rhythm, with its filthy talk and dirty beat, it was a fad, the big bands were coming back, Calypso was replacing rock and roll, the music was dying. But from the end of 1953 to 1955, the conquest began, took hold, and was complete. Before the rise of Elvis Presley, without a single rock and roll act being presented on network television, the new music became the dominant sound throughout young white America.

As early as 1952 the Clovers' "One Mint Julep" had broken out of the ghetto rhythm and blues category to win a place on some pop music charts. A year later, a "race" ballad by Sonny Till and the Orioles, "Crying in the Chapel," became an enormous hit; an RCA staff man heard it, and got singer June Valli to "cover" it; in other words, to record her version of the song, which had more acceptability in the pop field, and which became a fair-sized hit. Three other songs reached the pop market in their original versions: "Good Lovin'" by the Clovers, "Money Honey" by the Drifters, and "Shake a Hand" by Faye Adams.

Early in 1954, the Crows' record of "Gee" began to hit the pop charts, with more visibility than any past rhythm and blues record. *Cashbox* noted that "one of the great surprises of the current record season has been the great strength which the Crows' waxing of 'Gee' has shown in the pop market." By May, the Drifters' "Such a Night" and the Four Tunes' "I Understand" were hitting the mainstream charts. The signs were starting to appear faster now. Joe Turner's "Shake, Rattle and Roll" was a top seller in Philadelphia; the Chords' "Sh-Boom" was the most played song in Boston juke boxes. And the white record world was starting to get the jitters. The sensibility of the Brill Building world was like that of the French nobility in the early 1780s; they still had the wealth and power, but from somewhere down the hill strange sounds were coming, and they did not augur well for the people at the top. The Brill boys were still putting out the real hits: "I Get So Lonely" by the Four Knights, "Make Love to Me!" by Jo Stafford, Dean Martin's "That's Amore," Julius La Rosa's "Eh, Cumpare!", the Hilltoppers' "From the Vine Came the Grape" (it was a good year for Italians). But the wave of the future was turning toward the backstairs of the music world—to the black music.

Rhythm and blues, *Billboard* could write in the spring of 1954, "is no longer the stepchild of the record business. Recent years have seen it develop into a stalwart member of the record industry . . . It is no longer identified as the music of a specific group, but can now enjoy a healthy following, among all people, regardless of race or color."

California juke box operators were reporting that in teen-age hangouts, pop records were being played less than the rock and roll stuff. In traditionally Latin music locations— West Texas, New Mexico, Arizona—demand for rhythm and blues was rising. Negro radio stations in New York and Chicago were finding that 20 percent of their listeners were white—mostly youngsters who could not find the music being played on "white" stations. Pop music stations in Los Angeles were turning over twenty hours a week or more to the new music. The kids wanted Ruth Brown and the Clovers, the Drifters and Joe Turner, they wanted the tenor saxophones, the heavy afterbeat, the infectious dancing rhythms.

And these artists—these sounds—were not on the big labels like RCA, Columbia, Mercury, Capitol, and Decca. They were on Atlantic and Chess and Imperial and Peacock and Savoy, the black-named, black-oriented labels tucked away in the sidestreets of the record industry, which had been havens for rhythm and blues performers. So, failing to have the artists, the white companies found another way of capturing the appeal of rock and roll: they stole it.

Well, not in the legal sense. When a company wants to record somebody else's song, all it has to do is pay a royalty to the publisher and it's legal. But a 1951 court case opened a far wider door to the white world's assault on black music. In that year, Decca Records—a major company—had covered a song called "A Little Bird Told Me" and had allegedly used almost exactly the same arrangement; the same use of instruments, the same phrasing by the singer, the same grouping of sounds which can mean more to a record's success than just the words and music. In that case, the judge ruled that musical arrangements are *not* property, and not subject to copyright protection.

Beginning in 1954, the major record companies walked right through that door. They might not have the artists or musicians, but they had ears. They could gather the background phrasing of groups—the "ya-da-da-ya-da-da-ya-da-da-ya-da-da-*bomp!*" of the Chords' version of "Sh-Boom," and hand it over to Mercury Records' Crewcuts to cover and make into a hit. Johnnie Ray could listen to "Such a Night" by the Drifters and cut his own record. Buddy Morrow covered "Lovey Dovey" by the Clovers; Joe Turner's "Shake, Rattle and Roll" was turned into a million-selling single by

Bill Haley and the Comets. June Valli covered "I Understand," originally by the Four Tunes.

In this effort, the major record companies had two enormous advantages: first, the major companies had far better distributing resources; they could place the record in major stores far faster than the small, independent companies, which historically had lines only into the ghetto market. In fact, so wide was the discrepancy that a big company could often put a "cover" version of a song into stores *before* the original version ever reached the market. Second, records were dependent on air play for exposure; and most disc jockeys on "white" stations did not like the raw energy of rhythm and blues. By temperament and taste, they would be far likelier to play an RCA artists' diluted version of a rock and roll song.

And yet the black sound still survived this onslaught—essentially because it was those versions that captured the excitement and power that had made rock and roll so successful. Alan Freed aided the smaller companies by generally refusing to play cover versions, and by making the preference for original versions a near-ideological cause. For Freed himself, the rise of rock and roll meant a major leap into national prominence. In the spring of 1954, Freed left Cleveland to join New York radio station WINS at an unprecedented salary of $75,000 for an 11 P.M. to 2 A.M. show. Although the move was delayed for several months because of a near-fatal auto accident, Freed hit the big city like a bombshell. By August 1954 he was syndicated to five stations. By December he had staged his first live show in New York, at the Brooklyn Academy of Music. It grossed $150,000—an unheard-of sum for a live show. A few weeks later, Freed staged a "Rock and Roll Jubilee Ball" at the St. Nicholas Arena, with Joe Turner, the Drifters, the Clovers, the Moonglows, the Harptones, Red Prysock, and the Buddy Johnson orchestra. The twelve thousand who danced and sang and cavorted for hours let New York City know that this music was a good deal more than a fad—it was reaching something deep within the American teenager.

Each night, sprawled on my bed on Manhattan's Upper West Side, I would listen to the world that Alan Freed created. To a twelve- or thirteen-year-old, it was a world of unbearable sexuality and celebration: a world of citizens under sixteen, in a constant state of joy or sweet sorrow. The rhythms of the fast-tempo songs were hypnotic; you could not lie still when Little Richard screamed out "Tutti-Frutti" or when "Shake, Rattle and Roll" came bouncing out. New to sexual sensations, driven by the impulses that every new adolescent generation knows, we were the first to have a music rooted in uncoated sexuality. In a sense, the editorials in the Archdiocese papers that demanded a stop to this obscene music were right; having been aimed for decades at an *adult* audience, rhythm and blues music was a powerful dose of sexuality for a thirteen-year-old. To parents, remembering the sweet sounds of Benny Goodman's clarinet or the mellow brass of the Dorseys, the honking tenor sax and the vibrating electric guitar and the insistent drum beat were fearful engines of immorality, driving daughters to strange dance steps and God knows what else.

Even more stirring than the incessant beat of the fast music was the slow sensuality of the rhythm and blues ballad—the so-called "celestial ballad," filled with eternal pledges of love evoking the stars, the sun, and any number of stray planets.

Take the Penguins singing "Earth Angel," perhaps the single most-remembered rock ballad of the mid-1950s; or the Five Satins describing what it was like "In the Still of the Night"; or the Nutmegs, bewailing "A Story Untold" of lost love; or Johnny Ace, the first romantic rock star, who killed himself playing Russian Roulette backstage during a rock and roll show in 1954, giving his song "Pledging My Love," with its promise of eternal love, a special pathos.

And beyond the agonizing vows of love, affecting beyond measure to a junior high school witness to breakups and betrothals on an hourly basis, there was the existence, unconfirmed by any sense other than faith, of another region of teenagers, far away, who were linked to us by this music.

Alan Freed would bring their world to mine each night as he read "dedications" to the songs from faraway places with strange-sounding names: Bayside, New Dorp, Huntington, Erasmus, Riverdale, communities of streets without numbers.

"To John, from you-know-who. I want you, but you want her. Listen to the words of this song—and go back to her."

"To Mike from Fran. Going steady for five weeks . . . and forever."

"To the kids of Miss Epstein's class. Good luck—and may our friendships never be broken."

Somewhere, somewhere there really were candy stores with juke boxes, where the kids ate Pop's hamburgers and danced after school the way they did in those Jane Withers movies. Somewhere, there were parties with close dancing. (Bill Haley and the Comets recorded a song called "Dim, Dim the

Lights" which had more capacity to stir the glands than all of
I Am Curious.) Somewhere there were kids who spent their
time with each other, touching and laughing and running
around to all this music . . .

"Turn that damn thing down!"

My father has always been a fair and gentle man, but in
the face of Little Richard or Fats Domino, he abandoned himself to rage.

"You're going to turn your brain to mush!"

Francis of Assisi become Spiro Agnew. My adolescence is
a continuing replay: the door swinging open, the dark, fur-
rowed brow, the flash of anger, the sullen retreat. Like a
river of troubled water, rock and roll music was the boundary
of a house divided.

Worse, there was a fifth column, a corner of my mind
which told me: you know, of course, they're right. It *is* crap
and your brain *is* turning to mush. One of the authentic scars
of my life—far more vivid than a broken date or a broken
zipper—is buying a rock and roll album with my parents during a shopping trip to Union Square. We walked into a record
store, and there it was, on Specialty Records: "Here's Little
Richard." On a yellow background, a tight shot of a black
face bathed in sweat, the beads of perspiration clearly visible,
mouth wide open in a rictus of sexual joy, hair flowing endlessly from the head.

"Oh my God," my mother said.

Come on, I thought, let's just buy it and get out of here,
come on . . .

"We better make sure it isn't scratched; let's play it first,"
my father said.

The saleslady smiled indulgently. From the phonograph, ripping through the store, came the shouted beginning of "Long Tall Sally."

"Jesus Christ," my father said.

I muttered something vague about "authentic gospel roots . . . tradition of Afro-American . . . folk," but what I was saying inside was something else: look, it's *my* music, I like it, and you're not supposed to listen to it, anyway.

And that, after all, is what I was doing in the line outside the Brooklyn Paramount on a chilly dawn, surrounded by six-foot, seven-inch hoodlums who were going to kill me. It was a refuge from ridicule, a liberated zone where everyone else liked the same crap I did without shame or guilt. In those days before scholarly encomiums to the Beatles in *Partisan Review*, before even Presley, Ed Sullivan was not presenting rock and roll stars. They were rarely seen on television outside local teen bandstand shows, and when they did appear, it was an embarrassment. They did not belong there, vulnerable to our elders' outrage. They belonged here—apart from them and with Us.

Self-defense was a vital part of the magic of rock and roll. Without question, the Elders were out to rid the country of this music, born in the black nation they had shunted off, away from our eyes, hiding the sights and the smells we did not want to face, the sounds of pain and joy now flooding the airwaves, infecting the bodies of their children. We might dance happily to a song observing that Miss Molly sure liked to ball, but the Elders knew that Miss Molly was not just dancing "at the house of blue lights"; it was their conviction that with enough of these records, we might start balling *after*, not during, the Sock Hop Ball.

Their concern for our morality predated the rise of rock and roll. Eric Goldman's history of the postwar years tells us that: "After the outbreak of the Korean War, [juvenile delinquency] mounted so swiftly that about a million children a year were getting into trouble with the police . . . Whatever the form of teenage trouble, the whole situation was showing peculiarly disturbing trends. The age of the children who went astray was rapidly dropping . . . The offenses were growing more serious . . . It was no longer possible to dismiss the child in trouble as something which did not happen to nice people. More and more, it was the son or daughter of the manufacturer who ended up in a jumble."

The same impulses that had shot parents out of the small towns and familiar neighborhoods of the prewar years had broken down the familiar barriers. The cop on the beat and the corner grocer, the small town sense of communality, had been wiped out by the insane genius of the suburbs and high rises, which provided *neither* community *nor* privacy. The children were reaching into new corners of America, linked to each other by radio and television, and separated from their parents by a life style which drew parents and children further and further from each other, even in physical terms. They did not know what was happening to their children and they did not like it. Watching them writhe and twist to sounds they thought of as primitive was another nail in the coffin of the Hardy family vision of life as it was supposed to be.

The music was just as strange, just as foreboding, to the men who had charted the musical tastes of America for the years since the Depression. The disc jockeys, the record executives, the "A & R Men" (artist and repertoire men, who selected the songs and helped create the arrangements of singers), none of them had grown up with a concern for rhythm and blues; they had grown up to swing and light jazz, and the crooners. They saw rock and roll music as a disreputable stranger, trekking uninvited into the front parlor of their home, leaving muddy footprints on the Oriental rug.

At first, the Elders treated the music with scorn.

"It's this year's hillbilly kick," scoffed Jerry Marshall of New York's WNEW—a "good music" station. "Maybe next year it will be Hawaiian music." "The big question," asked *Cashbox* in March 1955, "in the music business today is: 'How long will it last?' . . . It is our guess that it won't."

Variety, the show-business trade weekly, was particularly quick to seize on reports of the music's death. The paper was geared toward the Broadway stage and the Hollywood studio, to the nightclub comic and the big band sound; much as the New York *Times* of 1918 predicted the collapse of the Soviet Government once a week, *Variety*'s wish was father to the thought. Rock and roll had to die.

In early 1955, *Variety* noted a teenage survey in which 70 percent of New York adolescents said they didn't like rock music. "If the drop since January continues," the trade paper wrote, "it will be gone by June." In April, *Variety* observed that "the fade of the rhythm and blues tunes from the pop lists is happening faster than originally expected." At about the same time, Joe Carlton, A & R head of RCA, said the company would do no more rhythm and blues. He liked the music, but, he said, "I think the time has arrived when different type songs will again be wholeheartedly accepted by the public. As far as RCA-Victor is concerned, we will make our own trend."

Only a few months later, RCA signed a singer out of Sun Records in Nashville, named Elvis Presley.

At Mercury Records, Hugo Perrette and Luigi Creatie announced the death of rock and roll, proclaiming that their singer Georgia Gibbs would cut no more rhythm and blues tunes. Within a year, Mercury had established itself as the all-time rip-off king of the field. Georgia Gibbs recorded two LaVern Baker tunes, "Tweedlee Dee" and "Jim Dandy," copying Miss Baker's arrangement so exactly that Miss Baker wrote her Congressman asking for protective legislation.

In addition, two Mercury groups—the Crewcuts and the Diamonds—were kept busy covering every conceivable rhythm and blues tune by a black group on an independent label. Both groups' hits—"Sh-boom" by the Crewcuts and "Little Darlin'" by the Diamonds—were copies of other groups' original hits.

When it began to dawn on the Brill Building set that rock and roll was not a six-day wonder, they began to get angry. They could not latch on to the secret themselves. They tried everything. Kay Starr had a hit with the "Rock and Roll Waltz." The Ames Brothers, rooted in the late '40s slicked-down-hair-white-tux crooner set, were posed in a finger-snapping motif as a trade paper ad read "You ain't heard rock and roll till you've dug the Ames Brothers . . ." Alan Dale recorded "Rockin' the Cha-Cha." But the kids were buying the Cleftones and the Clovers, the Drifters and the Orioles, and Frankie Lyman and the Teenagers.

Confusion turned to petulance.

"How about some records for adults that don't rock, roll, wham, bam, or fade to flat tunes?" moaned WMFM disc jockey Bob Tilton. A Tucson jockey wrote at the end of 1955 ". . . with the tremendous upsurge of r & b into the pop group—the almost complete absence of good taste, to say nothing of good grammar—this has been the worst and certainly the most frustrating 'pop' year I have ever known."

Esthetic complaints were one thing; far more serious was the accusation that rock and roll was obscene, a menace to the morals of the young. Part of the reason for this sense was the source of the music: niggertown, the other side of the world, where men went to buy forbidden pleasures. Part of the feeling was in the sound of the music: raw, frenetic, basic. Part of it was the fact that, on occasion, rhythm and blues music was pretty strong stuff. A group called Hank Ballard and the Midnighters, for example, had sold a million records under the counter with a ditty called "Work With Me, Annie," including the immortal lyric: "please don't cheat/ give me all my meat." (The song, cleaned up, became a hit single on pop charts as "Dance With Me, Henry.") Later, the Midnighters cut "Annie Had a Baby (Can't Work No More)" and "Sexy Ways."

The response of the Elders was fury. WCBS disc jockey Bob Haymes, in a letter reprinted in the New York *Daily Mirror* and attacked by Alan Freed, called rock and roll "poor music, badly recorded, with lyrics that are at best in bad taste . . . and at worst obscene . . . This trend in music (and I apologize for calling it music) is affecting the ideas and the lives of our children."

"Perhaps," sniffed *Variety,* "the rhythm and blues thing has snowballed beyond control, because there are any number of independent diskery-labels which neither know nor care about ethics and concern about juvenile delinquency."

And a Los Angeles disc jockey put the final word on the matter. ". . . *All* rhythm and blues records are dirty, and as bad for kids as dope."

Swiftly, pressure mounted, within the record industry and from government, to curb the menace. A disc jockey commission in Houston, Texas, established a black list of rhythm and blues tunes that could not be played, including "I Got a Woman" by Ray Charles, the "Annie" songs, "Good Rockin' Tonight," "Winehead Baby," and the tender "I Want a Bowlegged Woman." In Somerville, Massachusetts, Police Lieutenant Thomas O'Brien ordered a list of songs removed from local juke boxes on grounds of obscenity. A Bridgeport rock and roll dance was canceled by police superintendent order. He declared that "teenagers work themselves into a frenzy to the beat of fast . . . music." And Chicago radio stations received fifteen thousand letters from teenagers protesting smut, as part of a church-run campaign dubbed a "Crusade for Decent Disks."

Without question, however, the central focus of complaints, the major figure in the rock-is-juvenile-delinquency equation, was the opening of the movie *Blackboard Jungle* in the spring of 1955. The movie, set in a New York slum school, portrayed teenagers as murderous rapists, as likely to pack a switchblade as a slide rule. A year earlier, Bill Haley and the Comets—ironically an all-white group who had started out as

a country music combo called the Saddlemen—had recorded
a moderate hit called "Rock Around the Clock." MGM chose
this song to open the picture. Horrified adults and foot-tap-
ping teenagers watched the camera move in on a schoolyard,
the ducktailed, T-shirted rocks cavorting and slouching about,
as the song played on.

The exposure made "Rock Around the Clock" a number
one hit—ultimately, the largest selling rock and roll record of
all time. When the movie was shown in Europe, it made rock
and roll a worldwide phenomenon. But in the minds of the
grownups, rock and roll was indelibly stamped as a cause
and effect of the criminal impulses raging among the young.

And night after night, it was Alan Freed and Us defending
ourselves against the onslaught.

"It's the 1 percent of the bad kids who are making it rough
for the 99 percent of the good kids," Freed would say, and
the theme became part of our cause. When Freed began to
make rock and roll movies in the mid-1950s—with plots out
of the I've-got-a-great-idea-let's-put-on-a-dance-and-build-the-
new-gym school of cinema—he stressed this theme that the
good kids liked rock and roll music. Coupled with this defense, the ban on rock records, the attacks of our Elders,
pulled us into a kind of a sect. To journey to Brooklyn was
not simply going to a show: it was an act of faith.

Of course, nobody knew that or talked like that at the time.
There was no self-conscious Woodstock spirit, no notion that
this was a spirit in which we could live out our lives. We
knew we had to grow up sometime, to be like Them. No, the
Paramount was a temporary refuge, not a path to a different

life. We were here because . . . well, it had a good beat and
you could dance to it.

My first journey to the world of the rock and roll show was
not out to Brooklyn, but to the safer regions of the New
York Paramount at Times Square. Alan Freed had taken a
big gamble, breaking his Christmas-Easter-Labor Day cycle
to put on a Washington's Birthday show in 1957. To shorten
the odds against conquering the citadel of Dorsey, Goodman,
and Sinatra, Freed had booked two big acts: Frankie Lyman
and the Teenagers, and the Platters. And he chose this occasion for the premiere of his movie, *Don't Knock the Rock*,
with Bill Haley and the Comets and Little Richard.

My friend Alan and I got there about 6:30 A.M. The line
already went past McBride's Ticket Service plate glass window down Forty-third Street toward the offices of the New
York *Times*. By the time the doors opened, the line was blocks
long. The show broke all of Sinatra's records. It also broke
McBride's plate glass window. The kids danced in the aisles.
They stomped so hard to the beat of the music that the Fire
Department evacuated the balcony. They cheered the good-
guy grownup in the movie, who said in effect, "Gee, I don't
see anything wrong with the music. I kinda like it." They
told Middle America, through the pictures in the next week's
Life magazine, that the conquest of rock and roll was complete.

At about 9 A.M. at the Brooklyn Paramount, a ticket-taker,
alone and afraid in a world he never made, edges into the
booth. The line begins to rock, slowly, ominously. The doors

open. Ushers flank the line, chanting "Admission is $1.50. Have your money ready, please. Admission is . . ."

The enormous, cavernous theater is filled as it has not been since television. The horrible Randolph Scott western or two-bit horror flick begins. Interminable hours later, the movie ends. Cheers. The newsreel comes on. Groans and boos. The newsreel ends. Cheers. *Another* newsreel—a feature on pet shows or women's fashions—comes on. Boos and shouts. The newsreel ends. Cheers. The lights go out. There is movement behind the curtain. Anticipatory shrieks. The announcer: "And now—the Paramount Theater is proud to present—Alan Freed and his rock and roll revue!" Yaaaaayyyyy!

The lights go on, red and blue and yellow, as the Alan Freed All-Star eighteen-piece orchestra plays "Night Train," one of Freed's trademarks. The band—as Freed has told us endless times—has great tenor sax men, Sam the Man Taylor, Big Al Sears, Panama Francis. The song ends and Freed walks out to ear-splitting roars, grinning widely from a slightly misshapen face, permanent reminder of his auto crash and the months of plastic surgery. His voice is throaty, raspy, electrically charged.

"Hiya!"

"Hiiii!"

"This is yours truly, Alan Freed, the ole king of rock and roll."

The acts. In a sense, they are all the same. Four or five singers, outlandishly dressed, in flaming red tux jackets, purple pants, yellow shirts with velvet ties—this in a time when charcoal gray was a bit daring. There are always two mikes—one for the lead singer, one for the rest of the group, including (always) a bass singer who supplies the doo-bobba, doo-bobba doo line, one falsetto to surround the reedy lead voice with logistical support in the form of descants.

The steps. They defy description. In a tribute to symmetry, the guy on the left puts out his left hand, the guy on the right puts out his right hand, and the guy in the middle puts out both hands. Fingers snap and wave, legs flash out and up, in mirror-image perfection. Now the hands switch, the feet shuffle in tempo. The tenor sax break begins. The singers spin completely around; they do splits. They gesture with the words.

"You know"—point out

"In my heart"—point to the heart

"I pray"—hands together in prayer

"We'll never part"—hands separate, heads shake no.

Many of the acts have completely faded from memory. Some of them—now gaining a new lease on professional life through the 1950s revivals—I will never forget. Winnie Winfield, lead singer of the Harptones, softly singing, "I want a Sunday kind of love/a love to last past Saturday night . . ."* Fred Parris, and the Five Satins, singing "In the Still of the Night," Herbie Cox and the Cleftones bouncing their way through "Can't We Be Sweethearts?" and "Little Girl of Mine." Together with a hundred other groups, they define my adolescence with precision: the Charts, the Dubs, the Del-Vikings, the G-Clefs, the Willows, the Monotones, the Ravens, the Crests, the Paragons, the Jesters, the Schoolboys,

* "A Sunday Kind of Love." Words and Music by Barbara Belle, Louis Prima, Anita Leonard, Stan Rhodes. © Copyright 1946, by MCA Music, a Division of MCA, Inc., 445 Park Avenue, New York. N.Y. 10022. Used by Permission. All Rights Reserved.

the Teen Chords, the Teen Queens, the Royal Teens, the Bachelors, the Students, the Elegants, the Platters, Frankie Lyman and the Teenagers, the Tune Weavers, the Dream Weavers, the Moonglows, the Five Keys, the Chords, the Drifters, the Clovers, the Vibrations, the Mello-kings, the Mello-tones, the Skyliners, the Penguins, the Innocents, the Crickets . . . all of them standing in the garish spotlight and singing back to us the music we had taken as Ours.

All the while, back at WINS, Paul Sherman kept up a constant hype. Normally a straight, solid square d.j., he would raise his voice twenty decibels when he subbed for Alan Freed, telling us endlessly that "Alan's at the Brooklyn Paramount right now with a show that is just un-be-*liev*-a-ble, you've just gotta catch this one." If you were home listening, you felt the existence of a party, the best party in the world, and everybody was there except you.

By 1959 Alan Freed was at the top of the heap. He had moved from WINS to WABC, after charging that WINS had failed to give him moral support when a touring rock and roll revue he was m.c.-ing had turned riotous in Boston. He was host of a Channel 5 Bandstand show, a New York afternoon show which was at times outdrawing Dick Clark's network *American Bandstand* show. His movies, his Paramount shows, all were bringing in fortunes. But 1959 was also the beginning of the end. In the wake of the quiz show scandals, payola—the practice of paying disc jockeys money to push certain songs—exploded as a national issue. Freed had, in the early days, been given author credit for a share in such hits as "Sincerely" by the Moonglows and "Maybelline" by Chuck

Berry. The hearings threw doubt on just how much Freed had contributed to writing the songs, and how much the author's royalty cut was a reflection of Freed's power to influence rock and roll hits. He was driven off the air in New York, drifted to the West Coast, where he found and lost several jobs. In early 1965, facing criminal charges for perjury, Freed died of a liver ailment.

At about the time Freed was driven off the air, rock and roll had in fact begun to die—although not in the way that *Variety* and the Brill Building crowd had hoped. The beat was there, and so was the noise and ferment. But by now white America had taken the music as its own. Under the influence of Dick Clark, whose face looked like it had been preserved in Saran Wrap every night, the Philadelphia sound— shlock rock—took over. Frankie Avalon, Danny and the Juniors, Fabian, they became national celebrities with songs which had neither wit nor power nor sexuality. Fabian, who, legend had it, was observed sitting on his front stoop by a record promoter and who had no voice at all, smirked out of record store windows across America, his hair doused with Bardol. Frankie Avalon filled the airwaves with "Dee Dee Dinah" ("you're kinda naughty *but*cha naughty and nice"). And the sounds of Chuck Berry and Fats Domino, the city sounds of the groups, faded and stilled.

There were a few who remembered. In Hibbing, Minnesota, and Liverpool, England, they had listened to the hard rock of Little Richard and the driving guitars of Chuck Berry and Bo Diddley, to the rhythmic, infectious beat of Buddy Holly and the Everly Brothers. And when Dylan and the Beatles came to power, they fed the sounds of rock and roll

into a new generation; sounds infused with lyrics far more
explicitly subversive than those that had sent our parents
fleeing in terror in the 1950s. What our parents had thought
they heard from our radios, the Rolling Stones threw at them
with shameless bluntness a decade later: "Bet your mama
don't know you bite like that," "Come on, honey, don't you
wanna live with me," "Let's spend the night together." The
unspoken fear of trouble had turned into a generational war:
by the thousands, the children were parading out of the
mainstream, into the hills, into the cities, into the streets.
And as they left they took with them the music that had been
born out of outrage and pain, the music we had heard and
cherished and shielded from the Elders. Some of us stayed behind, some went shuffling after the younger ones, tentatively,
one step at a time. And we, too, kept with us the music that
had now been coursing through America for fifteen years,
renewed, strengthened, and possessing the power to wipe out
all of the inducements and threats of the Elders.

The Brooklyn Paramount no longer exists. Its physical shell
is now part of Long Island University. The New York Paramount has been leveled for a new skyscraper. WINS is now
an all-news station; Paul Sherman now reads the bulletins
of crisis and intrigue solemnly and soberly. There is nothing
at any of these places to remind anybody that Alan Freed
once existed.

And yet, fifteen years after Freed first came to New York,
I attended a 1950s rock and roll revival at the shiny new
Felt Forum in Madison Square Garden. Approaching the
entrance, I saw the Others: a little plumper, some with bald

spots where their pompadours used to be, but with the grunts and hostility still in place. Most of them had married Fran; at least, the hair curlers and the kerchiefs were still there. Many of them wore lapel flags and Honor America buttons. Instinctively, I removed the peace button from my jacket. Terror does not die easily.

We went in together and sat together. When the M.C. announced that this show was being dedicated to Alan Freed we applauded together; and when Fred Parris and the Five Satins came out and sang "In the Still of the Night," we sang together and stood together and cheered together until they sang it again.

OPENING DAY

There are six of them, not yet fifteen years old. Their hair is short, sideburns ending at the top of the ear. They wear tennis sneakers, T-shirts, nylon jackets, chinos. Clutched in their hands are brown bags, one with the telltale spreading oil slick of a tunafish sandwich. They are dancing the Rite of the Subway: shuffling up to the edge of the platform, leaning dangerously over to peer down into the tunnel, seeking to pull the train into the station by sheer force of will. Nothing. Just the echoes of tennis shoes slapping on the concrete platform of the Fifty-ninth Street IND station, as they pace impatiently from the rusting soft-drink machine to the overhead clock with the blinking bottle of Palo Vieja Rum, the Rum with the True Flavor.

Ronald and his friends are restless. School is in session, but Ronald and his friends are not. It is Opening Day at

Yankee Stadium—1970. And even though it is 10:45 A.M., even though it is four hours and fifteen minutes until game time, Ronald and his friends want to get the day started.

A squeal far down the tracks; an echo that quickly becomes a rumble—a train is coming. Ronald and his friends run up and down the platform, looking for a deserted space. Suddenly, excitement turns to disgust. The train is new, steel-shiny, and that is terrible, because that means it is an "A" train, and the "A" train does not go to Yankee Stadium. Only the "D" train, always blackened by soot and dirt, its windows streaked with tracks of filthy rain, its bamboo-weave seats ripped out, scars of ink from day-old *Daily News* racing pages staining the floor, only this train goes to Yankee Stadium, cutting like an invisible wound underneath Harlem. And when you are twelve years old, with a brown bag lunch and tennis sneakers, and $2.40 in your pocket—enough for admission, a hot dog, an orange drink, and two tokens—the first inevitable fact of life is that the "D" train never comes first.

So Ronald and his friends groan and pace, and punch each other on the shoulder as two more "A" trains insolently rumble through the station. Finally, a few minutes before 11 A.M., a blackened "D" train finally pulls into Fifty-ninth Street. Ronald and his friends race on, bouncing from seat to seat, and watch the local stations speed by the windows as the express roars on to 125th Street. As we pass by 110th Street, one of Ronald's friends points out the window and yells: "Fifty-one blocks to go!"

One-hundred-and-tenth Street was where I began my own journeys to the Stadium, fifteen and twenty years ago. First

with my father, then with my friends, we would walk the
unsettling half dozen blocks east, from the comfortable fa-
miliarity of upper Broadway, along the southern border of
Morningside Park, to Eighth Avenue and 110th Street, the
southeast border of Harlem. We would walk quickly, nervously, past the auto repair shops, service stations, and bo-
degas, waiting for the train to take us to 125th Street and the
relative assurance of crowds pushing into the "D" train. We
would crowd in, belly-to-belly, clutching bulky Sunday
Times against us, juggling our brown bags from hand to hand,
laughing uneasily as the sudden jolts of the subway threw us
against each other. A sudden sense of anticipation would
touch us as we pulled into 155th Street, the station embel-
lished with orange tile bordered with black, black-lettered
signs on white wood stating, "Polo Grounds."

That ancient, rickety stadium, perched on Coogan's Bluff
on the Manhattan side of the Harlem River, looked across the
water, as a duke's fortress might look out enviously on the
castle of a far more powerful rival, at the white concrete coli-
seum, its huge sign proclaiming simply, "Yankee Stadium.
Home of Champions." And, as the subway tunneled under
the Harlem River and our ears clogged, as the fragmented
discussions through the noise of the train grew louder, the
proclamation of the Stadium was echoed by the certainty in
our minds: we were going, on this weekend day in the early
summer, to see the Yankees win.

The Yankees won. The Yankees always won. Through my
childhood and adolescence, through puberty and pimples,
through the discovery of emotions and passions and rage and
exultation, that once central fact was an Eternal Verity. It
was not some fantasy of immaturity, like faith in the infalli-

bility of a father or the good will of strangers. It was a quantifiable truth. From the time I was six years old—when I first began to follow baseball continuously—to the time I was twenty-one, the Yankees won every pennant race but two. Fourteen pennants and ten World Series. To root for any other team—certainly any other team in the American League —was to be taught the lesson of Sisyphus. Each April, with faint hope tinged by certain resignation, those all-but-anonymous teams, no more authentic challengers than the Harlem Globetrotters' stooge teams, would begin pushing the stone up the hill. Sooner or later, perhaps by Labor Day, perhaps by mid-August, the Yankees, sitting on top of the mountain, would hurl the stone back down the hill.

And it was not simply *that* they won, but *how* they won, with a quality of expectation no more to be doubted than the income of an heiress clipping coupons. In their white executive pin-striped suits, the corporate emblem of New York austerely pinned to their hearts, the Yankees won with a serenity that made passion seem the vulgar display of lesser breeds. Let the St. Louis Browns, now the joke of the American League, cling to memories of the 1930s, the Marx Brothers antics of Pepper Martin and Dizzy Dean. Let the Brooklyn Dodgers, fated to lose World Series after World Series, swap tales of Babe Herman catching fly balls with his shoulder, or sending three men to the same base. For the Yankees, Joe DiMaggio was symbol enough; standing calmly in the endless acres of Yankee Stadium's center field, framed by the monuments and flagpole, moving with serenity before the batter swung, his long legs moving with the grace of a slow-motion film, somehow, always, reaching the long fly ball. DiMaggio always made the catch. The Yankees always won.

I was five years old the first time I went to Yankee Stadium, hanging on to my father, overwhelmed by the crowd in the subway, watching and feeling them push to the subway doors as my ears unclogged and we reached 161st Street and River Avenue, the signs of black letters on white wood reading, "Yankee Stadium." We walked up the stairs, as the older kids and the grownups ran past us, up the exit stairs, out into the sunlight latticed through the Jerome Avenue elevated subway line. Across the street were a cluster of baseball diamonds, with wire backstops and green wood bleachers.

"Is that where the Yankees play?" I asked my father.

No, he laughed, and pointed to an enormous concrete building, blocks wide. In there.

In *there? In* there? That's indoors. You can't play baseball indoors.

Around we walked, past the nuns sitting silently on wooden chairs, holding baskets into which an occasional passer-by would drop a coin, crossing himself as the nun mumbled something to him. Through Gate 6, the General Admission entrance, a pause at a wooden stand no bigger than a carnival barker's for a scorecard. Then up the inclined ramps, pushing uphill, past ramp after ramp, until we reached the upper grandstand and I saw, through the pillars and the crush of people, the unbelievably bright outfield grass, and the cluster of ballplayers batting, pitching, and catching under a brilliant sun.

It was, I remember, one of the most ludicrous games ever played at the Stadium, as though Puck had been umpire. The

Yankees beat the St. Louis Browns 20–2. All three Yankee catchers—Yogi Berra, Charlie Silvera, and Ralph Houk—were hit by pitched balls, and so outfielder Hank Bauer wound up catching. Tommy Byrne, the Yankee left-hander known through Mel Allen to a generation of fans as "that *goooooood* hittin' pitcher" and known to his teammates as "Wildman," balked three times. Balls took crazy bounces; throws went into dugouts and stands. And all through the carnage, my father shook his head, and said to me again and again, "You know, this isn't usually the way they play this game."

Never mind. It was enough to bring me back, again and again, always to feel the certain excitement when the "D" train pulled out of 155th Street and went under the river, always racing up the stairs at 161st Street and River Avenue, always running the full length to Gate 6, always racing up the ramps for that first glimpse of a sunlit ballfield. It was enough, too, for others; from 1946 through 1950, the Yankees drew two million or more people every year to the Stadium. It was, in my mind, the best possible way to spend a Sunday: reading the *Times* sports section, running down the batting averages for every player in the league, munching the tuna-fish sandwiches, sticky with the oil saturating the white bread in the sunlight, waiting for the Yankees to win.

As I try vainly to keep up with Ronald and his friends as they dart past people and fly up the exits, something strikes my eye this Opening Day of 1970, something I have never really noticed before: the neighborhood of Yankee Stadium. All the years before, the surroundings of the Stadium had seemed the merest ephemeral backdrop: a bar or two and a steam table

cafeteria along River Avenue, half hidden by the Jerome
Avenue subway; access roads to the Major Deegan highway
and the Willis Avenue bridge; the pennant and souvenir ven-
dors, as permanent to me as the lampposts. From inside the
Stadium, looking out past the bleachers, you could see a tenement or two, with enormous Gem Razor signs on the fronts
of the buildings, and the faces of people peering out over the
roof for a free look at the game. Out past the elevated subway stop, the Bronx County Courthouse, built in the Mus-
solini-Art Deco style of decades ago.

Now, shortly after 11 A.M., with no crowds and only a
brace or two of policemen, the neighborhood of Yankee Stadium stands out. It is one of those permanently transient,
broken neighborhoods of New York, the kind that line the
East River past 110th Street, with parking lots and deserted
warehouses, and enormous signs of long-bankrupted businesses painted on the sides. Here, hard by Yankee Stadium,
is Nationwide Auto Auction and Econ-o-Car headquarters,
their names painted up and down the brick walls. Across from
the General Admission gate is Baseball Joe's—a long clapboard lunch counter, with rain-faded mockups of frankfurters
daubed with off-yellow mustard, a hamburger turned rancid
by twenty years, a chocolate milkshake. "Eat at Baseball
Joe's," the sign beseeches. Not at eleven in the morning,
thank you.

When the Stadium first opened, in April 1923, the Grand
Concourse and the surrounding neighborhood were in the
flush of a renaissance. Property values soared; Babe Ruth hit
a home run; and the Grand Concourse Plaza Hotel, where
the visiting ball teams stayed, was an autograph hound's

paradise, and a symbol for every parent with a son nearing
Bar Mitzvah age, or a daughter who had finally snared her in-
tern. The neighborhood now is dying; the Concourse Plaza
is now a welfare hotel, to which the city pays hundreds of
dollars every month to house a family in legal squalor. And
the Yankees—come out and say it—the Yankees have stopped
winning.

The Yankees began playing baseball as the New York
Highlanders. In 1904 they lost the pennant by one game. In
1921 they won their first pennant; in 1923, their first World
Series. In all that time since the first victory fifty years ago,
the Yankees never went more than three years without winning a pennant. In the years of my lifetime, until 1964, they
had lost only six. Now, suddenly, the magic has stopped. Five
years have gone by without the Yankees winning. They have
known the ignominy of finishing in last place, a possibility
completely beyond rational understanding in my childhood.

Worse, the Yankees have been losing because they have
stopped hitting. With Babe Ruth, the Yankees changed baseball into a long-ball game; hitting was to the Yankees what
wit was to Shaw; no matter what else was missing, the
hitting was there. For the team not to hit 200 home runs in
one season was a bad year. In 1969 the entire team hit 94.
Look at it this way: in 1961, the year Roger Maris broke
Babe Ruth's record with an asterisk, Mantle and Maris alone
hit 115 home runs. So ingrained was the tradition of Yankee
power that ballplayers who, on other teams, would have carried the hitting load by themselves had to play in the shadow
of titans: Gehrig and Lazzari under Ruth, Heinrich and

Keller under DiMaggio, McDougald and Bauer under Mantle. Now, the hitting is gone.

So are the fans. The two million home spectators have vanished. The Press Guide says that in 1969 1,067,996 fans came
to the Stadium; and given the fact that Press Guides are at
times as accurate as the body counts from Indochina, it is at
least possible that in the year 1969 less than a million fans
paid their way into the Stadium for the first time since the
end of the Second World War.

The Stadium itself seems untouched by the decline in the
fortunes of the Yankees. Newly cleaned and painted for its
48th Opening Day, it is an appealing collection of brilliant
colors: the ticket windows, rounded turrets which look like
Moslem guardhouses, are bright red; the white concrete inside
sets off the bright blue seats. But there is, inside, one powerful reminder that things have changed: the sign that is not
there.

All through the 1940s and '50s, New York baseball was
surrounded by the smell and taste of sin: each of the three
metropolitan ball clubs was sponsored on radio and television
by beer and tobacco companies. Indeed, it was possible to
guess the team loyalty of fans gathered around a bar TV by
the beer they ordered and the products they smoked: Chesterfield Cigarettes for the Giants, Lucky Strike and Schaefer
Beer for the Brooklyn Dodgers [they called it "Dodger Beer"
in Flatbush], and for the Yanks, White Owl cigars and, for
more than twenty years, Ballantine Beer. So frequently were
these brands connected to feats of athletic skill by New York
announcers—a home run was "a White Owl wallop" or a
"Ballantine blast" at Yankee Stadium, a "Chesterfield clout"

at the Polo Grounds—that a generation of New York's kids could have contracted lung cancer or cirrhosis of the liver out of sheer enthusiasm.

But the Ballantine Beer sign, running the length of the enormous scoreboard, is not there. Ballantine Beer does not sponsor the New York Yankee broadcasts anymore.

It is about 11:15 A.M. as I stand in center field of Yankee Stadium, looking at the spot on the scoreboard where the Ballantine Beer sign used to be. Here, 450 feet from home plate, is one of the distinctive features of the Stadium: a trio of monuments, which used to mark the continuing tradition of Yankee greatness. Today, after five years of pennant-less mediocrity, they suggest overwhelmingly a sense of a lost past, a mocking reminder of a better time rather than present strength.

The cluster of monuments, lined up in front of the flag-pole, celebrate great Yankee names: Miller Huggins, the manager who won the first Yankee pennants and World Series ("He made priceless contributions to baseball and on this field brought glory to the New York club of the American League"), Henry Louis Gehrig ("A man—a gentleman —and a great ballplayer"), and George Herman "Babe" Ruth ("A great ballplayer. A great man. A great American"). Each bears a bronze plaque with the likeness of the ballplayer. Babe Ruth's also bears graffiti, from John, GM, and MF.

Ten feet back, against the center-field bleacher wall, are plaques honoring the late general manager Edward Barrow ("molder of a tradition of victory") and the late owner of the Yankees, beer king Jacob Ruppert ("gentleman, American, sportsman"). Several feet to the right is a plaque honoring the 1965 Mass that Pope Paul VI celebrated at the Stadium. Looking at the plaques and monuments now, for the first time in years, I am struck by how much they appear, in the midst of the bright green turf and the stillness of the empty ballpark, like tombstones and memorials in a cemetery.

We used to argue a lot about those monuments, sitting in the upper-deck General Admission stands, in sections 2 or 4 directly behind home plate, watching the Yankees take batting practice in the hours before the game was supposed to start.

"How far do ya haf ta hit the ball to get it over those monuments?"

"Look, stupid. If it's 461 feet to center field, you got ta hit the ball 450 feet to hit a monument."

"Oh yeah? Then how come nobody ever did it?"

"Whaddya *mean*, nobody did it. Sure they did it."

"Yeah? Who?"

"Hank Greenberg."

"Dollar bet. No, come on, Ira, dollar bet."

We used to argue a lot about a lot of things that might happen, or should happen, at the Stadium. For example, there was the mystique of hitting a fair ball out of Yankee Stadium. With its three decks rimming the Stadium, its deep bleachers stretching from right-center to left-center field, the Stadium was so built that no major league ballplayer had ever hit a fair ball clear out of Yankee Stadium.

"There's only one place you could do it. Over the back of the right-field bull pen wall."

"No, down the right-field foul line."

"No, man, look. You haf ta get it over all those three decks along the line. So the trajectory means you have to hit like 480 feet. But the right-field bull pen wall is only about 12 feet high. So if ya hit it right on a line with the bull pen, you could do it with about 450 feet."

"No, look. How about the left-field bull pen?"

Jeers and groans.

"Look, stupid. The *left*-field bull pen is 80 feet further back. And besides, it's not lined up with home plate. You'd haf ta clear the left-field third deck to do it."

Then one day, on Memorial Day, 1956, against the Washington Senators, in the fifth inning, with two men on and the Yankees behind 1–0, Mickey Mantle came to bat, swinging left-handed, against Pedro Romas. As soon as he swung on that 2–2 pitch, we all knew it was a home run. The Senators' right fielder literally did not take a step, except to turn around and stare in awe. And suddenly, from the right-field stands, came an enormous cheer of shocked amazement: the ball had gone *over* the upper deck and, for an instant, the fans thought the ball had gone out of the ballpark. It hit the façade of the corniced roof, 107 feet above the field, and 18 inches below the top of the roof. The buzz of excitement went on for nearly an entire inning. And when we would come back to the Stadium, later that summer, and in later seasons, we would point out to right field and talk of what we had seen.

This, however, was an outsize feat. Looking back on the days—perhaps fifty, perhaps a hundred—that I spent at Yankee Stadium, the one that stands for the most, I think, is another Opening Day: this one in 1952.

It was not, really, an Opening Day—it was more like an inauguration of a new President in a small, secure Caribbean dictatorship. In those days, the Yankees would celebrate every Opening Day by hanging not only last year's pennant and World Series flags out—since they always won, there was always a flag—but the flags of all the other years. By 1952 there were enough to hang from the Stadium roof from the farthest reaches of right field back down to home plate and all the way out to left field.

The transfer of power was more than metaphorical. The year before, at the end of 1951, Joe DiMaggio had retired after fifteen years as the Yankees' center fielder. On this day, DiMaggio walked out to home plate, in a business suit, with his uniform folded, ready for presentation to the Hall of Fame at Cooperstown, New York, the number 5 shining clear and bright. From behind home plate I sat, dressed in my Yankee uniform with its felt number 5 on my back, under the official Yankee warm-up jacket, my eyes looking out under the visor of my official Yankee cap, my toes inevitably tangling up in my official Yankee baseball sox. We stand and cheer the old order yielding—and a few moments later, cheer the symbol of the new.

In 1952 the Yankees were heading into the last half of their journey to a feat which no baseball club ever achieved before or since: the winning of five consecutive World Series titles. (The club which had won four was, of course, the Yankees, 1936–39. The only club ever to win five straight pennants was, of course, the Yankees, 1960–64.) This day in 1952, the awards for the previous season were given out; and we knew without question the Yankee tradition would continue.

Who was the American League rookie of the year? Gil McDougald, New York Yankees.

Who was the American League's most valuable player? Yogi Berra, New York Yankees.

Who was the outstanding World Series player of 1951? Phil Rizzuto, New York Yankees.

Who won the New York sportswriters Page One award? Pitcher Allie Reynolds, New York Yankees.

The pageant approached the ridiculous. The top baseball executive was George Weiss, general manager of the New York Yankees. And the top sports broadcaster for 1951—Mel Allen, the voice of the Yankees, whose blend of southern drawl and Jewish wisdom taught generations of us to announce our own sandlot games, standing in Riverside Park, stepping past the dog droppings, intoning silently to ourselves, "and it's a drive to deep left field, that ball is going, going—no, Greenfield makes a *great*, leaping one-handed catch —how about that!"

I am sure that if they had given out awards for the best stadium franks, Harry M. Stevens, of the New York Yankees, would have won hands down.

There are no more Harry M. Stevens franks in the Stadium. The concession stands are now sleeky modern, with back-lit color pictures of shrimp rolls. Trefe comes to the Concourse. The back-packs of watery orange juice are gone too, carried by the high school dropouts; so vivid was the memory of those unwieldy tanks of ersatz orange drink, that when I saw Neil Armstrong step onto the surface of the moon the first thought I had was: "My God! Orange juice on the moon!" And the frankfurters—they don't call them frankfurters anymore, but Ballpark Franks; evidently a surrender to that universal cynicism which has now penetrated so deeply that a customer cannot reason for himself that a frankfurter bought at a ballpark qualifies as the Real Thing.

Looking around the Stadium, walking slowly back to the Yankee dugout from center field, I remember what has triggered this flood of other days; this sense, not of the excitement of a new season, but of sadness for something gone and irreplaceable. It was a radio ad for the Yankees; an ad which, lacking anything to say about the Yanks of 1970, was reduced to playing that fragment of the Simon and Garfunkel song: "Where have you gone, Joe DiMaggio, a nation turns its lonely eyes to you . . ."*

The Yankee Clubhouse: if there was a single place I dreamed of being as a child, a wholly inaccessible sanctuary, it was the Yankee Clubhouse. With a vision shaped by innumerable baseball books (for ages twelve to sixteen, read, precociously, from eight to eleven) and a hundred commercials for hair tonic and Desenex, I saw the clubhouse vividly and distinctly: tiled floors, metal lockers, with touseled players laughing, swapping jokes, and exchanging affectionate grins with the youthful batboy, whose whispered suggestion of a

* From "Mrs. Robinson" © 1968 Paul Simon, Charing Cross Music, Inc. Used with the permission of the publisher.

suicide squeeze into the manager's ear had pulled out the crucial game. You have one guess as to the identity of the youthful batboy, hailed as a hero in the sports columns of New York.

The clubhouse, however, is a spacious suite of rooms, with light green wall-to-wall carpeting, and a three-walled cubicle for each player, with shelves, hangers, and stools. The paraphernalia of the Vitalis-Desenex lockerroom, the showers, whirlpool baths, and treatment machines for torn ligaments, are in a room to the right. A separate office, comfortable and sedate, more in keeping with the workroom of a junior partner in a medium-sized New York law firm, is set aside for the manager.

The players enter the clubhouse from a flight of three or four stairs, which brings them quickly from the Players' Entrance of the Stadium into their sanctuary. They park at a special lot in Cromwell Avenue, just down from Baseball Joe's. Flanking the lot across the street from the Stadium, restrained by yellow police sawhorses, are pockets of kids, nylon-jacketed and Yankee-capped. They wave their scraps of paper and, each time a tanned, well-built, modishly dressed Yankee enters, the papers wave and a high-pitched buzz garbles out the name of the new hero.

"Ellis! Ellis!"

"Kekitch! Kekitch! Hey, Mike! Here!"

The players walk straight out the lot, sign a few pieces of paper, and move swiftly, straight ahead, to the Players' Entrance. Since the same kids are toward the parking lot, the same kids get all the autographs; one tiny fan, no more than eight years old and three and a half feet tall, keeps jumping up and down, waving a piece of paper which appears like the life jacket on a sea of taller, older bodies. There is, for all of his energy, nothing on his paper, and there will be nothing when game time starts.

In the clubhouse, something incongruous catches my eye. A bulletin board. More than the coffee break, more than the glass-steel office building, it is the bulletin board that speaks to me of corporate America; the mindless memoranda, the faded list of detailed rules for a crisis that will never happen again, the distant, metallic voices of people making decisions who never speak to the people who walk by and read, and note the new mindless lists to replace the old mindless lists, and shake their heads, and move on.

Here, just to the left of the clubhouse door, is just such a board; three notices, each dated April 2, 1970, each from the American League Professional Baseball Clubs, 520 Boylston Street, Boston, Massachusetts 02116, Joseph E. Cronin, President, are pinned to the cork.

Who wrote these rules I do not know; perhaps a graduate from a night law school, doomed to fail the bar exam, who now ghosts *obiter dicta* for Mr. Justice Cronin; perhaps a sleek, six-figure income general counsel declaims the order. They are models of the Death Voice of Corporate America. *Decorum, decorum über alles:* "All players of the club at bat must be on the bench except when they have some duty to perform as coaches, baserunner, batsmen, or succeeding batsmen . . . only pitchers and catchers will be permitted to stand in the bull pen during the game. *Exception:* a substitute player who will enter the game at the end of the half inning will be permitted to warm up in the bull pen . . . players who are participating in the game will not be allowed to lie down or sit on the bases when time is called . . ."

At one level, this dream of a spinster fifth-grade teacher for good posture and silence approaches a compulsion toward neo-religious subservience: "the succeeding batsman must occupy *and kneel* in the spot indicated." And kiss the plate umpire's World Series ring?

Ralph Houk looks like a manager. The sports lore of John R. Tunis and Duane Decker's Blue Sox books, the images of the fictionalized film versions of the lives of baseball stars, the back pages of the *News* and *Mirrors* and *Posts*, they have all taught us that a baseball manager is stocky, grizzled, leather-faced, with a hefty chaw of tobacco jammed in his cheek. Here is Ralph Houk, stocky, grizzled, leather-faced, looking like the ex-Marine he is, with an enormous wad of chewing tobacco jammed in his left cheek. He is standing in back of the batting practice cage, one foot propped up on the rail, one hand stuck into the back pocket of his uniform, staring straight ahead as his team warms up.

Ralph Houk was one of those Yankees whose existence in the early 1950s was a matter of doubt. He was a catcher, the third-string catcher on a team that never seemed to need him. Yogi Berra, a folk hero of undeniable ability and unbelievable syntax, was all but indestructible as the Yankee catcher. On those rare days when injury or a rest put him out of action, Charlie Silvera would back him up. Ralph Houk was a bull pen catcher, a warm-up catcher. And suddenly, in 1961, there was Houk as Yankee Manager; and, like clockwork, his teams won three straight World Series titles.

Like a successful commanding general, his battlefield triumphs a part of his country's history, Houk stepped out of the uniform into the business suit of general manager; and, from his new vantage point, he watched the machine fall apart. A pennant in 1964 under manager Yogi Berra, then a loss in seven games to the St. Louis Cardinals. The dismissal of Berra, and the hiring of Johnny Keane, St. Louis Cardinal Manager who had inflicted the Series defeat. And, in the 1965 season, complete collapse—a sixth-place finish, unheard of, unimaginable. By June 1966, Johnny Keane was dead and Ralph Houk was back as the Yankee Manager—and he has found that no manager can lead a team that bats .235 into a pennant, or even respectability.

Reporters and cameramen are wandering around the field, looking for Colorful Quotes, the Spark of Human Interest. A cluster of writers stand silently around Houk, watching him watch the hitters, one foot on the rail, staring through the wire batting cage.

"Do you remember your first awareness of the opening of the baseball season?"

"Prob'ly with the Eagles," Houk deadpans.

"The *Eagles?*" "What Eagles is this?"

Houk grins slowly.

"Eagles Lodge. Lawrence, Kansas."

General laughter.

"How many games did they play?" "Helluva team that must have been." "No lights, eh?"

"Naw," Houk says. "Twilight."

A photographer asks him to pose. Houk, still chatting with a sportswriter, slips his sunglasses off his face, into his hand,

and out of sight behind his back. Instantly, two, three, half a dozen cameramen cluster around. If one of their number is shooting at something, it must be worth while. A newsman is questioning his colleagues who talked with Houk.

"Whattid he say? Was he nervous about Opening Day or excited?"

One of the fundamental truths of childhood is that everyone is older than you are. Apart from an aberrational child entertainer, or prodigy at the keyboard, there are simply you and Grownups, all of whom are roughly the same age, except for really old people. Baseball players, of course, are Grownups too, only better.

Watching the Yankee players on the field, throwing a baseball back and forth, waiting to take their turn at bat, I am struck by the fact that I am older than all of them. John Ellis, a twenty-one-year-old catcher-first baseman who has won a large chunk of preseason press comment, looks like a dozen people from my college days. Affable, pleasant-looking, he could well be the treasurer of a reasonably popular fraternity at the University of Wisconsin. He, pitcher Steve Hamilton, and a few others are forming a pepper game behind home plate; a handful of players, grouped dangerously close to a batsman, field sharp grounders and throw the ball back to the batter, who in turn hits another shot right back at them.

The banter is casual, distant; the sounds echo back to my past: to twilight at a Summer Camp, between dinner and the Evening Activity, when the counselors with sweatshirts from Hunter and Brooklyn, NYU and Michigan, would get out the gloves and the forbidden hardballs, and swap tales of the lubricious evening to come as they swept the ball back and forth; to a Saturday morning on the first warm day in spring at college, when the Bermuda shorts and polo shirts were broken out.

"*Look* out there." "Comin' at ya." "Atta way to *go*, baby!" "Aaaayyyy! Way to *go!*"

From behind me, through the dugout, a voluble, reasonably off-key voice warbles the last Beatles song, "Let It Be." It is Mike Kekitch, the twenty-five-year-old second-year pitcher.

"Hey, meatball!" he yells good-naturedly to an old groundskeeper. "Don't you know we got a game today?"

"Yeah?" says the groundskeeper, Walter Brennan in a jacket. "So how come you showed up?"

In the midst of these young men, confident of their bodies in a way wholly alien to me, Elston Howard walks from the clubhouse tunnel into the dugout. Howard is one of the last links to a better time for the Yankees; a first-rate catcher-outfielder from the early '60s, the first black man ever to win a starting place with the Yanks. His face is weathered, calm. He squints out at the field.

"Goddam shadows gonna fall all over the dugout," he says. "It's gonna be tricky."

In the clubhouse a few minutes later, Howard talks about the old days, and the new team.

"I think we're on the way back . . . this year we added a lot of offense . . . I think we're gonna surprise a lot of people."

Not twenty minutes earlier, Manager Houk, talking with some reporters, notes that his team has youth and power.

"We're going to surprise a lot of people," Houk said.

The Stadium has people in it now. Ronald and his friends have waited outside for an hour and a half to buy six of the first General Admission seats. As batting practice begins, a few of his contingent race out to the short right-field stands, hoping to get a baseball. After half an hour of batting practice, one of Ronald's friends races back to the rest of the group, shouting hellos to the players from behind the dugout.

"Hey!" the messenger shouts. "Louis got a ball! Hey! He got a ball! Louis got a ball!"

"Next joke," says Ronald.

"He got a ball! Louis got a ball!"

"Cut it, will you?"

"Two-dollar bet," says the messenger. Inflation has touched us all.

"Yeah," says Ronald, "okay. Two-dollar bet." A growing uncertainty fills Ronald's eyes as the two pinkys reach toward each other, link, and pull. The messenger grins explosively.

"Okay, big shot, you owe me two dollars. Louis got a ball ten minutes ago. Munson hit it." Like a cue, Louis, flushed with excitement and smeared with dirt on his T-shirt, approaches, clutching a baseball in his right hand.

"Hey! You got a ball. Jesus."

"Lemme see!"

"Boy, Ron," says an observer. "You owe Mike two dollars."

"Look at that catch," says Ronald.

Understandable as Ronald's interest in the ballplayers is right now, many of his peers find the batting practice far less interesting than another source of attention: the growing press of recognizable radio and television reporters now moving through the stands, interviewing fans out at Opening Day.

If the kids are eleven, twelve, fourteen, fifteen, then they literally cannot remember when television was not a part of their lives. For them, the men and women who tell them what is going on are more vivid, more familar, and therefore more authentically celebrities than the people they are telling us about. Outside the Stadium earlier, the single biggest hand, the most authentic excitement, has gone not to any of the Yankees, but to Phil Rizzuto, former shortstop, now one of the Yankee broadcasters, as he entered the press gate resplendent in a fur coat, his gray hair styled to perfection. Inside the stands, a crush of people crowd the aisle where Melba Toliver, a feature reporter for Channel 7, is trying to interview a fan. As a man in a topcoat walks by with a cassette tape recorder, an eight-year-old boy shouts: "Hey! What channel?"

It is, to me, a matter of supreme self-restraint that the managers of baseball teams permit anyone with a television camera within two miles of a ballpark. More than anything else, television has destroyed baseball, stripped away its title of National Pastime, not out of malice, but by the nature of baseball and the nature of television.

Baseball is a slow game; leisure is built into it—the long waits between innings, the pauses between each batter's appearance at the plate, the time outs for hurried conferences on the pitcher's mound, the minutes of inaction as a pitcher and batter duel between them as the count runs to three balls, two strikes. It is also a distinctly linear game, an assembly-line kind of game. Each man comes to bat, like so many cans being filled on a conveyor belt, one after the other. The batter's job is to advance each man, step-by-step, around the bases, one after another. Every three outs, the machine shifts over. Unlike every other major sport, in which the action is electric, simultaneous, baseball is segmented.

To a spectator at a ballpark, this is part of the charm of the game. Excitement, at crucial moments, accumulates as the catcher and infielders confer with the pitcher. The between-innings rest is a time not only for a beer and a quick visit to the men's room, but also for second-guessing, analysis, and, above all, comparisons with other games. Because the fundamental fact about baseball is that it is a game of accumulation; statistics are as much of the game as the actual play. What did this pitcher do in past seasons? How has this batter been doing against this team, this year and in past seasons?

The moments of real action, too, almost demand being there. On television, baseball is a game either of a pitcher throwing to a catcher, or of almost minuscule animals running around. At the ballpark, baseball's moments of excitement are real. Take an example: two men on base. A batter hits a long fly into the outfield. As a spectator, you are watching everything at once, calculating possibilities. Will the center fielder reach the ball in time? If not, can the man on first score? Will the shortstop cut off the throw to the plate and try to nail the hitter as he tries to stretch a double into a triple? If the ball is caught, will the man on third be doubled up? Will he try to tag up and, if he does, will he be thrown out at the plate?

Television captures none of this. Baseball is, perhaps, the only major sport where a slow-motion instant replay adds almost nothing to an appreciation of the game. When a player hits a home run, we have *seen* it; there is nothing more to be gained from slow motion except that it looks slower. Television, then, is a device which has enhanced football and basketball, which is learning to come to grips with the incredible speed of ice hockey, but which simply emphasizes the slow pace of baseball without capturing its depth and subtleties. Add to that the incredible number of games televised any given year—more than two hundred in the New York area—and you have the spectacle of fans saturated at home with a game that, on a twenty-five-inch screen, isn't worth the time.

But the TV emissaries are here, like accomplices helping to report on the death of their victim. Outside the park, two camera crews are sitting and waiting, talking out the same conversation that camera crews seem to indulge in at every event they cover:

"We also have an option, there, if you retire early, like at fifty-five, you draw a high pension . . . I'll have twenty-seven years at sixty-two, and I figured out . . ."

Game time is nearing. It is crowded inside the Yankee Clubhouse. The players are exchanging autographs with each other. Houk walks in, spits a dollop of tobacco juice into a wastebasket, and goes into his office. In the midst of middle-aged reporters with sports jackets and ties and youthful athletes in their underwear, an old man, frail and perhaps past eighty, walks in. Nobody seems to know who he is—at least, none of the players. But some of the Yankee executives pay him deference. He walks over to the cubicle where John Ellis, the highly touted rookie, is answering the questions of reporters.

"John," the old man says weakly, "I've got a note here," and the reporters strain to read it over his shoulder.

"It's from Mrs. Lou Gehrig. It says: 'John: for thirty years I've been looking for Lou's successor (if not better). Today, I'm looking for you.' You keep that, John." The old man hands it to Ellis and walks away.

"Who was that old fellow?" somebody asks one of the Yankees. He shrugs and shakes his head. So as Larry McPhail, one of the general managers of the Yankees in their greatest days, and father of the current general manager, walks away, he is met by blank stares and an occasional warm hello from the older executives who remember a better time.

They used to do it right, this Opening Day ceremony. The pennants and World Series flags would fly. Mel Allen, the master of ceremonies, would introduce the World Series victors, officiate at the various player and manager awards, and call out the names of the Yankees from the last year as they received their World Series rings. Major Francis Sutherland's 7th Regiment Band would play patriotic music. Lucy Monroe would sing "The Star-Spangled Banner," and the color guard would raise the American and World Series flags. The Mayor would throw out the first ball, and everyone would boo. The Yankees would take the field, and everyone would cheer. If forty thousand people weren't there, it would be because it was raining.

Opening Day, 1970, is a bright, sunny day, chilly but not cold, but there are barely twenty thousand people in the ballpark. Mel Allen isn't there; he was fired as the Voice of the Yankees in 1964 after twenty-five years as their chief announcer. Lucy Monroe is not singing "The Star-Spangled Banner." The band is from Flushing High School. Only Bob Shephard, the Yankees' deep-voiced public address announcer, provides any link with other times. Whitney Young, Executive Director of the Urban League, throws out the first ball.

"What did *he* hit last year," a fan yells.

Robert Merrill, the Metropolitan Opera star, sings the National Anthem and the game is under way.

It isn't much of a game. The Red Sox, once traditional rivals of the Yankees and perennial pennant contenders, now simply another team, are the opponents. In the late '40s, the Red Sox were managed by former Yankee manager Joe McCarthy, and sparked by Ted Williams and Dom DiMaggio, Joe's younger brother. The Red Sox always came close. The Yankees always beat them.

By the fifth inning, the Red Sox have a 4-0 lead. Out in center field, the scoreboard is flashing out welcomes: Mrs. Babe Ruth, Ned Irish (head of Madison Square Garden), James Farley (F.D.R.'s Postmaster General and political advisor), ex-Mayor Robert Wagner.

In the sixth inning a flicker of excitement springs up. A hit batsman. A walk. A base hit into left field, a throw home that goes wild, and suddenly the score is 4-1, but the

Yankees have men on second and third with nobody out—
the single best position for a team at bat, since not even the
prospect of a bases-loaded double-play can spoil the sense of
anticipation. The crowd is cheering, stamping its feet, clapping.

Now Curt Blefary is up. The count goes to two strikes.
He swings and slams the ball deep into left field; it bounces
up into the stands for an automatic double and two runs
score. It has taken perhaps eight seconds, but it has been
eight seconds that a television screen will never capture:
the ball shooting into left field, the two Yankee runners
wheeling around the bases, the fielders moving to relay a
possible throw to home or third. The Yankees now trail by a
run, 4–3. One hour later, and one Yankee hit later, the game
ends with the same score.

With the last Yankee out in the bottom half of the ninth
inning, a curious and revealing reaction occurs: hundreds
of kids leap over the railings of the stands; from behind home
plate, from up and down the right- and left-field foul lines,
from the bleachers in the outfield, they elude the red-jacketed
ushers and pour onto the field, jumping up and down on the
pitcher's mound, sliding into home plate, and ripping up the
outfield grass.

"Look at 'em," a voice says. "Just like the Mets."

Exactly so. Three times in 1969, we watched on television
as thousands of jubilant kids pillaged Shea Stadium—after
the Mets won their division title, after they won the pennant, and after they won the World Series. Television
brought into these homes the sanctified ritual of celebration
—of wild pandemonium. To the celebrants today, it doesn't
matter that the team they rooted for did not win; it doesn't

matter that the Yankees might finish in fourth or fifth place; it doesn't matter that they have nothing to celebrate. They might have missed being at Shea Stadium last year, but, by God, they know how to do what they see on the tube.

Behind the lower stands in right field is a "Yankee Hall of Fame." Along a wall is a series of blown-up, lit-from-behind photos of Yankee stars from the past; by picking up a telephone, you can hear a tape-recorded message, either from the players, or from the people who remembered men like Ruth, Gehrig, Lazzari, Miller Huggins, DiMaggio, Tommy Heinrich, Charlie "King Kong" Keller, Berra, Whitey Ford, Vic Rashi, Allie Reynolds, and other players who brought pennant after pennant to the Stadium.

Looking at these pictures from ten and twenty and thirty years ago, remembering the scoreboard flashing out its greetings to the men who once held power in New York, I suddenly see the Yankees, the Stadium, the world of Sunday subways and brown bags, in a new context.

There are, in New York, living artifacts of other times; neighborhoods, buildings, restaurants which speak of cars with rounded hoods, women in feathered hats, nightclubs, the *Daily Mirror,* and Walter Winchell in six hundred newspapers. Ride in the dying breed of a Checker Cab down Park Avenue: as the avenue splits in two and weaves around Grand Central, as it speeds south past the Art Deco East Side Airlines Terminal, you will know what I mean. It evokes the Broadway Limited, with its red carpet and the white-toothed, nappy-haired Pullman porter; it evokes ocean liners, steaming into New York Harbor, as newsmen swarmed aboard to record the comments and predictions of notables; it suggests the Empire State Building as the symbol of power, with men like Farley and Wagner and Al Smith controlling the destiny of the city; a time before television and Astro-Turf.

The Yankees once did not need their own Hall of Fame; they sent out the players to fill the real one at Cooperstown; once they embodied their past in their present, stirring memories by what their fans saw out in center field or at the plate now. But the spark is gone; it may well be that there will not be another Yankee dynasty for decades. Indeed, with the collapse of the farm system—another casualty of television, for who wants to pay to watch Buffalo when you can see New York for free—it may well be that the Yankees as we knew them and relied on them will never appear again. And so now there are two more plaques on that cemetery in center field; plaques which honor Joe DiMaggio and Mickey Mantle, who once stood there themselves, providing the backbone for year after year of glory and honor. And so now the Yankees seek to sell themselves on what they once did, and what they may never do again.

Ronald and his friends are riding the Jerome Avenue subway downtown. At 149th Street, they will change for the Seventh Avenue express, which they will ride down to Penn Station. The Knicks are heading for a National Basketball Association championship, and they are hoping to cage tickets for the game.

"Boys," says one of the troupe, "that stunk."

"Ronald, you owe me two dollars. Louie got a ball."

"Yeah," Ronald says, twisting the subject again. "What a dull game."

THE FIRST DAYS OF TELEVISION

EAVESDROPPING ON THE ELDERS

TUNING IN

Tuesday night, 8 P.M. The shops are closing all over town, the bars crowding in, three and four deep. The service-station quartet sings: "We are the men from Texaco, we work from Maine to Mexico . . ." Street-corner pitchman Sid Stone, pork-pie hat and checked coat, hovering over his open suitcase: "Ya say ya not satisfied? Ya say ya want more faw ya money? (clap) Tell ya what I'm gonna do." Any second now, any . . .

And there he is, front teeth blacked out, boggle-eyed, staggering across the stage dressed like Cupid or an Easter Bunny, or—often—in a woman's dress, pearls, and wig, giving aid and comfort to a generation of transvestites, shotgunning one-liners into the audience, interrupting himself, stalking back and forth across the stage: "And now, ladies and germs . . . I fwcar, I'll hit you a *millllll*yun times . . . a whatthe*heyyy* . . . o.k., let's make up." "Maaaaake-up!" screams a stagehand, racing across the stage to belt him in the face with a powder puff. Coarse, vulgar, goofy-faced Milton Berle—and at last we did not need the sound of a studio audience, laughing at something we could not see to tell us something riotous was happening. It was right in front of our eyes . . .

The spotlessly clean house shines on the spotlessly clean street in a spotlessly clean neighborhood. Spotlessly clean Ozzie shuffles into the living room, hands in the pockets of his cardigan sweater, shuffling with infinite patience—a reasonable speed for a man with no visible means of support.

"Er . . . uh . . . oh, dear, have . . . have you . . . seen . . . the . . . the paper?"

Harriet bustles out of the fifteen-thousand-dollar kitchen, wiping her hands on an apron, with a smile hinting of an incipient migraine.

"Gee, dear, Ricky may have seen it."

A grimace of concentration, then a flicker of understanding crosses Ozzie's face.

"Uh, oh, well . . . gee, I . . . I was . . . hoping . . ."

The door flies open. A dark-haired, irrepressible boy, grinning irresistibly, bounds in.

"Hi, Pop. Hi, Mom. I gave the paper to Dave to give to Thorny to read." He flies out, winking and grinning.

Ozzie begins to frown.

"Oh . . . uh . . . well . . . gee, dear, I . . . I wanted to . . . to read the . . . the paper." Twenty-five minutes of this, and David comes home with the paper. The family crisis is resolved, and it is Listerine's turn to present another crisis: "He said/that she said/that he had Halitosis."

The man with the widow's peak, piercing eyes, and deep furrows in his brow is staring straight at us in his cramped studio, little more than a desk piled high with papers and three TV monitors behind him. Other nights he is chit-chatting with a movie star, or interviewing Julius Caesar just before the Ides of March. But not tonight. Tonight Edward R. Murrow is in earnest.

"We will not be driven by fear into an age of unreason, if we dig deep into our own history and our doctrine and remember that we are not descended from fearful men, not from men who feared to write, to speak, to associate, and to defend causes which were for the moment unpopular. This is no time for men who oppose Senator McCarthy's methods to keep silent. We can deny our heritage and our history, but we cannot escape responsibility for the result. There is no easy way for a citizen of a republic to abdicate his responsibilities."

A few months later, from a Senate hearing room, the sprightly face of an old Yankee, Joseph Welch, is a mask of controlled rage.

"Until this moment, sir, I never gauged your recklessness . . . have you no sense of decency, sir, at long last? . . ."

For almost half an hour, the man with the horn-rimmed glasses and the intense stare, broken by a quick smile, has been winding his way through a history of human hair. Now, as the midafternoon sun glints off Channel 9, he is into the climax.

"You say you don't believe Lanolin can make a difference? My friend, science says you're wrong. Because, friend, Lanolin is a product of the natural, scientific, God-given body chemistry of sheep. I ask you: *have you ever seen a bald-headed sheep?*" Even before we learn the name of the product [Charles Antell Formula #9] the pencil and paper is out. Damn right we've never seen a bald-headed sheep.

A silver-haired cowboy in a black and silver outfit swings off the white horse.

"Easy, Topper," he says endearingly, and strides into the bunkhouse of the Bar 20 Ranch to rouse his men.

"Lucky, round up a posse. Bart Slime's kidnapped the judge's daughter."

Gabby Hayes throws down his tin plate and wipes flecks of grub into his beard. He stamps his feet, swings his fist, and growls: "Wh-h-h-h-y, them dirty no-good varmints. C'mon, Hoppy, let's go get 'em." When Hopalong Cassidy fights, it is just. When he kills, it is necessary. What he stands for is right.

The frenetic, wild-eyed man is cavorting his way through the night on *Broadway Open House*. He laughs a lot. He sings a brassy, loud song: "Flash! bam! alakazam! Wonderful you walked by." He brings out a blonde with a stupendous chest. He reads a poem, breathing deeply. No one is listening. Everyone is watching. "Thank you, Dagmar," leers Jerry Lester. "That was big of you." Four gags about Gorgeous George.

Gorgeous George, his hair ludicrously curly and long, almost down to his *shoulders,* is locked in mortal combat with the Zebra Kid. At ringside, Hatpin Mary is in hysterics, urging mayhem and murder. Announcer Dennis James is painting a vivid picture of the carnage, occasionally snapping dog bones against the microphones to suggest even greater carnage. The next day, James will be in the studios of Channel 5, flagship of the DuMont Television Network, hosting a show called *O.K., Mother,* which showers sewing machines on middle-aged women whose fondest desire is to grab Dennis James onto their laps, so they can hug and kiss him.

The hearing room in Manhattan is somber, the audience tense. We can see the craggy face of Estes Kefauver, the slightly built, moon-faced Committee Counsel, Rudolph Halley, asking questions whose content—blackmail, extortion, murder—is belied by his near-comical lisp. The camera shifts, not to another face, but to a pair of hands playing with a pair of eyeglasses. A million irons rest on a million ironing boards. A gangster and a Senator are face to face, and it is in our living room the moment it is happening.

THE ARRIVAL

So totally, so completely has television conquered us that it is difficult to remember the images of twenty years ago;

it is as if they have been buried in an avalanche of color pictures and instant replays and the immeasurable trillions of projections that have flooded our living rooms and our minds. There were seven thousand television sets in use in 1946. There are nearly ninety million today. For this country, now discovering the anguish of a lost sense of community and a growing sense of our isolation from each other, television is the single common experience we know we share with our countrymen, other than birth, lust, taxation, and death. By the time we reach adolescence, we have spent twenty thousand hours watching television. Apart from sleep, we will have done nothing else so consumingly.

I am part of the last generation that remembers when television began. For our younger brothers and sisters, it was there from the day they were born, as natural a part of the environment as chairs and walls, and far more absorbing. For postwar America, however, television was a kind of spoil of war, a down payment on the wondrous world promised our parents in all those magazine ads they scanned in barracks and foxholes, or during coffee breaks on assembly lines. Work, win, defeat the inhuman foe, said *Life* and *Look* and *Time* and *Ladies' Home Journal,* and we will give you a brave new world of high-speed trains, push-button homes, a paradise built by the technology now harnessed for war. Television was a marvel of the 1930s, perfected and demonstrated in time for the 1938 World's Fair. But the War froze the development of television; and thus, the children of the War Baby boom became the younger generation to first gaze on the miracle of television; a device which was to prove the most subversive of influences upon the young; not because of violence or sex, but because of what it showed us of the way our Elders really thought and spoke and acted when not conscious of the pieties with which children are to be soothed and comforted. But a moment, please. There is time enough for that.

For the War Babies, the new era began the Day They Brought the Set: an enormously awesome machine, covered with dials and wood, encasing a screen of seven, perhaps ten inches. Our parents, their faces a blend of excitement and fear, bit off words we were not supposed to hear as they twisted dials back and forth, praying that by such homage they could wipe away the dreaded Vertical Flip from the Stromberg-Carlson or the Philco. We were ordered across the length of the room to guard against damage to the eyes; like masturbation, television was a prime suspect in the battle against blindness.

It seemed to happen all at once, this conquest of television. At first, nobody owned a television set; that was a seminal fact of postwar life. It was always an uncle, or the lady downstairs, or the class klutz, shut out of parties, forced to play right field in ballgames—until his home became the after-school salon for *Howdy Doody* or *Uncle Fred's Junior Frolics* (Uncle Fred Sayles also being the vice-president and general manager of Channel 13 in New York, as well as its wrestling announcer and quite possibly typist). Then, slowly at first, then in a rush, the sets began to appear in the homes of the rest of us, and the new-found Best Friend sank back into obscurity. And we, huddled at the far corner of the living room, started to tune in the world.

BUT FIRST, A WORD FROM OUR SPONSOR

"There are some things a son or daughter won't tell you . . . Do you expect him to blurt out the truth—that he's really ashamed to be with the gang—because he doesn't see the same shows they see? . . . How can a little girl describe the bruise deep inside? . . . Can you deny television to your children any longer? Youngsters today need television for their morale as much as they need fresh air and sunshine for their health."

—From a 1950 newspaper ad by the
American Television Dealers and
Manufacturers' Association

THE CONQUEST

By the end of 1947 there were a million television watchers in America, mostly in the East, where NBC had established a four-city network. Apart from sports events, and an occasional Presidential speech, there was little worth watching. "Television," *Life* magazine wrote at the end of 1947, "has cruelly disinterred some of the hoariest acts in vaudeville. It has concentrated on its screens some of the worst aspects of radio. For lack of money or know-how, it boggles neither at impossible dramatics nor sword-swallowers nor witless chitchat."

Radio was still the dominant medium; the networks knew that it would be years before America bought enough television sets to persuade advertisers to pay large sums for the right to sell their wares on television. Through 1948, NBC was losing $13,000 a day on television; and the same hour of studio time on a Sunday night that cost $27,215 on network radio, cost $1,510 on television.

It would not be this way for long; it could not be. Television was a device that fit too perfectly into the mood of America after World War II. We had lived pressed against each other for four years: in training camps, on battlefields, in troopships and trains, the women linked together in offices, plants, and factories. Now we wanted Out; we wanted that patch of land, that house with a yard, that sense of ease and quiet away from each other. We had watched those movies with handsome men and beautiful women marching together, arms linked, with flags behind them and a patriotic air easing the burdens of faraway death and crowded living. Now it was time to separate, to find that new car and that home in the suburbs.

Television was both cause and effect of our national separation. It was a machine for people who do not need or seek the face-to-face company of other human beings. No need to drive to a movie theater or playhouse, no need to find conversation at a neighborhood bar or social club in a densely populated city community, or in the extended-family atmosphere of a small town, where an illness, a marriage in trouble, a good report card was common knowledge. Our parents could retreat to a new community, linked to work by highways, linked to a world of excitement and entertainment by a magic window. We could have isolation and communication at the same time.

And had anyone been prescient enough to instruct America as to the kind of society it was shaping in this postwar euphoria—had someone, for example, been wise enough to say, "Wait a moment; when you spend your evenings huddled in your own homes, you are unraveling the fabric of a neighborhood; kill the bars and social clubs and movies and soda fountains for late-night snacks, and you are pulling people off the streets, rendering your own communities havens for thugs; you are, further, losing human contact and, by turning life and other people into electric objects, to be summoned and dispatched at the flick of the wrist, you are lessening the collective estimation of human worth"— had anyone spoken such words in the late 1940s, would anyone have listened? No matter. No one spoke those words.

Instead, the first glimmering of something special on those picture-radios, and America turned to television in a rush; further feeding our atomization. In the fall of 1948, Milton Berle was featured in the *Texaco Star Theatre,* and television had its first super-attraction.

"Berle's farcical antics were, of course, invisible on radio, but may be a natural for television," *Newsweek* magazine theorized before *Texaco Star Theatre* went on the air; Philip Hamburger, the *New Yorker's* despairing critic of early TV, described him as "acutely repulsive." What made Milton Berle, of course, was that he was *visual.* For Americans used to radio comedians, dependent solely on jokes, ad libs, and timing, the idea of a man dressed as a woman careening across a stage, throwing pies in somebody's face, being brought directly into their living rooms was something fresh and exciting. It was not a use of television, in the sense that Ernie Kovacs and Sid Caesar would use TV to develop a new kind of comedy; but it was different enough to seize the national spotlight. As with Amos 'n' Andy a generation earlier, Milton Berle was for a time an institution. Movie theaters could not run shows at 8 P.M.; stores gave up late hours on Tuesday nights; bars, often the only establishment with a television set, found business leaping at 8 P.M. on Tuesdays, with crowds packing every square inch of space. And most important, at least to the people who ran the fledgling television networks, people started buying sets.

If Berle was a kind of outlandish burlesque, another key source of TV sales was starkly realistic: a Senate committee's hearings into organized crime. Day after day, Channel 11 in New York kept its cameras at a hearing room in lower Manhattan, where Senator Estes Kefauver was chairing a hearing into the practices of organized crime. We could hear Virginia Hill describe how she got her fur coats by being "friendly" to the right people; we could laugh at a mobster named Frank Erickson as he stammered: "I refuse to answer on the grounds that it might intend to criminate me." And we could watch Frank Costello, supposedly a top figure in organized crime, nervously jiggle his glasses as the camera, focusing on the hands and never on the face, added to the air of mystery.

Almost 70 percent of the sets in New York were tuned to the crime hearings; and around the country, local stations picked up Channel 11's feed. It caused a spurt in television sales; it made Estes Kefauver a nationally known politician; and it helped to complete the conquest of television of America's leisure habits that the Milton Berle phenomenon had begun. At the start of 1949—the first full year Berle was on NBC—radio accounted for 81 percent of broadcast audiences, television for 19 percent. By the end of the year, television was grabbing 41 percent of the broadcast audience. In May 1950, Baltimore became the first city in America where more broadcast hours were spent watching TV than listening to radio. By 1950's end, television had taken control: movie attendance among adults was down 72 percent; reading was down 29 percent; nightly radio use had dropped from three hours, forty-two minutes, to twenty-four minutes a night; and people were staying home 40 percent more often. It was possible to begin shaping an answer to the question: What did America do in the second half of the twentieth century? We were watching television.

PEEKING THROUGH THE OPEN CURTAIN

From the birth of mass communications, we have understood its revolutionary implications. Kings, presidents, nobility, captains of industry, can be seen posing around the new wireless; Marconi's latest refinement; DuMont's cathode rays; Morse's telegraph. (Presumably some courtier of Asia painted a portrait of a warlord beaming down on the genius who perfected rice paper, though this is pure conjecture.) The new communications would be a window on the world, a means of binding humanity together by enabling us to get to know each other, erasing distinctions built up and maintained by barriers of distance. (The fact that our worst wars have come in an age of constantly increasing communications is unsettling; but it is no doubt a quirk of fate, rather than a consequence of being better able to hear each other, thus honing our capacity for dislike and revulsion into a fine instrument.)

Of all those with great power, who welcomed new communications as a tool for the freedom of the human mind, only one seems to have spoken with total candor. Albert Speer, Hitler's architect and confidant, noted during the Nürnberg trials that mass communication and information had been a critical instrument for consolidating totalitarian control; it was impossible for the clear command of a Maximum Leader to be diluted through passage of time or length of distance. Every wish of the Führer was sent instantly across the length and breadth of the German Empire; no local official would have time or space as a refuge from which to undermine, say, the Final Solution of the Jewish Question.

America had seen, in an earlier generation, the capacity of radio and mass magazines to impose tastes on a national audience, and to obliterate the regional tastes of a sprawling nation. The American Tobacco Company, for example, was founded as a consolidation of dozens of small, locally distributed tobacco companies; with a common brand name, they could be advertised and sold nationally. A smoker, lured to cigarettes by the promise of sex and adventure in the pages of *Liberty*, could buy Lucky Strikes in California, or North Carolina, or Boston. Local brands could not afford the cost of advertising on a national medium; no more than local humor could withstand the onslaught of Amos 'n' Andy or Jack Benny. America was laughing at the same jokes in Grand Rapids as in Manhattan, and at the same time.

What all this suggests is that television should have been

a part of the pattern of increasing control of tastes and opinion; a source not of the greater freedom of which rulers speak when a new tool for the amplification of their voices is discovered, but a new source of blandness, and imposed acquiescence to the will of the Elders.

Ah, yes . . . And that explains why the first generation of television's children packed Sproul Hall in Berkeley in 1964 and were arrested by the hundreds; why they spent their summers in Lowndes County, Alabama, trying to register Negroes; why they formed the first core of resistance to the Vietnam War; why they and their younger brothers and sisters threw off the clothes, the life styles, the music, the politics, the assumptions of the Elders, with a fury and thoroughness never seen before. Let us try another explanation; an alternative to the idea that a powerful mass medium such as television automatically imposes what it shows on its audience.

How does a child lose his innocence? How does it happen that we discover that our father is not the strongest man in the world, that our mothers are not the most beautiful, that the homilies our principals speak at assemblies may not truly represent their innermost thoughts on Fair Play and Democracy? It happens, in large measure, through a process of Eavesdropping, deliberate or accidental; a series of events in which our Elders speak to or about each other in words they do not want us to hear: the coloreds are taking over the neighborhood; the boss is a liar and a cheat; the minister has been spending a *lot* of time with the young widow; the gym teacher and the dietician . . . the gym teacher and the *assistant* gym teacher . . . How many sudden, violent arguments in the kitchens of relatives during Thanksgiving dinner, hurriedly hushed because "the children are listening," does it take before a child understands that the people we are supposed to love and cherish are not held in such repute by those instructing us of our familial obligation? How many dark looks across the turkey and references to past good deeds betrayed, does it take before we start to perceive, no matter how dimly, ominous currents of hatred coursing through the existence of our Elders?

With the coming of television into our homes, the Eavesdropping, the look at a way of life supposed to be shielded from our eyes, became a nightly occurrence. Simply by switching on a dial, we could watch the Elders portray life the way they really thought it was, unfiltered by pleasant illusions. An effectively totalitarian society—one, that is, with the capacity to impose thought patterns on the young, instead of merely the desire—would have mandated a television set with a dial impossible to adjust to grownup programming until a viewer had acquired the requisite strength (special exemptions, of course, for the aged and handicapped). That way, children would have been restricted solely to programming properly calibrated to their tastes. (As we shall see, this would have proved futile, given the content of early television's children's shows, but it would have demonstrated an understanding of the potential threat of television to national stability.)

As it was, however, we could at will tune in the world of the Elders and learn about our society in a way that was to threaten its survival a decade or so later. I am not now talking about news shows, such as the *Camel News Caravan*, with dapper John Cameron Swayze greeting us with what sounded to me like ". . . ladies and gentlemen, and good evening to you" (why, I wondered, didn't they let him begin with a complete sentence), and rugged-faced weatherman Clint Youle, and its reminders to "take the Camel 30-Day test" and see how soothing a cigarette could be to the T-Zone. I am talking about what we learned about America from the entertainments; how we saw America as the Elders really saw it.

· We learned that dishonesty, fear, and pretense were the dominant values of domestic life, from endless episodes of *I Love Lucy* or *My Little Margie*. If, for example, Ricky Ricardo or Vern Albright called to say he was bringing an Important Person home to dinner, it was a reason to lie— about life styles, wealth, or tastes. An honest difference of attitude would risk the Big Contract; better to lie to outsiders. And if (as always happened) Lucy (or Margie) burned the roast, they didn't greet Ricky (or Vern) by explaining, "Gee, I'm sorry, but I burned the roast. Let's go out to eat." No, they bought Chinese food, and pretended it was a special Oriental banquet. And Lucy (or Margie), with the help of Ethel and Fred Mertz (or Freddy) would dress up as Chinese waiters and waitresses, with false teeth in their mouths and wigs and funny hats, and do anything except face a minimal domestic crisis with a shred of grace.

· We learned that Negroes could be maids (Ethel Waters or Louise Beavers as *Beulah*) or fools posturing with each other (*Amos 'n' Andy*) or bug-eyed elevator operators or porters (as in *My Little Margie* or *The Stu Erwin Show*), but that Negroes did not live on the same block, in the same neighborhood, probably not in the same town with the white who came into our homes every night. Not Chester Riley, not Molly Goldberg, not Luigi, not Mama, not My Favorite Husband, not even Jim Anderson, the utterly fair-minded father of Bud, Betty, and Kathy, none of them ever had a black for a friend.

· We learned that among men and women, the division of labor was fixed and rigid. Men worked; women ran the home. An ever-popular comic diversion of our domestic comedies was to place a bumbling, idiotic father in charge of the kitchen for a weekend; or laugh as Joan Caulfield (*My Favorite Husband*) tried to hold down a job while taking care of the house. Single women, of course, could work: as teachers (Eve Arden in *Our Miss Brooks*), as secretaries (Ann Sothern in *Private Secretary*), as models (Marie Wilson in *My Friend Irma*). Except for comic relief (the riotous premise of *Dear Phoebe* being that a woman could write sports and a man give advice to the lonely) through role reversal, men and women *knew their places and kept them.*

· We learned that, for the Elders, the proper relationship between man and material possession was blind, slavish greed. Every day on *The Price Is Right,* a curtain would open and a busty model would be lounging alongside a gleaming appliance.

"Yes!" the announcer would scream. "It's an all-new, Giant 16 Foot Cubic Freeze-o-Rama with—"

Moans, screams, grunts from the audience; the contestants would stare transfixed at this wonder, in tears at the prospect of actually attaining possession of this key to paradise.

"Ooooh, I want that, I *want* that, oh, Bill, oooh . . ."

Then the bidding, inching ever closer to the magic number *without* going over the *actual retail price*.

"Freeze! Freeze! Higher! Higher!" the audience screams, as crewcut, calm, collected Bill Cullen supervises the madness. Then the winner, who responds to his (or her) new wealth with civility:

"Ah, ha ha HA, ha ha HA, I won, I won, I *won*, ha ha hahahahahaha!"

• And, in the higher celestial realms, we learned first that wisdom was fungible, a commodity exchangeable for enormous sums of money and national adulation. It was the American dream come true: a shoemaker winning $32,000 for his knowledge of opera; a Marine officer exchanging his cooking information for $64,000; a twelve-year-old stock wizard carrying home $250,000; and best of all, an intellectual heir to a great tradition of letters and learning, Charles Van Doren, straining week after week through the labyrinth of complex knowledge, his fortune building up with every twist of his brow, every fearful summoning of all he knew—until the day we found that his contortions were no more authentic than the grunts and aches of Gorgeous George and Haystacks Calhoun; more aesthetic, perhaps, but just as fraudulent.

We learned much, much more, of course: the efficacy of violence in settling disputes, the need to use guns and fists in pursuit of justice; from the commercials we learned envy and a thirst for acquisition. At least, we learned that the Elders believed that happiness was mechanistic: a pill could cure any distress, a hair tonic could infuse sexuality not just into your hair, but into your body and personality; we learned that danger lurked in every orifice of our bodies; that we might at any time risk betrayal from hair, face, breath, teeth, gums, underarms, torso, feet; that here, just as in our domestic comedies, it was necessary for pretense to replace honesty.

Well, we know this. What I mean to dissect is the way that television unconsciously showed the War Baby children the way we thought we were living, or wished to live. Whether our Elders understood that television was a weapon of Eavesdropping for us, a means of learning truths about the world that other generations might take far longer to perceive, I doubt. What is clear is that the world of the seven-inch DuMont was a world where grownups did not do what they told us to, and did not live by the precepts they taught us. We as a generation received the earliest lessons in hypocrisy in history; and those lessons were lodged deep in our memories when the War Baby generation began to turn toward contempt, then open resistance, of the Elders. So, too, were the lessons we learned from the shows that were aimed at us.

AND NOW, KIDS, HUH-HO, LET'S SMASH THE STATE!

Screaming children, puppets with their faces frozen in a rictus grin; Buster Brown and Poll Parrot Shoes, clusters of tots in paroxysms of hysteria, and genial grownups who led us in games and songs and told us to say our prayers, brush our teeth, and demand the products of the sponsors.

Howdy Doody was the king, of course, as early as 1947. His show each night at five-thirty was the last bright flicker of adventure before dinner and the headlong rush to bedtime. Bob Smith, later Buffalo Bob Smith, chief of the Sigafoose Indians, was the Good Grownup incarnate. He was our guide to songs, games, and wondrous characters—both real (Princess Summerfallwinterspring) and puppets—Dilly-Dally, Flub-a-Dub, and Howdy himself. But what we forget is that there was also a running plot to the *Howdy Doody* shows—adventures, mysteries, and once a Presidential election.

And deep within this frolic and fun, surrounding the precepts of well-behaved children, was a fundamental lesson that our generation appears to have taken to heart, to the lasting sorrow and pain of our Elders: *the villain was always a Grown-Up in Authority*. The two most frightening members of the Howdy Doody cast were Phineas T. Bluster and the Inspector. Bluster, the white-haired, stern-visaged, top-hatted figure of Authority, the kind of man kids threw snowballs at in Norman Rockwell illustrations. And the Inspector! What blacklisted leftist children's writer, what craftsman burning with a hatred for J. Edgar Hoover, what foe of the Truman Doctrine or the House Un-American Activities Committee spawned this figure of fear? Everyone from our gym teacher to the ushers at baseball games, chasing us out of box seats, to the faceless figures in the outer edges of the Principal's Office—*all* of them were the Inspector.

Ah, but for every oppressor, there is a liberator. At *Howdy Doody* it was Clarabelle the Clown, as silent and as mad as Harpo Marx, with his own fright wig, his own horn, and his own seltzer bottle, darting in from offstage to creep along the front edge of the Peanut Gallery, to avenge the spirit of freedom.

No, it was not to Howdy Doody that we looked for our champion, that freckle-faced, white-toothed Howdy Doody, whose name caused no end of scatalogical snickering in the schoolyard. He was . . . to be blunt about it . . . a fink, telling us to wash our hands, listen to our parents, and look both ways before crossing the street. Clarabelle, the first Yippie, was the true hero of the show. Where did the War Baby generation get the inspiration to hurl marshmallows at Strom Thurmond and a pie at Clark Kerr. From the works of Lenin? From a footnote in Marcuse? Nonsense. From the inspiration of that genuine free spirit, that revolutionary foe of authority and good conduct, from Clarabelle.

And this sense of sticking it to the Dumb Grownups was not aberrational with *Howdy Doody*. Think back on *Buster Brown's Gang*, with Smilin' Ed McConnell (later replaced by gravel-throated Andy Devine of "Hey, Wild Bill, wait fer me!" fame). After the serial with Gunga Ram, elephant boy, lisping his way through what seemed to be Van Cortlandt Park, after the Midnight and Squeaky duet (a drugged black cat and a cadaverous mouse playing "Pop Goes the Weasel" on harmonium and drum in a brotherhood lesson) came the moment of truth.

Standing by a grandfather's clock, Smilin' Ed would chortle, "Pluck your magic twanger, Froggy!" (That line became an instantly hilarious punch line during later adolescent discussions of self-abuse.) From a cloud of smoke a gremlin, mighty like a frog, would appear, bouncing back and forth and growling, "Hiya kids, hiya, hiya, hiya." Almost imme-

diately, a Dumb Grownup—as distinguished from Smilin'
Ed, the Good Grownup—would emerge, always a symbol
of authority, constriction, and pomposity. One week a super-
cilious French headwaiter; the next week a prissy spinster
music teacher, lorgnette, hair in a bun: the next, an effete
grammarian. Insidiously, Froggy the Gremlin would interrupt the syrupy lecture, tricking the Dumb Grownup into
repeating naughty remarks.

Dumb Grownup: So, then, little children, I went to the
Opera with Madame DuSnob, and I—

Froggy: —put a spider down her back.

D.G.: Yes, and the spider was so funny, and— Oooh, ooh,
you horrid, naughty thing you!

Froggy: Har, har, har.

Oh, sure, Smilin' Ed reminded us about visiting the church
or Sunday School of our choice, but only *after* the Dumb
Grownup had managed to throw a pie in his own face.
Think on this, as you reflect on the fires licking at the
ROTC building a decade later, as you watch teenagers hurl
contempt and obscenities at their Elders amid the deceptive
calm of a university. We had, six days a week for ten years,
watched Dumb Grownups make fools of themselves. Why,
then, blame Mao or Che or Dr. Spock; somebody bring a
conspiracy charge against Froggy or Clarabelle, or the network executives who let us look so unblinkingly at the world
of the Elders, and you begin to have some idea of the real
culprits.

AND NOW, THIS WORD

The cigarettes marched, jumped out of the packs, spelled
out names and slogans, lit each other's fire, square-danced,

all to the infectious jingles. Lucky Strike, the first great triumph of the radio age, Lucky Strike, the product that had driven our parents mad with the endless repetition of radio slogans ("Lucky Strike Green has gone to war!"), now began hypnotizing the first generation of television viewers. At school we mocked the chanting of auctioneer F. E. Boone: "at sixtyandaoneandaonethatstwoandatwo,two,-andatwo*sold* American." We knew what L.S./M.F.T. meant before we could read. At the age of two, my sister would while away the evening hours by hauling herself up in her crib and singing, "Be happy, go Lucky, Be happy, go Lucky Strike, Be happy, go Lucky, go Lucky Strike today." No other company so eagerly hammered the American television viewer insensible as did Lucky Strike. George Washington Hill would have been proud.

The commercial, however, was not the only source of selling that the advertiser had as a weapon. Television, like radio before it, was a commercial medium, a communications source supposedly owned by the people, regulated in the public interest by a federal agency but in fact controlled by private corporations of enormous wealth and influence who prospered by selling time to other private corporations of even bigger influence and greater wealth. The corporations that ran the networks understood the sensibilities of the corporations that bought time. They were, after all, respectable businessmen.

It was, for example, important for a national sponsor to have national acceptance. No region could be offended. Thus, early dramas concerning prejudice on *Playhouse 90* or *The United States Steel Hour* or *Goodyear Theatre* could not deal with bigotry against Negroes; it would have risked the position of both network and sponsor throughout the South. So we had dramas concerning people of unidentified ethnic origins, or those afflicted by cleft palates rather than dark pigmentation.

It was important to maintain a respectable, acceptable image for business and the free enterprise system. Thus, at the end of 1952, General Foods dropped *Life With Luigi*, a heart-warming look at a band of lovable, simple-minded Italian immigrants (as distinct from *The Goldbergs*, a heart-warming look at a band of lovable, simple-minded Jewish immigrants and *I Remember Mama*, a heart-warming look at a band of lovable, simple-minded Norwegian immigrants). Why? Because of alleged subversive plots. In one show, Luigi battled a utility company trying to cut down a tree. In another Luigi bought a share of stock in a big business, and proceeded to demonstrate irrational and inefficient behavior on the part of the management. These shows, in other words, questioned the American Way of Life. The star, J. Carroll Naish, professed puzzlement, in part because he had always considered himself a Taft Republican. But General Foods knew subversion when it reared its ugly head.

Subversion, in fact, was a constant concern of the corporations that bought and sold access to the public airwaves. Back in 1947, when three temporary FBI agents left the department to fight subversion for profit, few broadcasting executives gave them a second glance. Soon, however, their publication, *Counterattack*, was listing the names of specific actors, writers, directors, and performers, along with their un-American activities, such as appearing at rallies in support of Henry Wallace, or belonging to Spanish Loyalist committees during the late 1930s. By itself, the publication, and its hard-cover product *Red Channels,* would have meant nothing. Even the support of people like Ed Sullivan and right-wing columnist Jack O'Brien would have meant a flurry of letters and little more.

What did make a difference was the attitude of the businesses that sold their products on television. To have their dog food, or refrigerator, or automobile enveloped in controversy was the worst thing that could happen. A business community whose reaction to boat-rocking was sheer panic— Ford Motor Co., for example, once ordered a show to paint the Chrysler Building out of the Manhattan skyline, and the American Gas Association bleeped the word "gas" from a reference to Nazi gas ovens, thus leading the audience to surmise that six million Jews had perished in electric ranges —such a community was not likely to sit by while talent it was paying for was accused of pro-Communist activities. This unease was heightened by the actions of one Laurence Johnson, a supermarket owner in upstate New York. He threatened to display products sponsoring "suspect talent" in his supermarket with a large sign explaining the pro-Communist quality of the product; and, through the American Legion and Chamber of Commerce, he promised to begin a national campaign.

Faced with this kind of challenge, the defenders of the American Way of Life—General Motors, DuPont, Metropolitan Life, R. J. Reynolds Tobacco—did the only possible thing: they collapsed. In the early 1950s, actress Jean Muir found herself dropped from the TV cast of *The Aldrich Family.* Her crime was having sent a telegram of congratulations to the Moscow Arts Theatre on its fiftieth anniversary. And in 1952, Philip Loeb, who played Papa Jake on *The Goldbergs,* was dropped from the show after *Red Channels* listed him as unacceptable.

"The livelihood of twenty people are at stake," Gertrude Berg, the creator and star of the show explained, adding that she was certain the charges were unfair. Loeb took his own life some time later.

It wasn't that the business enterprises were necessarily right-wing. Their response would have been the same had the national climate been swinging leftward, with a tight-knit group of true believers rooting out "protofascists" within the entertainment industry. The point was quiescence—a respectful silence when the sales pitch was made. An advertising agency chief explained this in a 1954 letter to Elmer Rice, who had suggested turning his Pulitzer Prize-winning play *Street Scene* into a TV series. Replying that the play was entirely too involved with gloomy, depressing people, the executive wrote:

". . . the American consuming public as presented by the advertising industry today is middle class, not lower class; happy in general, not miserable and frustrated."

In other words, if our family dinner conversations were punctuated by shouts of anger and bitterness, if icy silences hung over living rooms rather than the easygoing jocularity of Ozzie, Harriet, Dave, and Ricky Nelson, if family disputes were resolved by physical violence or imprecations of murder, rather than by the Socratic dialogues of *Father Knows Best,* if 90 percent of the American people never saw anything remotely resembling their families on American television, that was *our* fault for not living up to the models shaped for us by companies who were selling their products with the implied promise that enough acquisition would bring us the peace and ease of the Nelsons and Andersons.

A BRIEF DISCOURSE ON TASTE; OR:
YOUR HUSBAND IS DYING, SO HERE'S
A REFRIGERATOR

They really chickened out when push came to shove. Oh, yeah, Art Baker would peer out of a Skippy Peanut Jar and bellow, "You asked for it," and they *did* show a one-armed paper-hanger at work, a man wrestling a bear, a man wrestling an alligator, a six-hundred-pound cowboy on a horse, a sword-swallower, a goldfish-swallower, and a man being pounded on the head with a sledge hammer. But did they show a man being electrocuted? They did not. Did they show a woman being burned at the stake? They did not. And people—lots of people—had asked to see that.

No, on early television human suffering had to take more subtle forms than fried flesh. For instance, the kind of suffering we saw every weekday morning on C.B.S., during which Ralph Hall and Warren Hull—or perhaps it was Ralph Hull and Warren Hall—would comfort an emaciated, sob-racked woman:

"And then, Mrs. Masoch . . . when the truck . . ."

"So (gulp) . . . right after Billy lost his hearing . . . (choke) . . . a Bungalow Bar Ice Cream truck crashed into our living room and our . . . little terrier Rusty fr-froze to death . . . And the (sniffle) landlord said we'd have to . . . get the chocolate off the wall or . . . we'd be . . . evic-(sob)-ted . . ."

Ring! The audience cheers with joy.

"Heartline!" yells Warren, yanking a phone out of a giant heart. "Yes—oh, wonderful! Mrs. Masoch, Clyde Manheim of Manheim's Fruit Farm is lending you six migrant workers so you can clean up your house, and he's throwing in a bushel of grapes!"

They never missed on *Strike It Rich,* the show that proved that out there in America, a generous nation was waiting to shower largesse on the have-nots of our society. It was a seductive vision; the Traveler's Aid Society reported five cases a day of destitute families showing up in New York, hoping to appear on *Strike It Rich,* confident that a Heartline telephone call would pay for a kidney operation or a prosthetic limb.

For audiences with stronger stuff, N.B.C. offered us *Queen for a Day,* with Jack Bailey as host—the last man in America to wax his mustache. The special treat of *Queen* was *competition.* Mrs. Fenster's gangrenous leg could not stand on its own: it was put head to head against Mrs. Wagoner's husband's insanity—until Mrs. Morris' leukemic six-year-old wiped them out, set and match. It was the audience, in keeping with the democratic way, that decided, through its applause, which contestant was most pathetic. Dying relatives were sure winners; poor people who asked for a small stake to reclaim their own lives were sure losers. It was a generous audience; but it demanded total, abject helplessness before it made a lucky woman Queen for a Day: transformed via ersatz ermine and an ornate throne, and showered with kitchen ranges, vacations, and new clothes. (There was no Heartline for the losers; competition is, after all, competition.)

Even famous people took their lumps in our living rooms. Each week, Ralph Edwards, oversized book in hand, surprised a famous celebrity by sneaking up to them at some preset function, dragging them into the *This Is Your Life* studio and revealing their life story to the nation. Assuming the honored guest did not go into cardiac shock, Edwards would duck into a echo chamber and intone key moments in the life of his honored guest. Here is his gift to Lillian Roth:

"Confusion, distress, and tragedy walked by your side, even as you rose to the top—and soon all glamour was stripped from you as drink follows drink, and you sink into a stupor that was to last for sixteen years. These are the years to come before us . . . in just a moment."

Cut to an ad for Hazel Bishop No-Smear Lipstick.

Even 1950s television, however, had its limits to compassion, understanding, and generosity in the face of suffering. Thus, the king of such shows only lasted a brief time. It was called *Stand Up and Be Counted*, hosted by Ralph Baxter. Every afternoon, a victim, seen only in silhouette, told her story. One day I found out my son was a . . . He swears he's going to change, but meanwhile I . . . my problem is, do I turn my son in, or protect him, knowing that the shock may kill his grandfather, but the shock of his arrest may do in my mother.

Following the recitation, members of the audience, each an instant Rose Franzblau, would offer their judgment, with other members of the audience reacting something like *The Price Is Right* crowd.

"I say, keep your child. He belongs at home."

"No, no, turn the kid in!"

"Well, I think that the law is the law, and your son belongs behind bars."

"Freeze!" a misplaced *Price Is Right* fan would scream.

After several moments of this consolation, a collective decision would be made by audience vote, with the Victim presumably honor-bound to accept the advice of the studio audience. Whether this was another example of Communist subversion of television, with People's Courts being given a hidden tryout on network television, was never determined.

SMOKIN' ROCKETS!

The walls were crowded with levers, rods, dials, charts, maps, Naugahyde padding, oscilloscopes, and triggers. The danger was mind-boggling: Dr. Pauli, head of the dread Astrodial Society, whose avowed goal is the destruction of the Earth, has just kidnapped the universe. Only Captain Video and his faithful Video Rangers can stop them. On goes the visored cap, the lightning bolt uniform, the ray gun. Off they go, streaking across space in pursuit of the vicious Dr. Pauli. Back at home, we tune in the adventures of another member of the Video Rangers, who bears a suspicious resemblance to Johnny Mack Brown, or some other Western movie star of the 1930s.

It is 2355. Tom Corbett, Space Cadet, is flying to Alpha Centuri. Roger, the wise-guy radioman, is getting on Astro's nerves—Astro, the engineer, being the son of Venusian colonists and sensitive to ethnic slurs. Commander Strong warned them about this kind of dissension back at Cadet Headquarters on Earth . . . But no time for that now. Because Alpha Centuri lies straight ahead, and it appears populated solely by prehistoric monsters.

And for the militarists, here is Buzz Corey of the Spa-a-a-a-ce Patrol, enforcing collective security for the United Planets of the Universe on his Terra V rocketship, along with wisecracking subordinate Happy; the lovely Carole, and Tonga, once-villainous alien since rehabilitated by the Brainograph. Everything's super-modern here, including the jargon: "He's lost his gyroscope." "Smokin' rockets!" "Aw, go blast off."

How prosaic it seemed, years later, watching Neil Armstrong (now that was a name they should have thought of) gingerly put his foot down on the moon; how wearying listening to the computer print-outs and exchanges of numbers across a quarter of a million miles of space. And how revealing that a substantial minority of the American people did not believe the moon landing had actually taken place. For years we had watched Corbett, Corey, and Captain Video striding across Jupiter, or Galpha-Z-120, armed only with a pure heart and that quick energy from a Powerhouse Candy Bar or box of Kellogg's Corn Flakes. Well, that had come to us on the same medium as Armstrong's, and if Corbett, Corey, and Captain Video were hamming it up in some studio, why was it any more likely that Armstrong was laughing up his space-insulated sleeve in a top-secret corner of a TV studio at WJZ-TV, clamoring over his papier-mâché rocks?

FOLKS, BELIEVE ME

They made everything work. Tools that no mortal human being could manipulate slid like magic in the hands of Happy Haupt, king of the pitchmen. My single lasting impression of New York's old WATV (actually Channel 13 in Newark, New Jersey), apart from Uncle Fred's Farmer Grey cartoons, were the ads for home devices: Chop-a-Matics, with hands going like lightning, reducing every fruit, vegetable, and food-stuff known to man into neat geometric patterns.

"It slices, it dices, it can chop an onion, it can shave an ice cube, it can trim your nails, turn a radish into a likeness of Thomas Jefferson, and, friends, call right now, and we'll throw in an encyclopedia, a pool, and a car, for $12.98."

Storm and screen windows, looking as formidable as a guillotine, were snapped, spun, and whisked into place night after night, without the loss of a single hand. Dishware, eighty-nine pieces, was offered to the first hundred people who phoned in for a price so low that the earthenware must have been packed by slaves. Salesmanship: Hi, folks, I'm Rex Marshall . . . Dick Stark here for Chesterfields.

But at its best, it was an art worth a king's ransom. Arthur Godfrey in his heyday earned fifteen hundred dollars a minute when he was on the air, because he had the knack of relating to an audience the way television demanded; not by talking to a mass audience, but by reacting one to one with his viewers. It was *me* he was talking to, chuckling after a more-than-occasional double entendre, holding up a package of Lipton's and observing casually, "Try it. I don't know. Maybe you'll hate the stuff. A-heh, a-heh, a-heh." His on-the-air family was large and diverse: the exotic Hawaiian Haleloke, the Chordettes, romantic singers Frank Parker and Marian Marlowe (would they marry someday?). He was a part of our family. Not even that day in 1953 when he fired Julius LaRosa on the air ("that was Julius LaRosa's swan song with us. He goes now out on his own . . . bye-bye") could he erase that magic sense that he was on friendly, intimate terms with our hopes and daily troubles.

There were others we believed, those from the "Chicago School" of television, relaxed, informal, casual, with Dave Garroway as the King, bidding us farewell with a lazily up-raised arm and the incantation "Peace." But eventually Garroway yielded to televised boxing, and Studs Terkel, the great interviewer-author from Chicago, lost his *Studs' Corner* show. Somehow, in those days, the sense of relaxation clashed too dramatically with the frenetic quality of pitches elsewhere, as if the sound of a real human voice rendered the dominant voice of early television too noticeably crass.

The danger of a Garroway-Terkel kind of television was that it could remind us, if carried too far, that the voices we heard on television were not the voices of ordinary Americans; that the dilemmas of television's families were not those we were wrestling with: a sense of growing frustration, an impacted sense of economic stagnation in what TV told us was an increasingly affluent society; an unexpressed desire for solitude and ease in a consumer market which demanded stimulation, irritation, dissatisfaction as a spur to higher sales and profits. It was a quality we could find rarely: in the lighthearted children's humor of *Kukla, Fran and Ollie* or *Pinhead and Foodini*, for instance, which constantly held an adult audience searching for the sound of a simple human voice. It was not heard that frequently in early television, any more than it is heard today.

SIGN-OFF

Yes, there were moments of grace and wit and courage. Mary Martin and Ethel Merman sitting on two stools and singing for an hour; just sheer show-biz talent. Sid Caesar, only twenty-six when he began on network television, with a stable of brilliant young writers and cohorts, Carl Reiner, Mel Brooks, Howie Morris, Imogene Coca, Neil Simon, Gary Belkin. The cheerful anarchy of Ernie Kovacs, and his electronic wizardry; *See It Now*, and grim-visaged Edward R. Murrow facing down Joe McCarthy or telling the story of an Air Force officer stripped of his security clearance because of his parents' reading matter.

Yet what remains of those images that force their way back to the surface is a collected set of remnants of witlessness and outright stupidity; a self-portrait of a country coming out of a war for preservation and heading into a time that did not turn out the way it was supposed to. We laugh because there is no other way to come to grips with what we saw those thousands of hours. We watched. We remembered. And in a sense we are still trying to come to grips with what we learned about America at the knee of the seven-inch DuMont.

Book 2

FEVER

A FEVER IN THE BLOOD

POST-MORTEMS ON THE DEATH
OF THE CAMPUS PASTORAL

A moonlit Friday night in late October. Somewhere above
the colonial brick buildings, suspended ethereally between
the rustling oaks and the full, silver moon, a chorus of blazer-
clad, earnest young men and robed women is singing. The
hearty, full-throated voices of the men are cradled by the
descants of the women. Along a walkway bisecting a broad
campus greensward, a cardigan-sweatered girl, page-boy hair
bouncing on the nape of her neck, clutches her books to her
breasts and looks up shyly, adoringly, into the eyes of the
pipe-smoking young man, who is gazing with affectionate,
lust-free fondness at her.

In the distance, music and cheers resound. The youthful

couple strolls over to the Friday Night Pep Rally, now building to a frenzied climax. As the cheerleaders hurl another
pile of wood on the flames, the band strikes up the Fight
Song, and the chants of "Beat State!" grow. At the fringe
of the crowd, the ruddy-cheeked, white-haired professor of
classics takes a thoughtful puff on his pipe and strokes the
suede elbow patch of his tweed jacket. He is trying to maintain a serious demeanor, but his wife Martha, a woolly afghan
hugging her shoulders, spots the twinkle in his eye.

"Hey, Prof!" yells Squeaky, class cut-up, pushing his beanie
down over his tousled head as he gallops over. "How 'bout a
locomotive?"

"Yeah, yeah!" the crowd of collegians urges, grinning,
clapping, and nudging each other with their elbows. Prof
shakes his head, protesting, but his grin and the twinkle in
his eye—now more like a laser's gleam—gives away his true
sentiments.

"I believe, my dear Squeaky," says Prof, "I shall oblige
your most earnest entreaties." He leads a ferocious cheer, cli-
maxed by the roar of thousands. Suddenly, there is a com-
motion down by the Lake. Melvin, the scrawny bookworm
with the horn-rimmed glasses and the face like a pink Nes-
tle's Crunch Bar, Melvin, the embittered outcast who has
threatened to wreck the entire Weekend by revealing that
the star halfback is a functional illiterate—thus jeopardizing
his scholarship and his eligibility—Melvin is tossed into the
Lake, emerging, indignant, sputtering, but unhurt to the
raucous laughter of students, Prof, and Dean.

Yes, U. will beat State on the morrow. And, when the
glow of autumn yields to the white blanket of winter, there

will be Christmas parties; young men will rest their elbows on fireplace mantles, smiling down on their pinmates and future brides who sit by the crackling fire, their legs drawn up under them, waving out of the frosted, holly-wreathed windows to the mufflered carolers winding their way down Fraternity Row. Then spring, picnic outings, canoes gliding down the river. And finally, Commencement, with black-robed graduates, eager, solemn, happy, standing by proud parents, clasping their diplomas as the Mixed Chorus in the Sky swells.

Thus the Pastoral of the Campus: born somewhere at the beginning of the century, enshrined in a hundred movies, a thousand *Life* magazine photos and Coca-Cola ads, attractive enough to survive two wars and a depression, broad enough to absorb the mythological figures of twentieth-century American youth: flappers and raccoon coats, bobby-soxers and zoot suits, the button-down passivity of the 1950s, the coolly concerned, respectfully dissenting, responsibly committed student of the early 1960s—and finally plummeting to a violent, fiery death in the last half of the last decade, a victim with so many other myths of insufficient credibility.

That the Pastoral of the Campus could survive as long as it did was a function of its breadth and winsomeness. It did not depend on a particular length of hair, or style of clothes or politics. It was necessary only to believe that a university community was a privileged, insulated Way Station along a predictable path toward Life; warm-spirited enough to indulge the excess hormones of the Young, serious enough to instill a Respect for Learning and Values, hardheaded enough to equip the Next Generation of Leaders with the tools to run our factories, produce our goods, write our laws, heal our sick, and overcome the inevitable if disconcerting habit of the Young to tell their Elders to go to Hell. Years later, we would look back at our residence in the Pastoral with a bittersweet wistfulness at the swiftness with which youth flies, and— with a generous check dispatched to the Alumni Endowment Fund—turn back to the business of being grown up.

The pervasiveness of the Pastoral swept beyond those generations of alumni who fondly remembered a sense of fellowship and ease they may well never have lived through; it reached out to embrace those who had not yet even set foot in the Groves of Academe. On more weekday mornings than I can remember, in the inexpressible wickedness of an empty apartment and a nonexistent, not-going-to-school-today headache, I would watch armies of tap dancers, musicians, football players, good-natured profs, ill-natured deans, and impossibly sweet girls frolic across the campus. As a Senior in high school, I retained an absolute belief that the moment I walked onto a college campus, my taste for Little Richard and the Cleftones would vanish, to be replaced with an addiction for Paul Whiteman, Kay Kayser, and the Andrews Sisters. Much as I had hungered for those Pop's Candy Stores in the far reaches of Sheepshead Bay as I listened to Alan Freed send greeting to the junior high school kids who kissed and necked at age fourteen instead of watching Saturday night TV with a bowlful of onion-sour cream dip, so was I longing for a world of continuing fellowship, good humor, and stolen kisses in the Phi Gam kitchen.

The War Baby generation was heading toward college after a decade when the Pastoral had so gripped the collegians of the Postwar decade that even the normal signs of hyperenergetic youth were absent. They seemed almost indecently satisfied. ("The employers are going to love this generation," exulted Clark Kerr, Chancellor at Berkeley, where the university-industry-government-military nexus seemed to be creating a new kind of educational supermarket. "There aren't going to be any riots.") One of their teachers, Professor Otto Butz, felt compelled to write an article he called "In Defense of the Class of '58."

"The American younger generation is in danger of being unfairly and tragically sold short," he wrote. Its elders "are misinterpreting its realism and prudence as ominous evidence of apathy and lack of idealism . . . I fully agree that today's youth are a down-to-earth and matter-of-fact lot. [But they do not] lack positive political convictions. It does not mean they are, as one educator recently described them, little more than 'gloriously contented . . . self-seekers on the American assembly line.' . . . These American youths have *not* lost their fire. All that has happened is that they have become too mature merely to show it off, feel self-righteous about it, or play with it."

Professor Butz, it turned out, need not have worried much longer. The coming generation was bringing to college more than crew-necked sweaters, madras shirts, and a furtively purchased package of Trojans. We had, for example, been obliged to carry with us—from high school on—the responsibility of preventing the conquest of the United States by the scientific genius of Soviet Communism. From that first day in October 1957, when Sputnik was launched, we were told that we were falling behind the Russians. We were dancing

the Rock-a-cha in the gym while Boris was fiendishly calculating the trajectory of an ICBM aimed squarely at Scars-
dale. We were thumbing through *The Amboy Dukes,* or
1984 (page 103) looking for the hot parts, while Niki and
Anton were designing death rays in the back of their kinder-
garten. When you are told at age fifteen that a missed home-
work assignment is a nail in the coffin of the American Way
of Life, you are going to take a more sober look at the
world.

We had, also, been provided a look at a society whose
honesty was in some doubt. All through the late '50s, mothers
had dragged their sleeping children in front of television
screens, pointing to a modest, curly-headed young man with
earphones on his head, and a countenance that wrinkled into
the tortures of the damned as he desperately sought to pull
the last drop of knowledge from his brain.

"Oh, ah . . . ooh . . . uh . . . could we come back to that
question?"

"Look," screamed a hundred thousand parents. "Do you
know who that is? That's *Charles Van Doren,* and he's
winninging $147,000! Because he studied!"

And all of a sudden it wasn't true. All of the respect for
learning fostered by the example of instant wealth, the genu-
flections to the world of intellect, now possessing talent
quantifiable, was a hoax. The fix was in. Once again, television had given the young a peek into the family closet,
and we heard the rattling of the bones. The same invention
that let us witness the stupidities of our elders, the greed of
our parents, now gave us a ringside seat to the corruption of

the learning process. It was a lesson we would remember later in the 1960s.

As the decade opened, there were stirrings; from different regions, flowing from different sources, but all pointing to a common lesson: it was possible to do more than whisper about mindlessness and unfairness. We could stand against them. A handful of New York City high school seniors refused to sign a loyalty oath that had been required of prospective graduates since the days of the Palmer raids following World War I. The rest of us cowards watched, waiting to see what form the retribution would take. A few weeks later, the Board of Education spoke: the loyalty oath was abolished. Ah, ha!

In Greensboro, North Carolina, a handful of deferential, well-dressed, Negro collegians sat down at a Woolworth lunch counter, demanding service that laws and customs prohibited. Within a month, hundreds of us in New York were standing outside Woolworth's, passing out leaflets and urging a boycott. Why we felt we had a cause in common with those North Carolina Negroes, I don't know. But we did, and so did high school and college students in dozens of other cities. (This picket line was an early lesson in the complexities of public opinion. One Saturday at 110th Street and Broadway, a sweet-faced, elderly lady, all decked out in cameo, bonnet, and lace, toddled up to me, smiled benignly, and murmured in a winsome brogue, "Well, now, and what's all this shit about?")

And out in San Francisco, a mob of Berkeley students— this in 1960, mind you—were demonstrating outside a building in which the House Un-American Activities Committee was conducting hearings; after hours of pushing and shoving, the police cleared away the students, dragging dozens of them down a long flight of marble stairs, head first: an object lesson in the occasional willingness of those in power to respond . . . harshly to folks who looked just like us.

By the end of 1960 we had a different kind of lesson in the possibility of our exercise of power: John Kennedy had been elected President. And while his campaign was scarcely an appeal to radical youth (it had to do more with Moving Forward, closing a Missile Gap that clamped shut the moment he was inaugurated, and combating a tendency among Europeans to believe Russia was stronger than we were), Kennedy was a startlingly different kind of Grownup in Authority. He was young, looking more like twenty-three than forty-three, compared to other politicians; he was virile, energetic, and seemed the only man in power capable of laughing with his eyes and belly as well as his mouth. More: he seemed to be holding out the prospect of doing something with our lives other than joining the first giant enterprise willing to offer paid vacations and a generous retirement fund. We could, according to Kennedy, journey to exotic foreign lands, saving people's lives and building new societies. While it was not clear to us what we could be accomplishing —it seemed like a huge slum-clearance project, with English Lit majors curing Yaws in Zambia by the force of our presence and the confidence of peasants—it did suggest at least another possibility. It meant we were supposed to count in the real world, now.

There were new books to read, C. Wright Mills assailing the timidity of his academic colleagues and putting his sense about the Castro regime into the mouth of a fictional Cuban peasant, James Baldwin searing the conscience of a white, middle-class collegian, and—perhaps more important than any other single work—Joseph Heller's *Catch-22*, offering a portrait of Yossarian, trapped in a madhouse of arbitrary slaughter, needless death, and insanity by memo. There were twenty thousand in Washington to protest nuclear testing (the White House fed them coffee and doughnuts), and a growing presence of collegians in southern towns.

Thus, a stirring, a questioning. But in the early 1960s, the Campus Pastoral was still secure, still capable of absorbing this new spirit within the myth of a stable, benign, university community, linked by shared values to the greater world beyond its borders. It required only a slight adjustment. A new scene: a student council chamber. Serious, youthfully sincere young men (and an occasional young woman), hair neatly combed, perhaps in a suggestion of a JFK wave, coats and ties, debate a resolution. Quotations from Jefferson and Lincoln; the spirit of the American Way of Life now come to embodiment among the Leaders of Tomorrow. Another scene in the Alumni Association promotional film: football team, cut to student in white coat peering into microscope, cut to prof holding pointer lecturing on Causes of the Civil War, cut to a debate on whether Negroes in the South should vote, with collegians packing around tables in the Student Union. Why not? There were plenty of other reassurances to go around for the concerned Elders: Yell Like Hell rallies before the Homecoming Game, big bands playing on Saturday nights for students weaned on Presley and Chuck Berry, 10:30 P.M. weeknight curfews for women

(12:30 P.M. on the weekends, 1:30 A.M. on two glorious nights each year); a dash of controversy fit. It was just the spice missing from the 1950s.

And it fit, too, because the college generation of the early 1960s embraced two tendencies that divided us fundamentally from our younger brothers and sisters: Emulation and Sanctuary. Emulation, in that our style, our mode of behavior, was modeled unquestioningly after the patterns of the Elders; Sanctuary because we believed the university a community morally superior to the outside world, which offered us protection from the consequences of our behavior, and which shared with us a determination to be better than the rest of Them. We were, in other words, part of the process in building a new Campus Pastoral; and we were probably as shocked as the Elders when it collapsed so swiftly and thoroughly a few years after we had helped create it.

Consider, if you are puzzled at the critical importance I attach to the politics of Emulation, the Student Conference—my playing field of Eton all through the late 1950s and early 1960s. We knew we were the Leaders of Tomorrow; every keynote speaker told us we were; we treasured Roberts' Rules of Order as though it were the Holy Writ, or at least *The Prophet*. A clever use of a Point of Order or a Motion to Adjourn was to us what a dunk was on the basketball courts of Harlem: the sound of our own voices was our fix.

And while our politics, at least in New York, might be liberal-left—at one high school Model Convention we nominated Adlai Stevenson for President and gave him a platform which internationalized the Panama Canal, doubled the minimum wage, abolished HUAC and the Connally Reservation to the World Court, and recognized Red China—the skills we employed, the style of argument, was an art acquired from a Congressional committee. We did it that way because that was the way it was done.

The Major League of the Student Conference, the Nirvana of every Meeting Freak, was the annual Congress of the National Student Association. Founded after World War II as a means of enabling the voice of liberal anticommunism to be heard in the world, the NSA operated in the early '60s out of a rattletrap tenement in downtown Philadelphia, in which every inch of space from basement to attic was clogged with battered desks, broken typewriters, Coke bottles, mimeo machines, pamphlets, magazines, books, and endless stenciled reports on the 8th International Plenary of the National Union of Students of Venezuela, many of them printed on blue paper bearing CONFIDENTIAL stamps.

The officers and staff of NSA led what seemed to be lives of incredible glamour. Armed with credit cards and passports, they worked all night, flew to distant nations for urgent huddles with African students, met with Congressmen, defended the Association from the Young Americans for Freedom, and testified before commissions and committees about Whither American Youth. It wasn't exactly clear what the NSA was doing for the students back on campus, but it was very busy doing it. And anyway, for us Meeting Freaks, its annual Congress, our Woodstock Nation, was reason enough for its existence.

We would gather each August, five hundred of us, on some large midwestern campus, sitting on either side of

long tables in some huge ballroom or meeting hall, taking
our turns speaking into microphones placed throughout the
room. The pronouncements fell like rain upon the wicked
of the earth.

"We condemn the oppressive, unrepresentative government of Turkey for its brutal suppression of the legitimate
aspirations of the National Union of Turkish Students, and
its reprehensible subjugation of the spirit of Ataturk." Once,
I think, we condemned the government of Afghanistan for
not *having* a student union. Each of our resolutions were
models of Emulation, containing a FACT PRINCIPLE, DECLA-
RATION, and MANDATE section, just like the United Nations.
We were particularly enthralled to see large numbers of foreign students in attendance, as though their willingness to
travel thousands of miles was itself proof of our importance
(the idea that the Third World's Leaders of Tomorrow might
be more interested in a free vacation to America than in listening to debates on civil liberties was, we were sure, a sec-
ondary consideration).

And every summer, as we argued and caucused and stayed
up into the night, and plotted to elect new officers of the
National Student Association, a curious phenomenon reap-
peared; a handful of past officers and staff members of NSA
would, as if by magic, return to the Congress, and take root
for the duration. They were part of a Young Old Boy network, elder statesmen of twenty-seven and thirty-one, who
(we told ourselves) were so pathetically obsessed with the
games of power and politicking they had known in their
youth that they had to come back each summer to breathe
the heady atmosphere of better days. Indeed, it seemed as if

these Young Old Boys were determined to be professional youths, something like the forty-two-year-old student leaders of the Communist bloc we used to laugh at contemptuously. (That, we told each other, was the difference between a government-controlled student union and our independent, self-sustaining operation.) Our forebears would take jobs in Holland, with the International Student Conference, in New York with the U. S. Youth Council, in Washington with the Foundation for Youth and Student Affairs, all these shadowy organizations whose only functions seemed to be attending meetings, and paying for the travel expenses of their officers.

In structure and style, then, this form of stirring among collegians was shaped and limited by the forms of our elders. There seemed to many of us no contradiction between speaking the words and singing the songs of revolutionary heroes, while we wore the clothes and played by the rules of a tweedy, highly structured assemblage of power speakers.

This same kind of contradiction was played out back at our campuses in the early 1960s. The issues that were capturing our attention were both worldwide and trivial; we could get as exercised over Women's Hours as over the testing of nuclear weapons. We believed, as much as any group of students in any school, that the administration was bureaucratic and dotish, that a host of rules and regulations were outrageous, that new buildings would wipe out woods and trees and grass for no good reason. But our essential understanding of the University was that it was a Sanctuary; enlightened, liberal, and superior to the outside world.

The enemy was clearly defined: a state legislature determined to tie financial support to political orthodoxy; a towns-people interested in overcharging us for fire-trap apartments and translating their jealousy into kicks and punches; and the Alumni, a curious populace who, instantly upon gradua-tion, transubstantiated from life-loving, good-natured people into crewcuts, bullnecks, and prefrontal lobotomies, demand-ing good football teams and quiescent, forelock-tugging stu-dents and teachers. Our fight was for higher faculty salaries, lower tuition, political autonomy, and the God-given right of the University to expand its good works into the neighbor-hoods of the surrounding community. The contest was clear: We, up on the Hill (literally, in the case of the University of Wisconsin), defending freedom and justice, against Them, at the foot of the Mountain, howling for our blood. That the University community was essentially our ally, we had no real reason to doubt.

This new Campus Pastoral was not as reassuring to outsiders as the Tap-Dancing-on-the-Table-Tops-at-Pop's was, but ul-timately it contained reassurance, continuity, order. The vision of junior John Kennedys, in sweaters and slacks, drafting telegrams of support to James Meredith might please ADA more than MGM, but there was no contradiction between cheering for equality and for the football team; no danger of breaking completely and angrily with the past.

I left this scene of tranquility in 1964. In the next half-decade, it all came apart.

It began in the streets of Dallas, in November 1963. We would learn later that the Presidency of John Kennedy was crippled by illusions and arrogance, a vision of global author-ity that would take root and bear its wretched fruit in Vietnam. But in those first years of the 1960s, we liked the President; we would watch his television press conferences and laugh at his quips and self-deprecating humor; we listened to his speech announcing the Nuclear Test-Ban Treaty and thought, "Maybe this thing is going to work out." To understand that this supremely confident, self-assured man could be slaughtered in broad daylight, his head blown off by some madman (or by some sinister consipracy; no one could be sure) was to understand the fragility of life, the powerful forces lurking just under the surface of life. What our parents learned in a War, or in a struggle for survival, we learned that November. No one was safe; if not John Kennedy, then definitely not any of us. There was more than hope and nobility in the outside world, more than a Peace Corps or a pursuit of excellence. There were killers out there too.

And in a sense, there were deeper shocks to come, hammer-blows to the confident security which characterized the Campus Pastoral. Many of our beliefs were stripped from us, exposed as nothing but shabby, smelly lies.

In the fall of 1965, as a camp follower of the National Student Association, I flew to Washington for a meeting at the new, incredibly plush, NSA headquarters—donated, we were told, by a wealthy gentleman who wished to remain anonymous. A good friend of mine, newly elected as an officer, was in a mysterious, bitter battle with others on the staff. A day later, he resigned. When I went in to see him in his office, he was pale, in a state of near-shock.

"There are things going on here," he said darkly, "that you would not believe."

"Oh, come on now," I said. "It's not as if this is some kind of Communist spy operation."

He laughed once, bitterly, and looked at me unblinkingly.

"No, not a Communist spy operation," he said, "but that's the general idea."

I assumed that my friend was shaken by the difficulties he had been through. But a year and a half later, I ran into an old friend from my Meeting Freak days, who was passing through New Haven. After one beer too many, one casual remark too many about the strange, weird world of the National Student Association, she let a chance remark slip about "CIA stooges," and suddenly, like some final summation by a detective in a B-Movie, I put the whole wretched picture into place. *That* was why the Young Old Boy network kept returning, year after year, to the NSA playground; *that* was why there was always money for plane tickets to the other side of the world; *that* was the purpose of those CONFIDENTIAL blue-papered memos on the sex lives of African students.

By sheer coincidence, the link between NSA and the Central Intelligence Agency broke into the open two weeks later; and suddenly I knew how people of my parents' age must have reacted when they learned that a committee to aid the Scottsboro Boys was a functioning cog of the Communist Party machinery. It wasn't that NSA meant very much symbolically, and certainly not politically; most of us knew how ludicrous we must have looked to a sane observer. But the knowledge that good friends had lied to me, and countless others, the realization that all of the rhetoric about "free, independent" student organizations, was bilge. Those Young Old Boys, all of them, knew fully of the ties between NSA and the Central Intelligence Agency; some of them, indeed, worked full-time for the CIA, not in a cloak-and-dagger, spies-and-bombs way, but respectably, responsibly, gathering information on political trends abroad. It was, they later explained, the only way to find financial resources to send liberal and radical young Americans overseas to meet with the Leaders of Tomorrow. No Congress would ever have authorized money for such a "left-wing" organization as the NSA, and we had to show the Asians, Africans, and Latin-Americans something other than the Communists, didn't we?

It didn't wash.

It meant, instead, that once again an institution simply was not what it told us it was. Its weaknesses were not matters of wrong policies, or wrong leadership, but structural; the heart of the NSA, the very precept which gave it any worth, was rotten to the core, just another shell game run by people in hidden halls, with hidden purposes. And what had made it possible was credulity; the willingness of people like me to believe in a charming, innocent Myth: just a bunch of kids, busting their little hearts to somehow stand together, independent, unafraid, to bring the truth, free of propaganda and official sanction. So much for the Principle of Emulation; so much for playing the game by points of order and coats and ties. For, far more important than the wholesale corruption of the National Student Association and its morally bankrupt leaders, the men we were emulating were themselves instructing us to trust them no longer. With the middle of the 1960s had come Vietnam, an event which cuts across the recent past like the jagged scar of a dagger ripped across a delicate tapestry. Television showed us Marines flicking

Zippo lighters open, casually burning a thatched-roof village; every day in the press, every night on the news, the words of the statesmen were torn up and reduced to pathetic little lies by what we could read and see and hear. And no one in the halls of Congress, none of the people whose style had seemed so seductive, so admirable, none of these people seemed to see the horror. None of the people in whose hands our destiny lay seemed able to speak words of simple, human outrage. No one seemed willing to risk a shred of political power to speak what so many of our countrymen were watching with numbed fury.

So we had to do it ourselves. And as we began, still playing out our roles in the Pastoral, with Teach-Ins, and scholarly lectures on the history of Indochina, and petitions urging the President to consider the possibility of negotiation, we set in motion—some of us deliberately, some of us unconsciously —the final destruction of the Pastoral.

Consider the elements in the equation:

First, the existence of Evil, aimed at us. Most generations may wait until they are committed to combat to discover that there are people in the world who wish them dead. We began hearing such truths from the veterans of Greene County, Alabama, and the Mississippi Delta; tales of shotgun blasts from pick-up trucks, obscene phone calls, and groups of voting-rights organizers trapped inside a church, waiting for the mobs with the lead pipes and ropes. Whatever excess fear may have tinged these tales was wiped out in 1964, when three young men—one southern black, two New York whites—were murdered by a mob which included the Sheriff and Deputy Sheriff of a Mississippi county. No debate here;

no all-night wrangling over whether we "deplore" or "condemn" Governor Faubus. This was for real.

Second, the possibility that the authority of the University may be tinged with that kind of Evil. The veterans of the southern crusades, and their more timid fellow travelers, had learned to view authority with the deepest kind of suspicion. At Berkeley, in the fall of 1964, they had confronted a University Authority that seemed to share at least some of the instincts of the southern law-enforcement community. After a series of demonstrations against companies that were supposed to be discriminating against Negroes, organized by campus action groups, the University suddenly closed off a parcel of its land to use by speakers, breaking a long-standing use of that land for off-campus political action. It was, by all judgments, an ill-conceived, foolish act. But in the eyes of the students, it was something more sinister. It was a clear sign that the members of the Board of Regents, with ties deep into the corporate-industrial power structure of California, were drawing the line on what students could do: when you start coming after our power, they seemed to be saying, we will tell the university to stop you.

Moreover, Berkeley was an institution—one of many—in which the student body's confidence was a fragile, decreasingly existent entity. The school was a symbol of Giantism run amok: lectures to huge halls of hundreds of students, separated from the instructor by the length of a football field; students and teachers who never met, never tested each other face-to-face; an education that seemed more at home in a cannery than a university, stamping out service modules for the System. Far more than a fight over a student's right to use a strip of land outside a campus gate, Berkeley was an inchoate explosion; a cry of betrayal by a constituency increasingly coming to identify an Enemy Within: a faceless, purposeless, soulless machine. And, as the Media's instant celebrity Mario Savio observed (long-haired, rhetorically outrageous, physical in his fury, a perfect commodity for the seven o'clock news), sometimes it was necessary to place your body in the gears of the machine, to force it to stop. And across the country, we watched police swinging their clubs and bloodying the heads of people who looked just like us, who seemed to be speaking to a sense of emptiness that—we began to understand—was not simply one of those pangs of late adolescence, but might be a consequence of the way the University was being run. Just a second with that Alma Mater, fellah, and can the Mixed Chorus: just what the hell is going on here?

"We fumbled, we floundered, and the worst thing is, I still don't know how we should have handled it," Clark Kerr said afterward. "At any other university the administrators wouldn't have known how to handle it any better."

Without Vietnam, it might have been possible to test that statement. With Vietnam, it became moot. The War and what it came to stand for put the last link in the equation:

Third: The possibility—or the certainty—that the University was nothing more than a link in the chain of responsibility for mass murder. The Berkeley rebellion of 1964 was unique not merely because it was the first explosive protest of "overprivileged" youth, but because it would be the last student uprising unconnected to the War in Vietnam for years. That uprising was about the quality of education; the organization of an academic community; free speech. Yet Berkeley had left a taste in the mouth of students across America; a sense that the community of scholars might not be what the Pastoral had taught. With Vietnam, the suspicions took on a darker hue. For that enterprise was not just a cozy acquaintance with the captains of industry and finance, or an aesthetically repugnant preference for high-rise classrooms to grass and trees. With Vietnam we were talking about something murderous, something totally antithetical to the University. And when the links between campus and war machine became evident, it was like cutting into a handsome patient on an operating table, to find a noxious cancer spreading through every part of the body.

Here is a Michigan State professor, teaching President Diem how to establish a secret police force; here is MIT taking a large chunk of its budget to run defense laboratories; tank gunsights are designed by an adjunct of the University of Pittsburgh; Cornell's Aeronautical Laboratory tests ammunition and radar; the University of California runs counterinsurgency programs with government money. In the first two or three years of escalation, the student community was as enraged with the behavior of the universities as it was with the government of the United States. Their teachers, those pleasant-faced men with bow ties, pipes, and monographs, had been part of that slaughter in Vietnam as much as if they had dropped the bombs instead of designing them, or herded peasants into relocation camps instead of setting up theoretical models for such camps. They were the soul brothers of those white-faced merchants of death, Bundy and Rostow and McNamara and Rusk, with their Rhodes Scholarships and pretensions of civility, whispering words of death into the ear of the Maximum Leader, dancing a jig when the U.S. began round-the-clock bombing of North Vietnam, in celebration that *their* scenario had been turned into reality.

Thus, the last stage in the equation which spelled the death of the Campus Pastoral. These communities, with their white columns and greens and air of calm and stately libraries with quotations from the Greeks, these places were steeped in bloodshed too, these institutions harbored the enemy as much as the Pentagon. We were in the presence of an enemy with no more scruples than a psychopathic murderer. It might be stated thus: "Those who hold power in America are killers; the Universities of America nurture that power, feed it and feed on it, are enriched by it. They too are killers. And their power, as much as Sheriff Clark's or Lyndon Johnson's, must be resisted by any means. Indeed, it is doubtful that such an institution even deserves the right to state its own defense, since a respectful hearing is a sanction in itself of the exercise of illegitimate power."

This was a dangerous equation, partly fallacious, incipiently totalitarian, capable of the most outrageous distortions. (Professor to students: "Please let me into the library." Student: "This library serves those who commit oppression and death on the Vietnamese. It cannot be allowed to function.") But it was subscribed to, in whole or in part, by a substantial minority of the student community in the last half of the 1960s. And it was an equation to which many universities had no response; their participation in the work of Vietnam had left them limply waving a tattered banner of "free speech." It was no defense. The scar of the War had tainted every value, every claimed noble purpose.

All through the mid-1960s a sense was growing that things were ripping apart; apocalyptic visions seemed to be tomorrow's headlines. Burned children in Asia; burned streets in New Jersey and Michigan; a President whose very energy and fearful power seemed impotent in the face of shattered boundaries of public conduct. A line from Yeats's "The Second Coming" was probably the most frequently quoted sentence in the speeches of politicians and analysts, trying to describe the sense of the times:

> Things fall apart
> The Center cannot hold
> Mere Anarchy is loosed upon the world.

To sit in the gothic library of the Yale Law School, surrounded by stained-glass windows and stone gargoyles, poring through dusty books of legal philosophy, grappling with eight-hundred-year-old concepts of order and liberty while the sense of anarchy deepened, was an exercise in schizophrenia. We were, it was understood, a special breed, World-beaters-in-Training, destined soon to sit at the feet of Congressmen and Supreme Court Justices, inhabiting the corridors of power, at a time when the assault on that power was building, an assault with which many of us were in open or covert sympathy. When I left law school, this sense of a two-level existence deepened as I went to work in the Senate office of Robert F. Kennedy.

By historical accident, and by his own character, Robert Kennedy was a source of fascination; heir to a martyred throne, super-star, a man born to wealth and power who had suddenly, violently been thrust from center stage. During the Kennedy Presidency, he had been for many of my friends and relatives a figure of fear and suspicion: a "real" Catholic (his brother's aura of detachment and self-mockery suggested that John Kennedy did not believe anything with religious fervor), the shadowy "hit man" behind the scenes, driven, compulsive, unredeemed by compassion or pity.

With the death of his brother and his election to the Senate, something seemed to change. Kennedy began to question the assertions of calm assurance. He seemed willing to challenge liberal and conservative cant: questioning the vitality of liberalism in front of Americans for Democratic Action, demanding something beyond welfare-state, big-government policies; doubting even his own insistence that the War in Vietnam was a noble, just cause. He suggested, too, something beyond office, coat-and-tie public service. The papers of the mid-1960s are filled with journeys, into the ghetto of Bedford-Stuyvesant, into eastern Kentucky, into the shacks of migrant workers in Texas and California. And there seemed the possibility in Kennedy of what was coming to be the first concern: an electoral challenge to Lyndon Johnson from within the Democratic Party.

I spent eleven months working in Kennedy's Senate office, and on his campaign. It was for me a descent into the maelstrom: the sheer combination of personal magnetism and potential power he radiated was enough to draw constant throngs of people into Robert Kennedy's orbit. Some wanted to be around him because they had clear, hard concerns and he had the capacity to get those concerns before the public.

Others were simply satellites; people with a compulsive need to be in the center of action, or to be part of this year's or this month's excitement. Proximity, for almost everyone, became a kind of narcotic. One young campaign aide on his first political trip, became literally hypnotized by Kennedy. He could not break away; he would start to go back to a local office to do some work, and find himself hovering near Kennedy, unconsciously tagging along on campaign stops. In a lesser sense, everyone who worked with Kennedy fell victim to the same disease.

The level of experience, the sense of excitement, anguish (Did he like the work I did? Will I be allowed to stay?) and potential, the importance of the stakes we were all playing for, was a drain on energy and will unlike anything else I have lived through. By the time the end came, on a June midnight in a Los Angeles hotel, the sense of rage, grief, and sorrow was leavened with a kind of resignation: it couldn't last, it was too demanding, too exciting, too hopeful. The black hats won, like they always would. And among the disaffected young, many of whom had turned away from him because he would not challenge Johnson soon enough, Robert Kennedy's death seemed a confirmation of a lesson they were coming to accept without question: *there is nothing ahead that is any good.*

By the end of 1968, that mad year with tanks surrounding the Capitol, and two murders of hope in eight weeks of each other, and the sudden end of yet another kind of Pastoral—clean-cut students canvassing for McCarthy standing, a few months later, in downtown Chicago, choking on tear gas and bleeding from the clubs of the police—

by the end of that year the bitterness seemed to be deeper, more entrenched than ever. And it was coupled with a mode of expression that was supremely ironic for America. Since the Second World War, America had purged its political Left, driven them into exile, or into the unaccountable caverns of the Central Intelligence Agency (which had more social democrats in its employ than any dozen universities). There were no radicals in Congress, none on the airwaves; except for I. F. Stone, virtually none in the public prints. There was no radical tradition in America to which the newly enraged young could adhere to; no political party, no spokesman, no pattern which seemed appropriate. The bitterness, then, had to be expressed existentially, moment by moment, using symbols wholly outside the comprehension of mainstream America. The music, of course, because rock and roll was the music of the Young, completely and uncompromisingly; clothes and hair, because they were marks instantly identifiable and recognizable, like passwords of disaffection. And thus, the very thoroughness with which the radical past was demolished made the radical present traditionless, directionless, impulsive, instinctive, for better and worse: nonideological yet moralistic, unfettered by old defeats and betrayals, unleavened by wisdom and prudence.

With the start of the Age of Nixon, I was curious to see how the tumult of the half decade since I left the University had affected the new student generation. Perhaps it was because of my own rootlessness, a hangover from a surreal eleven months working for Robert Kennedy, finding myself swept into the tidal wave of energy and hope of his search for the Presidency which crashed on a midnight in June in Los

Angeles; perhaps it was simply an impulse from a search-for-lost-youth category. Whatever the motive power, I journeyed three times in the first two years of Nixon to look at what I had recently been. This is what I found.

THE FEVER AT REST

COLLEGE EDITORS
IN THE HEART OF THE BEAST

Walter Cronkite is worried. No calm reassurance, no avun-
cular chuckles tonight; instead, an extra furrow, a grimmer
set to the jaw. Something is Happening. Behind him this
Thursday in February 1969 is a projection map of the United
States, dotted with pockmarks of explosions. A strike at the
City University in New York, false alarms and billows of
real, black smoke. Thousands of National Guardsmen occupy
the University of Wisconsin, repulsing a massive strike in
support of black students. Police patrols at San Francisco
State fight pitched battles with students and their Street People allies. Sit-ins at the University of Chicago, in defense of a
radical faculty member who is being fired. And everywhere,

everywhere, marches against the War, attacks on ROTC, harassment of recruiters for the companies that manufacture war products, rallies against secret defense contracts that help the government wage the War. For thirty minutes, fragments of violence dance across the screen in a hotel room in Washington; downstairs, several hundred collegians are gathering in convention. The topic chosen with exquisite irony: "The Economics of Social Disorder."

The College Editors' Conference of the U. S. Student Press Association is for me an alma-mater-social club, an enduring beacon of younger days. I had been one of its Elder Statesmen; I had written its Code of Ethics—be responsible, don't mix fact and opinion, apologize immediately for unfounded statements and personal attacks. For more than two years I had edited *The Daily Cardinal* at the University of Wisconsin, attacking fraternity racism, demanding justice for southern Negroes, freedom of speech for Gus Hall, and free grass—the kind that grew outside the Student Union, not the kind you smoked. Now I sit in my hotel room, looking at the front page of yesterday's *Cardinal*: nothing but a page of stark pictures, National Guardsmen, impossibly young and frightened, with fixed bayonets on the ends of their rifles (could they seriously mean to *use* those rifles on the students? Impossible); cops with gas masks facing a line of students.

And this editorial attacking the University:

"When will they see that the 'Great Liberal University' they claim to be saving has already been through one butcherous lobotomy too many? How long will the price of admission to the legislative chamber be paid for with student minds? How long? For striking students, and for all today . . . there can be no peace on this campus until the present order is hauled down, taken apart, and built anew."

What is this? Is this the same paper in which I fought so hard for decent chicken salad sandwiches? How did I come, so soon, to fall on the other side of the Generational Fault, watching the chaos as an outsider, married, with a job and a wallet full of credit cards, and a coat and tie? How did They stop being Me so completely and confusingly? It is time to find out What is it These Kids Today Want.

Washington's Shoreham Hotel is an odd site for such an inquest. A sprawling complex at the edge of Rock Creek Park, it features catacombs of meeting rooms and banquet halls, an enormous sunken lobby which could accommodate a ballroom scene in a Napoleonic epic, and a huge, curved desk behind which the understaffed, overworked clerical force gropes with waves of conventioneers, hurling toward them armed with pink reservation slips and a firm belief in the power of their Connections. ("Look heah, ah don' cah if yew can't fahn mah resavayshun, ah'm a puhsonal fren' of a Congressman, heah, honeh? An' ah *wahn* mah resavay-shun.")

Such is the size of the Shoreham that a national convention can be swallowed up as easily as a single guest. At any given moment, a Model United Nations, chock full of boys with slicked-down hair and girls with circle pins, can operate cheek-by-jowl with an American Automobile Dealers' Franchise Symposium; a high school Key Club will be swearing fealty to Yale Locks while a black-tie wedding party is gorging its way through the Chicken Véronique.

But now, it seems, an assistant manager with a wicked sense of humor has been at work. The College Editors' Conference has been lodged between the Chemical Marketing Research Association and the Kodak High School Coach of the Year Clinic. This Thursday the coaches have not yet arrived, and the Chemical Marketers appear to be planning a swift retreat as the long-haired, casually dressed collegians gather at the Shoreham. The lobby is—literally and spiritually—split down the middle; short-haired marketers stare across an instinctive no-man's-land at the editors. Five years ago, the gap would have been narrowed by the commonality of coats and ties. Not now. Tie-dyed chinos, jeans, army jackets, backpacks, and flowing locks mingle with a rear-guard handful of slacks and a stray sport jacket on one side of the lobby. Across the great divide, the Chemical Marketers mingle among short-sleeved white shirts, stiff collars, single-breasted grays, browns, and blues, horn-rimmed glasses and multiple ballpoint pens in outside pockets, some matching the cheap silver gleam of tie clasps.

They stare furtively, repeatedly, as though they were glimpsing a woman with one too many buttons loose across a bus, at the registration table for the editors. Stacked copies of the *Guardian*, hailing the impending victory of the people's struggle in Indochina; SDS position papers; tabloids from the State University of New York at Buffalo, headlining rent strikes and draft resistance. On the wall behind the table, a Student Press Association wall poster proclaims in six languages:

"We are the students of the global village. We have been born to power and affluence; but we seek instead to transcend these social, political, and economic provincialisms of older generations."

Facing such an exquisite summary of grandeur, arrogance, and self-consciousness, the Chemical Marketers are reduced to mumbling security blankets at each other. "Firestone is weak in marketing . . ." "PPC should have a really dynamic breakthrough . . ." "Well, at Polytechnical Services, we . . ." They wander back and forth, uncomfortably fingering their name tags which, in the context of the editors lurking nearby, read like caricatures in a morality play: Imperial Oil, Gulf, Reichold Corporation. Two men look especially uncomfortable; they bear the tags of Dow Chemical, for three years a principal target for the wrath of campus communities.

Since the outrage of napalm, manufactured by Dow, the antiwar movement has focused on the company as a symbol of corporate evil done in the name of profit. Recruiters for the corporation have been locked in, locked out, harassed, badgered, and physically manhandled by students demanding to know how they could work for a company which manufactures a substance that burns the skin off civilians. (I have always found myself in sympathy with the recruiters, men who are as much victims of fate as a Hitchcock character who walks innocently into a room to borrow a match and finds himself pursued by eight competing groups of spies and international criminals. One day this poor, bright young lower-middle management man found himself called into some office. "Ferguson," said the superior, "you're personable and fairly young. We'd like you to try recruiting. Try and find some dedicated young genius who wants to double the uses of Saran Wrap." And poor Ferguson, armed with an attaché

case full of graphs about major medical insurance, paid vacations, and profit-sharing funds, finds himself interpreting the
Geneva Convention to a hallway full of chanting, shouting
youths who probably use nothing but Cut-Rite.)

Some of the Marketers edge over to the editors' display
table. They leaf through the tabloids, the underground press
with expressions suggesting a child looking at six Brussels
sprouts which remain between him and his dessert.

"Hey, Harry," shouts one from across the DMZ. "Bring
back one of those papers with the . . . Anglo-Saxonisms."
Harry smiles weakly at a young woman.

"Got a party going tonight?" And then the uncertain,
nervous, pseudo-macho laughter of a man away from home.

The first real session of the Congress involves a report
from those student editors who have met with the men of
the new Nixon administration. It might be said that their
tone reflects disillusion, except that there was a lack of much
illusion to begin with.

One woman editor is reporting on her meeting with a
State Department lawyer. She speaks crisply, matter-of-factly.

"He was exceptionally noncommittal on every question we
asked him . . . he left us in a state of frustration. The whole
discussion centered on the Vietnam War, and he gave us the
run-around. He didn't obligate himself in any way." She
stops. Pause.

"I didn't know any more than when I came in . . .
(pause) . . . he was a very *nice* man . . . Well, then we met
with four junior executive types who said they were looking
for an open forum to bridge the generation gap . . . (pause)

. . . we promised we'd send them our campus newspapers."
She concludes to general laughter.

"I'm trying to think of what we learned," another editor
begins, talking of his visit to the Pentagon. "Well . . . they've
made a serious effort to integrate the Armed Forces. And
they've succeeded."

"Yeah," a voice from the back yells. "Those casualty rates
for blacks are sure integrated."

"This man worked in one specific area," the editor-reporter
goes on, "but . . . I'm not sure what it was."

A *Michigan State News* editor supplies the local Pentagon
color.

"It's unreal. There are guys riding around on go-carts,
guards everywhere. We asked the guy the tough questions:
what about race riots in Danang, what about separatism in
the Army, what kind of training could black militants use at
home for guerrilla warfare purposes, what happened to the
black soldiers who refused to go to Chicago for riot duty
during the Convention. And it was incredible. He just didn't
tune in."

"Instead of talking about college disorders and student
problems," reports a *Daily Californian* staff member of native
son Finch, "he kept talking about cutting off funds to
southern school districts. He just completely ignored the
problems of the campus today."

"Hey, man, listen."

Heads swivel. Chairs scrape. The interjection comes from
the back of the room, somewhere from a cluster of Freaks, all
of them jeaned, their hair longer, scragglier than the long

hair of the editors, pale faces, intense eyes. They are Street People, or underground press, or drifters looking for free food —there is no way of knowing, but the way they slouch, the glances they shoot each other, the space they preserve between themselves and the rest of the room, defines them as Separate.

"Look, man. What's the relevancy of what's going on?" the interrogator says, slowly, disjointedly. "You're not making an analysis of what's going on."

"We're here to tell you what we saw," says an editor. "You can make that analysis yourself from what we've said."

"But you're not relating any of this irrelevant stuff to the issues."

"How can we? Nobody said anything."

The Freaks shake their heads, laughing among themselves, and the session ends. But their presence stirs a sense of uneasiness among the editors, and the organizers of the conference. It raises a specter that haunts any gathering of the young these days: the Specter of disruption. The scene has been played out at commencements, conferences, symposiums, in classrooms and debates. The struggle for the microphone, the chanted obscenities from the floor, the rush to the podium for denunciations of the government, the speaker, the audience, the organization, the angry exchanges in lobbies. Psychologists, philosophers, historians, linguists, are demanding statements against the war, against racism, challenging the right of the Mainstream to be heard at all. In 1968, during this same student press conference, Disruption struck. Partially planned by the sponsoring editors in an affort to create an encounter session atmosphere, partly exacerbated by the cheerful nihilism of Yippies Jerry Rubin and Paul Krassner, flavored with a Washington guerrilla-theater group, the ordered structure of a conference—speakers, panels, questions from the floor—was demolished. Senator Eugene McCarthy, the official, authorized Hero of the Young, was interrupted and taunted from the floor; participants in a panel found themselves bombarded by the sounds and slide projections of chaos and death; costumed players cavorted in the lobbies. It was too much for some of the straights, including financial supporters of the conference like *Newsweek* and *Reader's Digest*.

Will it happen again? No one knows; but the Freaks are gathering again. Their sleeping bags are propped up against the walls of the lobby; the temporary headquarters of the U. S. Student Press Association is packed with lumber jackets, jeans, and backpacks. For the organizers of the conference, running from telephones to file cards to sheets of paper, coordinating airline schedules and agendas, it is no more than another natural obstacle, like rain on the day of a picnic.

The Freaks never walk alone; they drift through the corridors of the Shoreham in packs, often so silent, so unfocused in their stares that they bring to mind the automaton-pea pod-victims from *Invasion of the Body Snatchers*. It is not pills or grass; it is something beyond chemicals, and more unsettling.

Soon, however, it is apparent that they have been doing more than wandering through corridors. On Thursday evening, a one-page, two-sides mimeograph broadside surfaces around the convention. Entitled "The Pipe Organ," its masthead features a freehand drawing of a marijuana pipe bearing a startling resemblance to the male genitalia, and a fist with an upraised middle finger.

"Challenge Marxian cunnilingual featherbedding!" it declares. "Don't be afraid to get caught with your print-oriented military-industrial culottes down! OWNERSHIP? Partnership! CAPITALISM? Rock music! Economic BULLSHIT? Yippie! Yes, friends, YIPPIE!"

The reverse side announced a "Super Yippie St. Valentine's Day Contest," promising that "the person who writes the best article about the pig party will get to fuck Janis Joplin at her next appearance in your home town . . . feed some slop to the pigs! Bring some heavy shit . . ."

A word of translation. The next morning is planned for a speech and discussion with a spokesman for the International Association of Chiefs of Police: the "pig party." The broadside is urging some form of confrontation, preferably a marijuana "smoke-in" to raise the policeman's consciousness, or at least his blood pressure ("bring some heavy shit"). Late Thursday night, the suggestion for a police-student confrontation moves from the printed page to another format; a meeting with the stylized quality of a morality play.

Following a series of keynote speeches, a group of Freaks walks up to the stage of the Empire Room (sometimes ironies do not wait to be illuminated by a hardworking writer; sometimes they run up and hit you over the head with a beanbag). They are "led," to use a forbidden word in the lexicon of young radicals, by David Livingston, from the American Playground, a D.C.-based guerrilla-theater group. Livingston is something out of Godard's *Weekend*: a Mick Jagger-androgynous face, red headband, tousled shirt and jeans. His allies sit at his feet—literally—and wander about the stage, at times holding brief, urgent conversations with each other.

In the audience, some sitting, some milling close to the stage, is a larger group of relative straights. The room is divided; up front, radicals, Freaks, and their allies; straights in the center of the room; neutrals somewhere in between. The argument: whether—and how—to disrupt the talk by the police representative on the morrow.

"Let's go somewhere and talk it over," says an editor.

"Why are we going anywhere else?" Livingston asks. "Let's stay right here and talk about tomorrow. Anyone who asks a question of the police chief without bringing a bag of garbage—"

A Freak interrupts: "If I bring dope, will you smoke it?" he asks a straight.

"Where do you go to attack the pig power structure?" comes a shout from the stage.

"That's the third floor," answers a voice from the floor.

"Look," says a girl from Agnes Scott College, deceptively demure, "I want to hear you out. But I also want to hear what the cop has to say."

"You know what the cop is going to say," a Freak shouts. "You've heard it a hundred times."

"Well," she says, "I want to hear him. If I disagree, I'll attack him. But not until I hear him."

"I'd at least like you to ask him to answer your questions."

Livingston is trying to bring ordered chaos by consensus.

"Let's agree on how long we want the cop to speak for."

From his allies:

"A minute and a half."

"Three minutes."

"I'm not going to let him talk for a minute."

"You don't have that right," interrupts a straight editor. "You can't tell anyone else how long they have a right to speak for."

A Freak leaps off the stage and walks toward the clustered editors, his hands outstretched, his voice beseeching.

"Don't think of him as an individual. You have to judge him in the context of his role."

"He's irrelevent," shouts another. "He's a tool of the capitalist system!"

"Damn it," a neutralist shouts at the radicals. "She's got to *hear* the guy first . . . You're not going to change the system by shouting him down. You guys aren't doing any good."

At least one Freak agrees. He is restraining an agitated long-hair with a Villanova sweatshirt, speaking to him with quiet insistence.

"Look, they don't understand, man. She's got to be educated."

The words flow on, as if from some clumsy TV movie about campus unrest: "symbol . . . establishment . . . pig . . . free speech . . ." By the time the group begins to break up, it is clear that the Disrupters have not carried their case. This is, after all, 1969; the ritual of confrontation has played itself out on dozens of campuses this year alone. Last year, the editors were trapped by surprise and guilt. This year, they do not seem to buy the necessity of expressing political hostility through upheaval.

Which is not to say they are prepared to embrace a support-your-local-police policy. This becomes clear Friday morning when Bob Johnston, president of the U. S. Student Press Association, escorts Quinn Tamm, the director of the International Association of Chiefs of Police, into the Heritage Room. There are no signs of the Disrupters, although one of them, garbed in a pig's mask and passing out leaflets, is unceremoniously booted out of the doorway a few moments before the police spokesman appears. The audience is straight, curious, and, to put it mildly, skeptical.

The man they have come to hear, Quinn Tamm, looks like . . . ah . . . well, he looks like what a director of the International Association of Chiefs of Police should look like. In his fifties, well preserved, Tamm wears a no-nonsense blue suit and a head of very close-cropped bullet-gray hair. His sober face is grimly set; he knows his audience today is not as receptive as, say, the Indianapolis Rotary Club.

Chief Tamm is introduced to an indifferent round of applause.

"I'd rather sit here and answer questions," he begins, and then offers a few facts about his group which turns into some informal remarks which becomes a speech which approaches Hubert Humphrey with a good wind.

Both Chief Tamm and his audience know that his remarks are warm-ups, batting practice while he reads his listeners. It is the questions they are all waiting for. The editors have kept their bargain with their sense of fair play; now they will keep their bargain with the radicals. They have listened. Now they are questioning.

What about press coverage of recent police behavior?

"I'm not a great admirer of the news media," Tamm says with heavy sarcasm. "I have strong views concerning bias and law-enforcement. I call the press 'the Froth Estate.' In Chicago"—the audience stirs—"there was atrocious use of the news media. There weren't *any* pictures of cops getting hurt. All the emphasis was on a small group of misguided youngsters." The room is quiet, the tension visibly higher. The Topic has been raised: Chicago. Police swinging at anything that moved, friends returning to campus with horror stories of Grant Park and beatings in the alleys of Oldtown and Balboa Avenue. Chicago. What about the behavior of the police? asks an editor.

"Let me say something about Chicago," says the Chief. "I was very critical of the mass coverage. There were 188 police officers injured. If you hit me, I have a right to hit back. I've seen police officers injured. I've seen the weapons the demonstrators used. Now, if a police officer violates the oath of office, he should be punished. But I would have lost my cool in Chicago too."

A moment later, an icily cool questioner returns to the Topic.

"Everybody knows that City Hall controls the cops and the violence in Chicago," he says. "You oughta have some *pressure.* I think you or somebody from your outfit should have been in Chicago. *You* didn't see a whole platoon of officers sweep down on the kids . . . *you* didn't have a cop knock a camera out of your hands . . . why don't *you* get involved? Don't you care what those uniformed men are doing?" Faster, angrier now. "You have no idea of what they did. You say a couple of hundred cops were hurt? Well, a couple of *thousand* kids were hurt. What about them?"

Chief Tamm, angry and impatient: "Well, what were they *doing* there?"

Hoots, whistles, a softly spoken, "Oh, come *on*."

"Now look," the Chief continues. "I came here because I was invited, not to debate—I didn't come here to be insulted."

"Are you afraid to debate?" a girl asks softly.

"You ought to start *some*where," a young man says.

"Yeah, how about student reaction to getting hit?"

"Well," Tamm begins, "if you want a philosophical discussion . . ."

"It's the right of peaceful assembly!"

The audience is not heckling Chief Tamm, at least, not by the standards of the Street People or the Freaks. They are not calling him names, or lighting up joints, or chanting at him. No, they are almost pleading with Tamm, beseeching him for a response: *talk* to us about Chicago, *tell* us why you don't see what happened as an outrage. There is a long pause. At last, without a flicker of emotion, Tamm speaks as a machine might:

"Chicago is a glaring example of what shouldn't have happened. It shouldn't happen in a country like ours."

A moment later, the formal session ends; but the editors crowd around Tamm. What *about* Chicago, man? Do you *know* what they did? My brother . . . my roommate . . . There is no sign of insult. But there is no acquiescence. This man stands with people who beat up their friends. And they are not about to let him forget it.

Of course, Chief Tamm never had a chance. In the months after Chicago, a police official stands a slim chance of qualifying as a culture hero. But the speaker at 11 A.M. surely does. In the Diplomat Room, a large hall with crystal chandeliers, Louis XIV moldings, pink drapes, and the faint echoes of five-thousand-dollar weddings, a documentary movie called *Cassius le Grand* is concluding to the cheers of the editors, who have packed into the hall, applauding the filmed antics and boxing of the ex-heavyweight champion of the world, now stripped of his title for refusing to enter the Army.

As the film ends, the cheers turn into shouts and whoops of approval, because Muhammed Ali himself is there, surrounded by editors, black and white, seeking his autograph and shaking his hand. There are, in fact, more black faces here than there have been—or will be—at any session of the Conference, except for the Black Caucus.

The introduction is short and simple.

"I have no presumption in introducing the Champ, Muhammed Ali," and Ali stands, impeccably attired in a severely cut suit, his face unmarked, strikingly handsome. In the first row, three young black men stand for him, throwing the power-fist salute.

The questions are respectful, not probing. Ali is a special kind of hero, bearing a parallel to the Beatles. He has tasted all of the riches and perquisites of fame that can be thrown at a man, and he has decided to repudiate the ground rules; he is no longer playing Their game. The Beatles in 1963 were four cheerful young men, singing silly songs as the '60s version of bobby-soxers screamed and swooned. And then, after all the hype, the millions of dollars, the *Life* magazine covers, *after* the teen magazines had locked their images tightly into place, there was a whole new brand of Beatles music: *Rubber Soul, Revolver, Sgt. Pepper,* sitars, dissonances, atonality, words that bit like acid. There was, bursting through the packaging and exploitation and airport interviews with bubble-gum radio stations, unmistakable genius.

Mutatis mutandis: Cassius Clay, everybody's favorite colored boy, with pretty girls, jokes, humorous doggerel, brilliant footwork (or was it natural rhythm), an archtypical bojangles. And suddenly, on the very night of his World Championship, he stands with a new name, an alliance with the dark, mysterious Muslims, and a bitter indictment of white America. And finally, there is his refusal in Houston to take the symbolic one step forward in an Army Induction Center; and within hours, with no hearing, no trial, the political hacks of state athletic commissions have stripped him of his title and denied him the right to make a living; Clay-Ali has stopped playing the game by Their rules, and he is suffering the consequences.

Which is exactly why Ali seems so authentic a hero to so many collegians; his decision may soon be theirs. All through 1966, 1967, 1968, the Draft has been a cloud over the campus. This is no abstract debate over Negroes a thousand miles away; no commitment fulfilled on a Saturday afternoon outside of a Woolworth's in the security of a neighborhood: no faraway, deliciously exotic topic like independence for Algeria. No, indeed, the Draft means You, Him, Me, Us; are we going to go to Vietnam, and get shot at, and face down a mother and child with an M-16, are we going to abandon family, friends, and career for Canada, are we going to spend five years in jail? And Muhammed Ali has answered the question in a way most of these editors know to be right: he has given up wealth, fame, and perhaps freedom. That act, by itself, is enough to win the respect of this audience. For such is their sense about their country now, after a decade of Vietnam, that to refuse to participate in that venture is an act which demands instinctive sympathy.

The questions:

Will you stay in America if your conviction stands?

"If I left, I'd be branded a coward . . . I wouldn't take no plane to Florida, no," he says and the audience laughingly acknowledges his reference to a recent black militant's hijacking of a plane to Cuba.

What about Malcolm X, the voice of the Muslims, the man who converted Clay into Ali, who broke with Elijah Muhammed, who stood as a symbol of young black anger, and who met his death in 1965 in the Aragon Ballroom under a hail of bullets? The answer, which he has given many times before, is by rote.

"Which Malcolm X? Do you mean the one who was made famous by Elijah Muhammed, or the one who went hypocritical? Which one?" Now the laughter is nervous, uneasy. Malcolm, after all, is another campus hero, a man who stood up, said no to the rules, and died for it.

"Malcolm X was brainwashed by all those cameras. He thought *he* was the leader. He was destroyed by the cameras. He told me that he wanted to start a new movement. He wanted to start a rifle club. We admired him, fed him, clothed him. But we follow the teacher, not the student."

It is an uncomfortable moment, and, with the next question, Ali turns to a more humorous vein. Are you really the world's champion? he is asked.

"Well," Ali says slowly, with the faintest hint of a smile. "Liston thought *he* was champion of the world." Laughter. "Terrell and Patterson were used, and they paid *dearly*." More laughter.

What about alternative service? Would you consider that route?

"I'm doing it now," Ali replies, smiling. "I'm stoppin' riots."

Would you accept an enlisted man's pay?

"How much is that?"

"Ninety dollars a month."

Long pause.

"Oohhhhhh." Long applause. "No, I wouldn't take that oath."

Aren't the courts and the athletic establishment denying you your constitutional rights?

"You can say that and I can't," Ali answers.

Why not? asks the young white student, and no fighter ever walked into a cleaner left hook.

"You got the complexion and the connection."

When the press conference ends, Ali wins a standing ovation and ringing applause. Yet, a few minutes later, there is a curious footnote to the appearance of this defiant hero. All this Friday morning, the participants in the Coach of the Year Clinic have been arriving at the Shoreham; dozens of men with whom Chief Tamm would blend in without a flicker. On their ruddy heads, the crewcuts stand proudly erect. The inch-wide ties, the checked sport jackets, the black wing-tipped shoes, the slaps on the back, all speak to roots anchored irreconcilably in a society separated from the college editors by the Generational Fault. Unlike the now-departed Chemical Marketers, the coaches look at the long-haired students with outright contempt; they seem to be wishing for an act of provocation that will legitimize a paste in the mouth.

As the coaches mingle in the lobby, they immediately spot Ali; they surround him, pepper him with mock-cordial greetings and questions.

"It's Cassius! Hey, Steve, c'mere, it's Clay. How ya doin', champ?"

Within moments, without a word of protest at the use of his "slave name," Clay—for surely it is Clay now, not Muhammed Ali, moving, bobbing, shouting back answers and jests to questions—Clay is reciting his poetry about turning Joe Frazier into "the world's first colored astronaut."

"What about Liston, Cassius?" a coach shouts at him.

"Liston? That big ole ugly bear!" Clay shouts back, cavorting within the tightening circle. Not a word about politics, no reference to the Honorable Elijah Muhammed; a gesture, a punch or two, a fast version of the Ali Shuffle, feet dancing back and forth. With a zest that was nowhere in evidence during his press conference, Clay now demonstrates the skills he is no longer permitted to practice in the presence of those who most eagerly await his imprisonment; and it is impossible to tell whether Clay or the coaches enjoy the put-on the most; or, indeed, who is putting on whom.

In the early 1960s, we college journalists were Press

groupies, faithful followers of the *Front Page* school of news-papering. We laughed with A. J. Liebling's accounts of the Wayward Press, chuckled—but envied—the snap-brimmed, press-carded, tear-out-the-front-page movie reporters of the '30s and '40s, and spent hours arguing the relative merits of Bodoni Bold and Tempo Italic headline types. We coveted Chicago *Sun-Times* and New York *Herald-Tribune* page makeup books, for their fresh ideas, and cherished a hope of getting stories good enough to be picked up by the UPI wire, or—paradise!—mentioned, with credit, by the New York *Times*. Fittingly, these conferences were held in an arena which fueled our fantasies: New York's Overseas Press Club, with paneled meeting rooms, a smoky bar from which women were, of course, excluded, and pictures of great war correspondents.

The intervening five years have not been kind to such visions; the press, too, has been revealed as a timid, sometimes obsequious institution, willing to protect its profits but not its principles, transmitting official lies into credibility. A whole new stratum of information has been created: the underground press, chaotic, irresponsible, biased, sometimes obscene, yet also freewheeling, untainted by ties to illegitimate authority that seem to fetter the great engines of journalism. The TV networks, the commercial press, look a lot more like another Dumb Grownup, more properly greeted by a squirt from Clarabelle's seltzer bottle or a demonic practical joke by Froggy the Gremlin, than by hosannahs for the First Amendment and the fearless, crusading muckrakers. This Friday afternoon, an event which my contemporaries would have greeted with sheer delight—a chance to listen to representatives from the real live professional press—becomes instead yet another demonstration of the suspicion and hostility to authority.

There are five speakers on this panel: Edward Barrett, former Dean of the Columbia Journalism School and a perennial participant in these student press conferences; Jules Duscha, late of the Washington *Post*; Shelia Ryan of the Liberation News Service, a clearing house for the underground press; Randy Furst, of the leftist *National Guardian*; and Jim Higgins, of the iconoclastic York, Pennsylvania, *Gazette and Daily*, an independently owned, fiercely antiestablishment, small-town daily newspaper.

Barrett is first; a link to the days when *Reader's Digest* ran these conferences, packing the panels with East European émigrés explaining the inflexible nature of Soviet foreign policy, and the good works of Radio Free Europe. He speaks in defense of the objective press, with a good word for advocacy journalism, and a call for better education and higher salaries for journalists.

Now, Miss Ryan. Her credentials are belied by a soft voice and sweet face which touches her with an aura of innocence. Five years ago, she might have been asking big-university editors what to do about a Mother Superior who wouldn't let her run pictures of boys and girls dancing together. Now, a serape thrown over her shoulder, she speaks to different concerns: attacking the "aura of objectivity which is not in fact objective," scorning the link between university trustees making decisions which benefit their economic interests, charging that "the hands of the people are controlled by the major corporations . . . the whole engineering curriculum, for example, is geared to teach people to build machines which break down quickly."

The *Guardian*'s Randy Furst, intense, pale, with nape-length hair and a blue work shirt, echoes Miss Ryan.

"If you go to the center of any trouble-making institution, you'll find regular readers of our paper," he says proudly, "you'll find regular readers of our paper. And if you decide to go into the commercial press, go into it not with the idea of reforming it but with the idea of taking it over."

Now a clash erupts. Jules Duscha, now directing the Washington Journalism Institute, lights into Furst, and the underground press.

"He doesn't know anything about journalism, and he doesn't know anything about the Washington *Post*," Duscha begins. "Mr. Furst wants to turn all newspapers into journals of opinion . . . Before anyone criticizes the great newspapers of this country, they ought to know what they're talking about."

Duscha attacks the "authoritarian tendency of the radical press . . . If I were feeling mean today, I'd say the *fascist* tendency." He is particularly incensed at a *Daily Californian* editorial which called Ronald Reagan an "idiot governor." "Writing is of a low state," he says, "if the best you can do is to throw out four-letter words."

A few moments later, it is Jim Higgins' turn. Higgins looks like what Ernest Hemingway was groping for. He sports a full white beard, a fisherman's-net sweater, sport jacket, and pipe. He looks out on the audience with perpetual wry amusement. In age and in occupation, he seems distant from the young, disaffected panelists. But ideologically, he is one of them.

He immediately turns on Duscha.

"'Idiot' is a five-letter word, not a four-letter word," he begins. "But maybe the real question is whether Reagan is or isn't an idiot." From here he begins a cheerful, wholesale assault on the commercial press in general, equating its outlook with Reagan's.

"The conventional press is much more velvet-lined, but it is just as authoritarian," Higgins says. "The press assumes institutionally that everything is okay, but maybe things could be a bit better."

Jules Duscha interrupts.

"I'm an admirer of Mr. Higgins' paper," he begins, but it is no go.

"I'm an admirer of I. F. Stone, but not of the Washington Post," Higgins cuts in. "It wasn't the Post or the New York Times that defeated LBJ, it was the National Liberation Front. In fact, the whole war in Vietnam is rooted in the very foreign policy the Washington Post and every other paper accepts." The voice of the conventional press, says Higgins, is a voice that speaks "essentially to make money. That just isn't my measure; it's a moral measure of what's important. The Gazette and Daily has steadily lost circulation because we've opposed American foreign policy ever since the Marshall Plan and the Truman Doctrine." It is the unchallenged acceptance of the foreign and domestic policies of this government by the press, he concludes, that is one of the great obstacles to a better country.

Coming from a perspective of twenty years in the "straight"

press, Higgins' attack sparks the audience. Their response is intriguing: they listen, they are clearly on the side of the challengers, but there is no uproar. It is, instead, a placid acceptance of something they already know to be true: that the people in charge aren't doing what they claim to be doing, and are incapable of telling the truth about what they are doing. After Vietnam, after the secret defense contracts between campuses and the military, after the madness of 1968, the revelation that the commercial press is itself walking on clay feet is just another piece of evidence building to a case against the Powers That Be that seems irrefutable.

And the distrust runs even deeper; it runs, also, to people who might well be symbols of decency, but who speak with the style of the Enemy. Witness what happens on Saturday to Walter Reuther. If there is a figure in public life who has cleaved to principle, the President of the United Auto Workers would be a candidate for such recognition. He built his union up from nothing, taking on and defeating General Motors, the single most powerful private institution in America. He endured beatings, shootings, and an ambush by Henry Ford's goons which almost killed him. Reuther turned his back on the affluent life style of George Meany and other union leaders; the United Auto Workers kept alive the struggle for basic economic equity—universal health care, guaranteed annual wages—at a time when many labor leaders seemed to embrace liberalism's "affluent society" myth; and out of the union's Solidarity House came endless reams of research on the maldistribution of wealth and income, and the inequities in the tax code and wage scales. While Meany and Jay Lovestone were taking CIA money to foment strikes against left-wing governments, and endorsing a foreign policy somewhere to the right of Barry Goldwater, Reuther was arguing for a nuclear test ban treaty; while craft unions were excluding blacks, Reuther was pumping money into the civil rights movement and the work of Cesar Chavez.

Impressive credentials; but not here. For the American student community is not simply going through a political disaffection; it is stylistic as well. This student generation has never been offered any sense of an enduring radical tradition in America, in politics or the press or anywhere else. And in fashioning their own, out of necessity, they have adopted a cultural tone to their movement. Walter Reuther does not fit in; he is a stylistic remnant from another age. His speaking style, forged in union halls where a shout was the only way to be heard, is evangelical, as if speaking into the teeth of a fist-fight, not whispered into a television microphone. His rhetoric is straight out of postwar American liberalism: let us seize this wondrous technology and build a great country, building up the underdeveloped world, lest Stalin and Mao get there first.

Consequently, Reuther's student audience is not receiving him well; there is a kind of come-off-it-buddy snickering that greets some of his more effusive proclamations.

"For the first time," Reuther is intoning, his voice vibrating off the back wall, "we have the capacity of mastering our environment . . . we must build a social order to shift our resources . . . to free man to grow as a spiritual being . . . Computers can think at three-tenths of a *billionth* of a second . . . and new computers are a thousand times faster than that. Consider the technological impact of that revolutionary breakthrough! If you stood on the equator and took a step forward every time a computer nudged you, you could walk around the earth seven times in a second!"

"Yeah," a voice shouts from the audience, "and you'd probably burn a hundred Vietnamese kids on the way!"

"We're learning to work with machines," Reuther goes on, "but we're *not* learning to work with man. As C. P. Snow said—and I read him three times—" A mock whistle of awe, followed by derisive laughter.

"We spend billions of dollars for the ends of war. Why is it when we ask for jobs and housing, they give us a Fourth of July speech? Why can't we spend billions for peace?" he demands, and the audience is still.

A voice: "Why don't you go out on strike against NASA? Why doesn't the UAW stop building bombers and missiles in California?"

"It isn't just that simple," Reuther replies. "They'd just go to another factory. Now," continuing his speech, "the second great priority is civil rights."

"What about human rights?"

"I'm talking about the complete civil rights problem. We all know we have to reject violence." Hissing from the Freaks at the side of the room. "Now, I know something about violence. I've been beaten and shot. It doesn't solve any problems." Half the room applauds. "There are no simple answers."

"You've been bought off!"

"I've been beaten up by the ugliest cops in Detroit!" Reuther shouts back. "I was invited to come here, and I'll make my statements." And the audience applauds, as it does for every speaker from John Lindsay to George Wallace; no tactic adopted by the radicals on campuses is as self-defeating as the attempt to shout down speakers. It transforms every confrontation into a question of free speech, and there is still enough of the old fair-play sense among most students to defend a speaker's right to be heard.

"I've been pushed around by experts," Reuther argues. "I'm *against* the status quo! I'm not ashamed of my record!"

Edgar Z. Friedenberg, a gnomish, radical professor at Buffalo, wanders in and listens for a few moments.

"I've never seen Hubert Humphrey looking so well," he says dryly. "This may be the most important speech of 1949."

Reuther is heading into the home stretch.

"You can't solve tomorrow's problems with yesterday's ideas. We must judge ideas not by their source, but by their substance. Now, I've gone over this rather quickly . . ." Snickers, since he's been speaking for more than an hour.

The speech finally ends; the questions begin.

What about the Panthers? What about the black revolutionary movements within the United Auto Workers?

"What about Vietnam?"

"On Vietnam, I'm working with Dr. Kerr on 'Negotiations Now,' and . . ."

"Oh, my *God, Clark Kerr!*" shouts a straight. Reuther looks puzzled, not understanding the symbol of Clark Kerr; not the defender of academic freedom from the late '60s, but the paradigm faceless bureaucrat-authoritarian of 1964.

When the question period ends, Reuther is surrounded by students.

"I'll respect your picket line," one says to Reuther, "but I want you to respect mine."

"Look," says Reuther, trying to answer half a dozen questions at once. "When you go around smashing computers—"

"C'mon, cut it out! Who the hell goes around smashing computers? We're talking about sit-ins, occupations, peaceful—"

"Dammit, there's nothing peaceful about smashing a computer," Reuther answers.

"Will you stop with that goddamn *computer!*" a young woman pleads.

Standing by Reuther is a middle-aged aide, a man as obviously devoted to Reuther as he is shaken by the angry interrogation. He turns to every questioner in the cluster, first left, then right, to anyone who will listen.

"Come on, don't attack this man, he's put himself on the line . . . he's spent his *life* fighting for justice . . . *listen* to him, *learn* . . . he's . . ."

From which one may draw the undeniable moral that no conventional, reformist, uncharismatic, coat-and-tie figure can win the hearts and minds of the young. Of course. Except a few hours later, the college editors give their most enthusiastic response of the entire convention to Ralph Nader.

In dress, in demeanor, Nader could be a time-warp traveler from a 1956 college of engineering class; or, more plausibly, a holdover from the Chemical Marketing Research Associates, long since fled from this den of iniquity. His hair is dark, close-cropped, sideburns ending far above the ear; his suit is dark, rumpled, with narrow lapels; his shirt is plain old white. His speech is brusque, sober, with no hint of rhetorical flourish, wit, or even a mandatory opening joke.

Instead, Nader brings to his appearance a mountainous evidence of facts. He is so weighted down with folders, clippings, reports, mysterious files no doubt filched from the inner sanctum of General Motors, that it almost appears a battle for him to make it to the podium. And then the attack begins: facts . . . numbers . . . this many people died from industrial diseases in 1969 . . . this group of professional men has betrayed its own Code of Ethics for personal profit . . . here is what the stockholders' dividend from this company means in terms of pollution . . . this law was gutted by this Committee and these lobbyists . . .

The response from his audience is not knowing laughter or cheers; it is instead silence, attentiveness. *This* speaker has been into the belly of the beast; *this* man does not know the system's corruption from hunches or assumptions; *this* guy's got the goods on them. There are few challenges to Nader's credibility or honesty or motivation from the floor. Instead, there is a different kind of inquiry. What can we do? How can we help? What difference can we make? Their passion is not a function of style or charisma, but a passion ignited by the evidence before them that a single human being can not only face the Machine, but begin to understand it, to spot where it has gone wrong, and to suggest specific changes in its design and operation.

The success of Nader is linked to a broad kind of attitude that has run through much of the talk at this conference: the ethic of personal responsibility. Whether it is a university dean, an Assistant Secretary of State, a corporation vice-president, or a labor union executive, the ritual of inquisition between the Voice of Authority and the challengers takes the same route: don't tell us about the limits of your authority or the role you were hired to perform; tell us what *you* are doing to stop an immoral war/condition of oppression/injustice." Nader is a living embodiment of one man, defying the largest and most powerful institutions, yet anchored in a practical, almost casual emotional environment, in which reality, evidence, facts mean something other than a cloak for the latest government-inspected lie. He does not need the right clothes, the right tone of voice, because his fight has daubed him with a baptism of legitimacy.

Saturday night. The lobby is a scene out of a Hollywood commissary; tuxedos, lacquered hair, expense-account tans, and jeweled necks and wrists glide past huddles of high school coaches, clustering nervously by the coffee shop and registration table, waiting for enough of their comrades to venture a night on the town; they are decked out in button-down white dress shirts, pleated slacks, wing-tipped shoes, and ankle-length socks. Heading into a room far away from the tuxes and gowns go hundreds of the collegians, work-shirted, jeaned, drawn by the promise of a hard-rock band, whose amplified rhythms are sending mild shock waves through the hotel lobby.

From inside the dance, the sound is a tangible, oppressive reality, cutting through the smoky darkness, pounding off the low ceiling and the walls, lined with sleeping bags and half-sleeping Freaks propped up against the wall. It is rock and roll music, of course, but to me, a child of rock and roll music from my, and its, childhood, it is a malignant mutation of the music, harsh, lethal, stripped of its cheerful eroticism, bound up in sado-masochism and cultism. On the dance floor, seen through a haze of pungent-smelling smoke, bodies weave in rhythm, atomized, blank-staring, faces utterly without expression.

There is a sensation of hostility in the air, free-lance, undirected. It is exemplified by the Freaks, standing close to each other, passing joints back and forth, speaking languidly, laughing in whispers. The wall they have erected between themselves and Others is high and thick; it is the single most unsettling quality of these kinds of Freaks. The sense of openness, generosity, and free-spirited fun that was the advertised charm of the Flower Children is missing; perhaps it is not in season. Whatever the explanation, the quick laughter when a straight passes by, clad in tie and sport jacket, is far more reminiscent of first-graders pointing their fingers at an outsider, or fraternity jocks lounging together with obvious contempt for an Outsider than it is of a band of Love Children.

Or so it seems to me. But is this sensation a consequence of their attitude or mine? Wandering through the black room, it suddenly occurs to me that I am probably the oldest person in the room. Is that possible? *The oldest person in the room?* Inside I am, of course, nineteen, but the fact is that at twenty-six, going on twenty-seven, I am somehow in the older half of the country's population: married, credit cards in my wallet, a job on a city payroll, a tie knotted around my throat, a sense of responsibilities and self-imposed hesitations narrowing the way I live.

By the standards of the students here, I am not young. I

am, somehow, inexplicably, on the other side of that Generational Fault. It is possible, at least, that these Freaks, seemingly so hostile and malevolent, are simply regarding me—or
ignoring me—the same way my friends and I would have re-
garded—or ignored—a recruiter for an insurance company back
in the early 1960s, when we were at conferences like these,
infinitely younger than twenty-six going on twenty-seven.

A few hours pass; every fifteen minutes or so a hotel security policeman comes by, walks up to the entrance of the
dance, peers in, wrinkles his nose at the blanket of bittersweet smoke, and walks away, muttering into his walkie-
talkie. It is probable that the Shoreham security force has
never before been faced with the issue of arresting several
hundred of its paying guests for violation of the laws of the
United States; it is also clear that discretion is the better part
of valor; nothing happens and the red dots of lights pass back
and forth, back and forth, along the walls, like some firefly
sentry.

Eventually the music dies; the young men and women
drift out of the Club Room, back toward the lobby. There,
some of the coaches, returning from the bars or strip joints
or movie houses of Washington, are standing, talking quietly;
the formally dressed guests file out, occasionally stumbling
out of weariness or drunkenness close to the editors' registration table, still stacked with radical tabloids and underground papers.

"Filth," mutters a heavily jeweled woman, on the arm of
a lustrously tanned man.

"Yeah," he says, leaning over as he passes to see if that

front-page picture really exposes the pubic hair of a young
girl.

By 2 A.M. only the editors and the coaches remain in the
lobby. They do not talk to each other at first, but it is almost
as if an argument is raging, unexpressed but evident. Finally,
a Freak speaks to one of the coaches.

"Hey, man, you wanna play some football?"

"What?"

"Football. Football. That's what you guys are, isn't it?
Coaches? How 'bout a game of touch."

It is absurd, of course. But within five minutes a dozen
Freaks and coaches are tossing a miniature football through
the deserted back lobby of the Shoreham. The game is con-
stricted; no long passes, no wide sweeps. And, curiously, the
blocking, the hitting in the line, all accompanied by high good
humor, is unbelievably vicious. Coaches, straight students,
and Freaks, are hitting each other with barely controlled
fury, each time apologizing with a pat on the back, a laugh,
a grin of understanding. Into the night, they line up, snap
the ball, and tear into each other, playing with no referee, no
victories, no end zones, but with a clear understanding among
them about what is going on.

On Sunday noon, the conference ends. The final speaker
is Kenneth Boulding, a Professor of Economics at the University of Colorado and a famous "futurist," a man who was
warning of the ecological peril before most Americans had
heard of the word. He is a white-haired, engaging man with a
glittering wit so appealing that it erases, within a minute, any
notice of a marked stutter. He is speaking of the Burden of
the Future; and it is a brilliant speech, one of the finest I

have ever heard, combining wisdom, passion, and wondrously glorious puns and jokes.

After a warning that "the title is better than the speech," he speaks of the fact that "the old know that they have a very good chance of coming to an end before the world, whereas the young are not so sure. Under these circumstances, it is perhaps unfortunate that so many decisions which affect the future of the world are made by the old who are not going to be around to suffer the consequence."

Boulding draws two distinct visions of the future: first, "the existentialist, who takes the view, 'what has posterity ever done for me?'; second, the futurist, like the dedicated Communist, 'who sacrifices all pleasure for a grand vision of the future he will never see.'

"To enjoy the present and yet work toward the future; this is the delicate and difficult strategy which is most appropriate to our human condition. This is a good time to be alive . . . of course, it's always better to be alive than dead."

He speaks of the dangers we face: war, overpopulation, the "entropy trap," an endless waste of resources by which "we're ripping up the planet and flushing it down the toilet, and this can't go on forever. In the past, there's always been some place like Kansas, where we could go and start over. Now, there's nowhere to go. I mean, space isn't even for the birds. The damn speed of light—it's so *slow*."

He concludes by warning his audience to be careful of ethnic or national or generational identities.

"In all parts of the world today, it is illegal and immoral to be human . . . so don't be content with anything less than the *human* identity. What I hope for is a newer left, or "further up" which will combine existentialist passion against present wrongs with a more realistic grasp of the dynamic processes of the world."

What Boulding has done, at the very end of this conference, is to speak from the strength which so many of the young have come to doubt: the capacity to fuse past wisdom into a device which illuminates, and inspires, and amuses and teaches. Boulding has shown in one hour what many of these students have come steadily to doubt: the "relevance" of learning and study for a purpose beyond a piece of parchment and a job. But, as the hotel begins to empty this sunny February in the first days of the reign of Richard Nixon, the prospects for their remembering what one man—or a few more, like a Ralph Nader—have shown them, amid the turmoil of their college communities, and the perversions of the Academic values, does not seem very hopeful. For every Kenneth Boulding, there are a dozen Walt Rostows, Clark Kerrs, and McGeorge Bundys, uncounted new lies and corruptions, to further fray the remaining strands of trust between the young and the men who run their communities.

THE FEVER PEAKS

MAY DAY AT YALE

The cab pulls away from the ancient brick railroad station and winds through the broken streets, past the empty lots and the jumble of concrete, brick, steel, and pipes of construction sites: the new sports arena, the new national headquarters of the Knights of Columbus, the new elementary school. From the overpass spanning the Connecticut Turnpike, we can see a town newly rebuilt. Macy's and Edwin O. Malley's department stores, a shimmering Park Plaza hotel, now packed with newsmen and television camera crews, a shopping mall, a multi-tiered parking lot. Across Orange Street is the remnant of the old downtown: a musty newsstand-lunch counter stacked with piles of three-hundred-point-headlined tabloids screaming of eaten foetuses and lesbian whipping orgies; narrow retail clothing stores with three-dollar shirts, six-dollar slacks, and button-down collars; furniture stores, sporting goods windows, and men with dusty gray hair staring out of the streaked windows for customers.

Not far from the two downtowns of New Haven is the Green, separating the town from the campus of Yale. Six square blocks of pastoral insulation, the lawn latticed by walkways, dotted with two-hundred-year-old New England Churches, the Green is bordered with street names embodying the Eternal Verities: College, Chapel, Temple, Church, Elm—God and Nature at Yale. On the west edge of the Green stands the Old Campus; fully shielded from the outside world by the oldest buildings on the Yale Campus, now used to house the freshman class. The setting might be lifted whole from an English university, although it is doubtful that the British would have put a statue of Nathan Hale in the midst of their freshman campus.

In its sense of antiquity, however, the Old Campus, and Yale University, is decidedly British, as though centuries of stability have anchored these gothic walls deep into the earth. From the Law School, gargoyles leer down at the passers-by; the entrance to the university library is so like a cathedral that a supplicant for knowledge might find himself uncertain about asking for a book instead of a candle.

On this Tuesday in late April it is sunny, more hot than warm, California weather melting away the ingrained chill of a New England winter. Tall young men in blue broadcloth shirts and madras bermudas languidly sail frisbees back and forth.

The cabby, lean and tanned, his hands rough and his hair

pompadoured, looks out at the tranquil scene. He shakes his head.

"Yeah. It's really going to go up this weekend."

"Why do you say that?"

"Why? Well, when they kidnap four hundred rifles . . . and the fires . . . did you hear about the fires they set in the law school? And those animals coming in? All I know is, I'm getting far away from here this weekend. It's really going to go up."

As we drive past the "colleges" of Yale (each dormitory complex is a college, self-enclosed with an interior courtyard, drawing undergraduates inward, away from campus-wide activities) the streets are dotted with Mustangs, Chevies, and Volkswagens; undergraduates are carting out boxes of records, stereos, TVs, some books, and clothes.

"What do you mean, am I leaving?" one nervous young man snaps. "What the hell does it look like I'm doing? You think I'm gonna stay around and watch this damn place burn down—with me in it?"

Across the plate-glass window of Liggett's Drug Store at Broadway and Elm, where the campus ends and the student trade store begins, an enormous plywood board covers the window, with a paint-sprayed apology: "General Accident Has Cancelled Our Insurance." The Audio Den, whose tape decks and stereos draw lustful stares in calmer times, is boarding up its windows, its display stock already moved to safer quarters. Haig and Haig clothiers stands in the bright sunlight and watches a workman board up the windows as he chats with Bartlett-Hoffman stationery, his next-door neighbor.

"Let's drill a hole," Haig and Haig says. "When they come in, we'll hide in your place."

Bartlett-Hoffmann laughs uneasily.

At the Yankee Doodle, an eleven-stool luncheonette with the best breakfasts in town, a rangy, easygoing Yalie chats with Connie, a motherly, pleasant waitress, as they watch the plywood going up across the street at the Audio Den.

"You closin', Connie?"

"Yes. We open Monday."

"That's why there's going to be trouble," the student goes on lightly. "Every store's closing, and the kids will break in."

Connie slams down a rag. She is angry.

"Yeah? Suppose they go berserk and somebody fires a shot through the window and it hits the chef or one of the help. Who's going to save *their* lives?"

So it has come at last to Yale: the Fever, the mobs in the night, the tear gas blanketing the campus, all of those televised images sweeping east out of Berkeley, triggering the National Guard into armed occupation of the University of Wisconsin, hurling hundreds of New York City police into bloody pacification of Columbia, pitting shouting, screaming students around the automobile of Robert McNamara at Harvard. For almost six years the Fever has left Yale untouched. Oh yes, a peaceful vigil or two on behalf of a professor denied tenure, Teach-Ins against the War in Vietnam, a continuing alumni revolt over the chaplaincy of William Sloane Coffin, who has been arrested for participating in freedom rides and antiwar actions. Yale, however, has stood unscarred. Not a window smashed, not a class blocked, not a recruiting officer held captive. Perhaps the calm was because of its architecture; even in revolutionary times, it is difficult to organize the sacking of what appears to be a cathedral. Perhaps it is because of Yale's constituency in the mid-'6os; drawn from enough of the aristocracy to impose an ambience in which passion was not sophisticated.

Now, however, from pressures within Yale and outside the community, a national Community of the Disaffected is spreading the word through its networks: Yale is where you will be this weekend. Perhaps ten thousand, perhaps fifty thousand people, will come to rally for an imprisoned band of Black Panthers. The numbers, really, do not matter; it is not the size of the crowd that is drawing the focus of the great American Media Machine to New Haven. No. What has drawn five hundred newsmen and camera crews, and thousands of federal troops, guardsmen, and police, is the whispered second half of the message coursing through the Community of the Disaffected: *come to New Haven this weekend, because this weekend, May Day, Yale will burn.*

One enormous practical joke, that's what it must be. Some witty undergraduate, seeking to create the ultimate parody of '6os madness, has structured this May Day weekend. On Friday, May 1, the newsmen, camera crews, sound men, technicians, photographers, magazine writers, all of us will crowd the New Haven Green, looking for the rally that will climax as the torch is put to Woolsey Hall, and the corpse of Kingman Brewster is dangled from a lamppost. At a given signal, a hundred members of Skull and Bones, Fence Club, the *Yale Daily News,* and the football varsity, half in black face, will race out of New Haven's Superior Courthouse and pelt us with powderpuffs and the Whiffenpoofs, strategically perched in the trees above the Green, begin singing, "We're poor little lambs/who have lost our way/baaa, baaa, baaaa." After a rousing cheer, we will all adjourn to Mory's and drown our sheepish embarrassment with Green Cups, those ten-dollar concoctions of champagne and crème de menthe served in loving cups, while the colonial eating club (Men Only) echoes to the rich young voices of the Whiffs.

If these thoughts of mine this Tuesday in late April are irrational, are they any more irrational than the sights and sounds of this sunny spring day: plywood stretched across plate-glass windows, students packing their cars and beating a hasty retreat on the fear of burning and gunfire? In New Haven? At *Yale?* I spent three years here as a law student, and it is simply not possible that this drama of bloodshed and destruction is to be played out here. When you have eliminated the impossible, Holmes told Watson, whatever remains, however improbable, *must* be true. Therefore, my practical joke of a scenario *must* be true; because the idea of Yale as a setting for campus violence, based on my three years here, simply is impossible.

It was not, in those mid-'60s days, that Yale was outside of the ferment of student unrest; the difference lay in the style, the ambience through which discontent was expressed. The ideal seemed to be a sense of Cool, a kind of nonviolent James Bond quality, which precluded rushing enraged into the streets. Yale sent more than its share of students into the South in the early '60s, working on Aaron Henry's Freedom Democratic governor's campaign in Mississippi, working with COFO in the summer of 1964 registering blacks; Yale's own chaplain, William Sloane Coffin, was an early freedom rider; and a great many of Al Lowenstein's moderate-dissident efforts—all those ads in college papers and the New York *Times* calling for a negotiated settlement in Vietnam or a "reappraisal of our Far Eastern Policy"—could depend on Yalies for support.

What was different at Yale was that the final step in the erasure of the campus pastoral—the equation of the University and the Enemy—had yet to take place. While students were being dragged down the steps of Sproul Hall at Berkeley and battered across the Columbia University campus, screaming of secret defense contracts and university ties with the military, the campus at Yale remained calm. For one thing, there *was* no campus—no center of college power that served as a rallying point, other than a patch of concrete outside the small administration building along High Street. There was no student union, no student government, and no sign of a demand for either. Each Yale College, by its design, turned the undergraduate inward; to the interior courtyard, the separate dining halls, the reading rooms. A focus for common anger and energy was missing.

The greater source of calm, though, was rooted in an unspoken understanding at Yale: a sense that the university was, by its very existence, a part of the structure of power: not in the sense of an evil institution, to be battled and destroyed, but in the sense of a conduit into affluence, access to power, and easy, civil conversation with people who wield life-and-death power over money and lives.

I remember a specific event which characterized much of

Yale's mood in those years: a debate between William F. Buckley, Jr., and the Reverend William Sloane Coffin. In the afternoon of the debate, Buckley met with a group of student editors in the four-story gingerbread-slice home of the *Yale Daily News,* the self-proclaimed Oldest College Daily in America. The meeting was held in the Board Room, a part of the *News* unimaginable in almost any other college newspapers, part of the same feeling which impels the paper to call its chief a Chairman rather than an editor. The Board Room is pulled bodily out of an Auchincloss novel: paneled walls, a fireplace at the head of the board table over which a large portrait of Brit Hadden glares down. (Hadden, Class of '20, was co-founder of *Time;* the *News* building was donated in his memory by his classmate, Henry R. Luce.)

Along the walls is a photographic gallery of the paper's past editorial boards. The portraits paint a picture of power: Potter Stewart, '37, now Associate Justice of the United States Supreme Court; R. Sargent Shriver, '38, now director of the War on Poverty; William Scranton, '39, ex-governor of Pennsylvania; scores of others, running corporations, foundations, universities, occupying high positions in the epicenters of power in America. The faces from the photographs radiate a quiet assurance; we knew it then, the faces say.

The *News* staffers lounge with forced casualness in the moments before Buckley enters, all looking disturbingly alike, with tweed sport jackets, chinos or jeans, a careless tie or two. At one point the door swings open—dead silence. Buckley? No, it is not Buckley. It is a girl; blond, sweatered, happily self-conscious as she walks in beside the *News*man who can't keep the grin off his face. In these days before coeducation, the one presence guaranteed to rattle the Yale man attuned to casual acquaintance with power, is the presence of a young female on campus between Sunday and Friday. To touch a girl on a Thursday afternoon at Yale is something approaching sodomy.

By 7:30 P.M., it is clear that the Buckley-Coffin debate is drawing an immense crowd. Not because of any burning desire on the part of the Yale community to weigh the question of whether the federal government has a duty to promote equality as well as liberty; rather, because this debate is This Week's Event, just as Princeton Weekend was the official Event a few days ago, and the Harvard Game (the Game, in the argot of the Ivy League) will be the Officially O.K. Event a week or so hence. It is time, tonight, for the Cerebral Experience, spiced, hopefully, by juicy clashes of sarcasm and bitter exchanges.

As the hall fills up, about fifteen to twenty young men stand along the walls near the stage; functionaries of the Yale Political Union, a kind of Elephant Burial Ground for student politicians in a college with no student government. They are of a piece with their brothers on campuses the nation over, and with the annual pilgrims to the National Student Association: the boys who carried the flag in third-grade assemblies, the eager participants in whatever system promises money, glory, and good-citizenship awards. They have learned early that it is easier to get a slice of the pie than to complain about the recipe.

At Yale, however, or at least at the Political Union, there is another dimension to this play-acting; an increased emphasis on style. The Political Union is divided into "parties," and the members carry themselves with exquisite self-consciousness. The Party of the Right, for instance, has a coat of arms with the motto "Pour la Droite," and its members dress with exaggerated formality. It is, literally, sophomoric sophistication, of a kind found in undergraduates bowled over by the anglophiliac vocabulary of a teacher of English— or a celebrity-snob such as William F. Buckley, Jr.

This theatricality governs the entire debate. Just before the start of the proceedings, an enthusiastic furry-headed Yalie-bopper leans over to a friend and chortles:

"This is gonna be a real zoo."

Ah, yes. The Cerebral Confrontation summed up. One remembers that a few weeks earlier, a mob of Yalies, spurred on by a hyperthyroid news story, besieged a hall where experimental Japanese movies were to be shown, blocking traffic and howling, "Skin flics! Skin flics!" What do they hope for tonight? Do they think Reverend Coffin will try to beat up Buckley? Are they expecting the staff of the *National Review* to set fire to Battell Chapel. The confrontation may be cerebral, but there is something highly ectoplasmic in the hopes of the Yale man as scholar.

The debate is uneventful, except for the revealing tension that greets the vote on the proposition following the debate, with the "parties" polled as in a national political convention. The wild cheers which greet the narrow victory for the liberal side are evidently sparked by a confidence that an expression of belief by politically conscious Yale men is communicated by direct line to the rulers of the firmament, who will pause, nod, and follow accordingly. Following the results, a horde of Yalie-boppers flock around Buckley, seeking autographs and propinquity, and the body adjourns to Mory's. It has the aura of young men striving to behave like upper-class Brits: a fierce Clash of Ideas, bounded by civility and good-fellowship, concluded by a round of drinks. This is, of course, Emulation with a vengeance, an Upper-Class version of the early 1960s Campus Pastoral: Concerned Young Men, com-bining a firm grasp of vital issues of our time with the social graces. In this year of our Lord 1967, it is something close to an anomaly: the prospect, say, of Mark Rudd and Grayson Kirk or Mario Savio and Clark Kerr greeting each other after a campus riot over hamburgers and beer is not credible. It was as if Yale itself was like one of its colleges; surrounded by walls and held together by an interior courtyard, pulling its community inward, where lay good manners and safety.

Has this bastion of casual elitism really become the site for a May Day conflagration? Have three short years unraveled so many generations' worth of tradition and good behavior? (Vi-olence, of course, broke out at Yale on a regular basis, but it was the kind of violence understood by the authorities: a springtime food riot, a water-fight, a surging of Gonad Power by hundreds of more-or-less virile young men, occasionally met by an enthusiastic town policeman getting in his once-in-a-lifetime belt at the families who held his mortgage, paid his wages, and drove their Corvettes contemptuously through New Haven's streets, trailing an aura of privilege past his drab existence.) Is Yale going to burn?

"I was in Chicago in 1968," says a survivor of Gene McCarthy's campaign. "The tension is eight times worse than there. Last week there was a small fire in the Law

School library, and afterwards I heard some junior faculty discussing how the Law School would burn."

"There'll be sniper fire directed against police and Guardsmen by white radicals," predicts a women's liberation organizer.

"Don't forget," warns a young Law School professor preparing to leave New Haven—with his family—for the weekend. "It's not just black militants and white radicals and cops. We've got a lot of lower-class whites. You know, that Italian motorcycle gang, the Slumlords? There're going to be fights between the Weathermen and the Slumlords all weekend long."

"It will be," declares Abbie Hoffman on WBAI, a New York radio station with a large radical audience, "the biggest riot in history."

What is the source of this vision of inferno? At one level, it is a murder trial of eight members of the Black Panther Party, including Bobby Seale, co-founder and Chairman. They are accused of torturing and murdering Alex Rackley, a Panther member who—says the prosecution—was discovered to be a police informer and shot. The authorities say Bobby Seale ordered the murder, and the other defendants carried out those orders. The Panthers say Rackley was killed by somebody else, an *agent provocateur*.

On April 14, 1970, during the preliminary stages of the trial in New Haven, a brief courtroom scuffle broke out. The judge, determined to avoid a circus atmosphere, summarily sentenced two Black Panthers to six months in jail for contempt. It was these sentences, revoked a few days later, that outraged many on the Yale campus, and helped set in motion the furious tidal wave of energy now sweeping toward New Haven for May Day. What is behind this movement, however, is much, much more.

Begin, then, with Yale and New Haven. Even as Yale had its participation in freedom rides and antiwar demonstrations, so New Haven had its symbol of enlightenment in Mayor Richard Lee, who had created an antipoverty program which served as the model for the national War on Poverty, who had attracted more federal funds per person than any other mayor in America, and who had prodded local financial and commercial interests into rebuilding New Haven almost from scratch. He was, for many of Yale's students and faculty, a symbol of tough-minded liberalism.

Toward the end of the decade, however, the same Great Disillusionment that had taken root in New York, Chicago, Los Angeles, Newark, and Detroit exploded in New Haven in a mild-sized riot that shattered the city's self-confidence.

For Yale, the rising discontent among New Haven's black community was a new phenomenon; and one which created a new, much more personal sense of guilt, responsibility, and anger. Yale, after all, sits in the middle of a not-very-rich community, a constant symbol of power and wealth. A half-billion dollar endowment, a student body from some of the richest families in America, on a large plot of land which pays no property taxes to New Haven. It employs hundreds of members of New Haven's communities—black and Italian —at wages of less than a hundred dollars a week. What had begun to happen in the late 1960s was an understanding among a part of the Yale community that *they* were part of a privileged class; *they* were the ones for whom low-income neighborhoods had been torn down; *they* were eating on plates and in dining rooms cleaned by underpaid blacks; *they* were in a protected community, shielded by 2-S draft deferments, foundation grants, and parental affluence from the rats, the induction notices, the crime, the drugs, the sour smell of poverty that bordered their existence. The "oppressors" were no longer fat-bellied sheriffs with tobacco spittle and billy clubs. Now the villains were men in coats and ties, with flow-charts and computer print-outs; the same kind of men, many of them with Yale degrees and teaching posts in their pasts, running the War in Vietnam. The Yale community was vulnerable, primed for appeals to guilt as well as to justice. Could you send a check to Martin Luther King, or spend a few weeks in Alabama, knowing that sanctuary was a phone call away, and rest content? Could you admit a handful of middle-class blacks to Yale and let the silent poor move among you, cleaning floors and emptying garbage bins, and believe you were "part of the solution" instead of being "part of the problem"? Not likely. And not with the emergence of a new movement, tailored as if by design to meld with the guilts and outrages of collegial America: the Black Panthers.

In the '60s, when the civil rights movement erupted into prominence, the symbols generating sympathy from white, middle-class college kids were Negroes—not blacks, *Negroes* —who appeared, among other things, *better* than their white adversaries. NBC showed us film footage: polite, neatly dressed young men and women sitting at a Woolworth's lunch counter, reading Montesquieu and Kant, eyes lowered to the textbooks, while greasy-haired, fat-bellied, cigarette-smoking whites hooted, jeered, and threw dabs of ketchup and mustard. Birmingham and Selma offered us lines of prayerful Negroes, patiently enduring jail, water hoses, and police dogs, answering violence with spirituals and worship services, led by a young, earnest minister named Martin Luther King, preaching the gospel of love and nonviolence.

Whatever else the civil rights movement was, it was overwhelmingly *reassuring*; if not to southern sheriffs, then to collegial America. These were, after all, *our* kind of Negroes; patient, respectful, respectable. In style, they were of a piece with a vision of Negroes pumped out of leftist Hollywood in the 1940s; *good* people, *clean* people, in no sense a threat to life or wallet. They did not seek our money in dark city streets; they wanted only the right to vote and eat at Woolworth's. They were law-abiding (or at least, peacefully lawresisting) Christian patriotic Americans. And in form if not in substance, they suggested at one level a kind of servility. Wipe the sound track off the film and they might have been characters out of *Gone With the Wind*.

Toward the middle of the decade, however, a different kind of black American began appearing on television screens. Deacons for the Defense of Justice: a group of Louisiana blacks who drilled with guns, and said quite explicitly, if whites start shooting at us, we will start shooting back. (What? Shooting *back*? No more prayer services and stirring harmonies of "Let My People Go"?) Stokley Carmichael, exhorting a march to begin chanting the new slogan: "Black Power." (*Power*. A stirring of dread and uneasiness. Was this not what blacks had always possessed in the minds of whites? The power of ramrod sexuality, pulsing rhythms, sweaty muscularity? Consciously or not, the specter of blacks shouting "power" rather than whispering, "Justice, please," grazed an exposed nerve.) Then the summers: fragmented images, dark as the night, fleeing down city streets, hurling rocks through storefronts, frolicking with looted goods. (Where are the coats and ties? The prayers? The songs? And what are you doing half a mile from where I live and work? Why are you no longer in the comforting settings of dusty roads and clapboard shacks a thousand reassuring miles away?)

And finally, the Panthers, seizing a name surrounded by connotations of anger, violence, and blackness, and abandoning the last remaining links with quiescence by their rhetoric and symbols: marching into the California state legislature with rifles; drilling military-style with black berets, leather jackets, and clenched fists; fusing the street fury of ghetto blacks with the words of Marx and Lenin; facing down policemen on streets with *High Noon* overtones.

Only now, for a growing proportion of white college kids, the hero was not the one with the badge. From San Francisco's HUAC rallies in 1960, to southern sheriffs, to campus cops at Berkeley, to Columbia University, and, shatteringly, to the streets and parks of Chicago, 1968, students and police had yelled at each other, cursed each other, bloodied heads and twisted arms. Police were "pigs," subhuman, blood-loving enforcers of the System's will (even the War in Vietnam, at times, was a debate over whether we were to be the world's policeman, as if only police were suffused enough with the love of death to drop jellied napalm on children). America's campuses by the end of the '60s held within them a contingent of self-described revolutionaries who were ready for a movement overtly revolutionary, heroically militant, and prepared to enact, with guns and uniforms, a scenario of violence that seemed attractive to a younger generation coming to define itself as Outlaw. Moreover, the Panthers encompassed different *kinds* of attractions: they were black Americans, about whom guilt was felt—not entirely without reason—by the disaffected children of the white middle class. They identified themselves as Revolutionary, *and seemed prepared to act on that identity;* that is, they seemed to be "picking up the gun" within America; a dream seductive as a fantasy and frightening as a reality to an affluent youth. The Black Panthers were a kind of updated manservant: instead of cleaning up the young gentleman's room for him, they would kill a pig for the young gentleman.

And the fee for services, the gratuity exacted willingly from the collegial revolutionaries, was an uncritical acceptance of the worldview of the Panthers. A plank in their political platform called for the release of every black man and woman in jail as a "political prisoner." Right on! A member of the Black Panther Party arrested for a crime was a political victim. Right on! The styles and catch-phrases of the Panthers were absorbed whole into white radical ambience. "Right on!", the clenched fist (the "power salute"), "power handshakes" blossomed within this Community of the Disaffected. And the issue of the treatment of Black Panthers became a necessary part of the radical agenda, equal to, and at times surpassing, the intensity of Vietnam. It was, apart from the real issues of racism in America, apart from the actual incidents of police harassment against Panthers (and a case of deliberate murder by Chicago police against two Panthers), a case of expiation. White collegians could keep their stereos, their sports cars, their twenty-dollars-an-ounce stashes of dynamite grass, by cheering on the black struggle: in the bitter, hangover atmosphere of post-1968, when the energies of thousands of middle-class white kids had burned out with Robert Kennedy's death and Eugene McCarthy's indifference and Chicago's madness, the Panthers were a surrogate cause, sparked with an energy that the college Left has lost. In mood, in time, and in emotional climate, the preachments of the Panthers and the wants of the upper-income, younger-generation radicals were made for each other.

All very neat; but Fate is lurking in the wings. The very location for this trial, the Superior Court at the edge of New Haven's Green, is a fact which is turning this May Day into a potential holocaust. In addition to pricking the consciences of Yale's students, the setting of the trial is a perfect place for a mass demonstration. Less than two hours out of New York, and less than three from Boston, a New Haven demonstration can call on two concentrations of college radicals, street people, dropouts, and Weekend Counterculturists, disenchanted college graduates, who work by day as cab driver, waitress, editorial assistant, usher in a movie house, telephone repairman, welfare caseworker, by night and weekends into rock music, gentle dope, and Movement politics. Between New York and Boston live hundreds of thousands whose allegiance lies with the Disaffected; more than enough to make the prospect of one hundred thousand angry young people in New Haven a plausible prediction.

Then, too, the Elders have given this Community yet another cause for legitimate outrage. In the fall of 1969, eight

Movement personalities go on trial in Chicago for conspiracy to cause a riot at the Democratic National Convention. By the end of the trial in mid-February of 1970, a new contribution has been made to the Theatre of the Absurd: eight defendants, some of whom have never met, tried for acting in concert; Bobby Seale, co-founder of the Black Panther Party (and the principal defendant in the New Haven trial) shackled and gagged in the courtroom; an aging, wizened judge, acting as if played by a villainous Edward Arnold in a Frank Capra movie ("Our system isn't collapsing," Judge Hoffman said to Tom Hayden as he was sentencing him to fourteen months in jail for contempt. "Fellows as smart as you could do quite well under this system."); Abbie Hoffman yelling Yiddish imprecations at his namesake on the bench ("You shtunck! Shonda fer da goyim, right, Julie?); former Attorney General Ramsey Clark barred from testifying; lengthy disputes about the defendants' bathroom habits; and a post-trial speech by prosecutor Tom Foran to a group of cheering Rotarians denouncing the defendants as part of a "freaking fag revolution."

The five months of the trial, the lengthy contempt sentences dispensed by Judge Hoffman (four years for chief Defense Counsel William Kunstler, fourteen months to Tom Hayden), the self-evident symbolism of the cultural, generational, and political gulf between the defendants and the Court, is bound up with this May Day. For the principal speakers at the rally to defend the Panthers are the Chicago Seven; each of them (more or less) certified celebrities, each of them certified heroes. Among the Community of the Disaffected, and in lesser potency far, far into the mainstream of

America, there is enough distrust/contempt/suspicion of the United States government to make any political victim of that government a figure of admiration. Further, the combination of white radical-black revolutionary causes that surround this May Day is a rare event in post-'60s America: a sense of racial unity after a time when black activism has increasingly rejected not simply white leadership, but white *participation*. For a guilty community, conscious of racism but unable to be part of the effort to combat it, attendance at a Panther rally is a welcome invitation to affirm a continuing clear racial conscience.

Thus the impulses reaching beyond New Haven, along the spine of the eastern seaboard. What of Yale? It is here, within the gothic walls of a campus seemingly insulated from the fever of tumult, that the most astonishing response to the Panther Trial and the May Day rally has formed. With the full support of President Kingman Brewster, Yale University has suspended classes and is spending full-time discussing the Panther Trial and preparing to welcome the thousands of outsiders for May Day.

First, some skeletal facts. On April 14, Panther officials David Hilliard and Emory Douglas are sentenced to six months for contempt after a brief scuffle in the courtroom where the Panthers are being tried. For many students, the summary action strikes a strong memory of Chicago and Julius Hoffman. The sentences also enable the Black Student Alliance, local Panthers, and the largely white Panther Defense Committee to relate the trial to the Yale Community. The next day, April 15, four hundred students meet in Harkness Hall to call for a three-day moratorium on classes in support of the Panthers. On Thursday, April 16, the faculty begins debating the university's response to this demand. On Sunday, Yale Chaplain Coffin, himself a defendant with Dr. Benjamin Spock in a draft-conspiracy case, calls the trial "perhaps legally correct, but morally incorrect."

The next week sees Yale thrown into a fever of concern about the trial. Yale's Student Senate on Monday urges support for a voluntary student strike. President Brewster appoints a committee to investigate not only the trial, but an issue increasingly raised in connection with black student and faculty demands: Yale's relationship to New Haven's black community.

On Tuesday, the first dramatic highlight of the buildup takes place. More than forty-five hundred students pack Ingall's Rink to hear the Strike Steering Committee's "Five Demands"—an amalgam of issues, including a fair trial, a minimum wage for Yale workers; day-care centers for the children of mothers who work at Yale; Yale-financed housing for New Haven; and a cessation of the Social Science building, which is alleged to have links to secret defense-Pentagon-mind-control activities. A brilliant speech by Panther Doug Miranda ignites the crowd, and nine of the twelve resident colleges support the call for a strike. Wednesday begins the cancellation of Spring Weekend (set for the May Day weekend), and a call by Coffin for a nonviolent march to the courthouse in defiance of a court ban on demonstrations.

On Wednesday, April 22, the tension begins to build; students stay out of class; some disrupt an Earth Day speech by Ted Kennedy to demand his views on the Panther trial; and a student opposing a strike dissolves his group and demands that Yale be closed and evacuated for the May Day weekend.

On Thursday, Brewster drops his bombshell at a faculty meeting.

"I personally want to say," he says in a prepared statement, "that I am appalled and ashamed that things should have to come to pass that I am skeptical of the ability of a black revolutionary to achieve a fair trial anywhere in the United States. In large measure, this atmosphere has been created by police actions and prosecutions in many parts of the country. It is also one more inheritance from centuries of racist discrimination and oppression."

Faced with this declaration, the Yale faculty adopts the bulk of a black faculty resolution: it authorizes the "suspension" of normal classes through a "modification" of academic requirements. Yale's establishment, in other words, has legitimated the "strike," has become a part of it, and has, not so incidentally, defused the University as a symbol of unyielding rigidity. Nonetheless, the reports from Boston and New York are not encouraging. A theft of mercury; rifles hijacked; Boston Weatherpeople (Weathermen has been abandoned as male chauvinist) burying handguns from hock shops. By the time I arrived in New Haven on Tuesday, April 28, the paranoia has taken hold; the plywood is going up, the cars are being packed; the police are planning for any contingency, and the murmur is growing: Yale will burn.

The day's conversations suggest the sense of confusion, excitement, uncertainty, thoughtfulness, and sheer energy that surround the Trial, and the larger issues.

"This strike is all very vague," says Steve Cohen, a McCarthy organizer in 1968 and a leader in the Yale community for causes such as the banning of ROTC from campus. "You have a self-formed strike committee writing the five demands. Some are good, some aren't really related, and then all the radical hodge-podge has been added. I mean, this case against the Social Science department is absurd.

"And then you start asking, 'What is a political trial?' If there's any political element, it's in the nature of a distinction—as in not prosecuting a cop who kills a black man. But here, they're not being treated any differently than a lower-white-middle-class Italian. Is it self-defense? Maybe, but when a murder is committed you have to prosecute. Is there procedural inequity? None that isn't part of Connecticut's normal procedure. We've got the most liberal discovery rules in the country . . . a sensible judge . . . the defense even got cross-examination in a bail hearing, and that's unprecedented." Cohen is troubled, torn between his instincts and his judgment as a law student.

"The act for which they're being tried," he continues, "is murder, and brutal and sadistic torture. What's going to happen if the people of Yale find they've *trusted* this guy and it turns out the whole strike is about brutal, sadistic people. Distasteful as it sounds, you have to make an independent judgment of the evidence—that's what I try to say to the undergraduates. The general presumption around is that the Panthers were framed. And these Yalies have a funny kind of political sense. They have a notion of Kingman Brewster calling up the Judge and asking—or telling him—to free Bobby Seale."

I talked with some law students about the issue of revolutionary violence.

"When I see a picture of a burning bank in Santa Barbara, I *think*, 'It's terrible, it's wrong, it'll just bring more repression.' But I *feel*, 'Wow! Just once they got a taste of it!' "

"There's a line going around at Harvard and Columbia," another law student says, "about how we all gotta put Yale on trial. And somebody over at the Panther Defense Committee was saying, 'A trial implies a judgment and a sentence.' And when you add to all of that the fact that we've had fires in the Law School, and drawings in the Black Panther paper on how to clean rifles, and how to make a molotov cocktail . . . well, it's not exactly a teach-in."

Peter Almond, a former Yale student, came back as an assistant to Brewster after the New Haven riots; he is now working in the black "Hill" neighborhood, on leave from the University. Almond is a quiet-voiced, amiable fellow with a sense of inner calm.

"There's some real bitterness and resentment between parts of the black community and Yale. Some of them have a sense that the Yale kids equal radical crazies; a sense that what's coming is a circus, and one which will expose their kids—black kids—to the cops when the white kids go back home or back inside the gates of Yale.

"In fact, white lower-class kids are much more anti-Yale than anti-black. They know that Yale will run Standard Oil twenty years from now, and they'll pump the gas."

Almond is involved with planning the concept of student marshals, trained in nonviolence in the days before May Day, and used to contain whatever violence may erupt.

"But you have to be careful. Somebody suggested using black high school kids as marshals. For the black community, O.K. If they're supposed to marshal whites, it's naïve and dangerous. And most blacks know this, because they know *they're* vulnerable. You even have some blacks like a leader in New Haven's black coalition, suggesting a new conspiracy between the white establishment and white radicals, at the expense of blacks.

"But you know," Almond says with a grin, "this is very much a Yale crisis. Frisbee-catching in the colleges, relaxation. And it really isn't a strike. It *is* a moratorium."

Ernie Osborne, a black coalition participant, echoes this tension between black and white responses to the rally.

"Nobody wants to oppose the Panthers, because too much of what they say is part of the black scene. But most blacks don't really see the May Day rally as part of their scene at all, but more a part of the Chicago Seven. There's a fear that May Day obscures concern with our local Panthers in jail. And we also know that the white community is looking for a scapegoat. If there's trouble, the sense will be, 'Why didn't *you* stop these riots?' "

In the early afternoon warmth, William Coffin sits on the stoop of his house and chats about the trial. Coffin is a good-looking man with thinning hair, and a determined expression on his face softened by frequent laughter. As always, his phone rings constantly, and people keep coming to confer with him; he is attempting to keep together a joint student-faculty monitoring committee, to check rumors of organized violence and keep things calm. He is worried about the Panther Defense Committee, and the rumors that it has been "ambiguous" about the prospects of violence.

"When you have an organization that doesn't connect with New Haven or Yale, and when its speakers are being brought from the outside, you have increased problems. You could say it's explosive now, or you could say this is something quite beautiful—the concern, the organizing, the education." He stretches out, relaxing in a blue turtleneck, blue slacks, and cordovan loafers.

"The thing that you have to understand is that what's going on at Yale is *not* like Harvard, not like Columbia, not like Cornell, not like any demonstration. There's not one broken window, not one building occupied, but all the press emphasis is on demonstrations. You have headlines like: 'And Now —Yale.' The jerks. People here are cheering Brewster. Did that happen to Pusey at Harvard? To Kirk at Columbia? And then you have to ask," he sighs, "how did things get so intensive? Was it fear? Or was it real unity about some very important issues?"

Coffin retreats into the house for a few moments of consultation with members of his monitoring committee. Then he returns to his stoop, and his reflections.

"There's really an education going on here. Some very real discussion of the issues surrounding the trial. I would say not many people here have been enthusiastic about the Panthers. I mean, some of the rhetoric is a bit heavy. There may be sympathy for them as victims of injustice rather than as champions of justice. And of course, those contempt sentences were outrageous. That really triggered the concern, and by the time the Judge dropped the sentences, it was too late. But my main concern isn't the Rally. I want Yale to focus on the community; to turn away from the New Haven Green. We need a moratorium on business as usual in order to deal with unusual business."

Barry Scheck, who has been active in straight and Movement politics as a student, reflects on the emotions of the past two weeks.

"At first, the Panthers 'terrorized' the whites—not physically, but by putting the radical whites up against their rhetoric. As it started out, it was like, 'If you're a revolutionary, go get a gun.' There was one incredible night where Doug Miranda started screaming at us—and then a woman student stood up and said, 'We don't have to prove our manhood.' There was huge applause, and after this the blacks—Panthers and black students—began moving away from total rhetoric, into organizing the university.

"It was very tricky," Scheck goes on. "First, the white demands were originally more far-reaching than blacks. The blacks had a sense of their constituency; they didn't want white people telling blacks what they wanted. But thank God for the Black Student Alliance. The Panthers just couldn't sit there too long. They'd get sick and tired of all that talk. I guess the turning point was when Miranda gave a speech at Battell Chapel, explaining how he understood the position of students, how they didn't have to pick up the gun, but they had to help. That's where Miranda said, 'The Panther and the Bulldog got to move together!' He tore the place apart, and that's why you see this . . ."

He points to some students wearing T-shirts, with stencils of a Panther, a Yale Bulldog, and the slogan "Solidarity."

"Then the black students, who began by severely limiting the role of whites, really opened up. And it began to jell. But it took a lot of hard work to convince people that if we didn't shut down Yale and open it up, Yale will be trashed entirely."

What about the issues in the Trial?

"It's very confusing," Scheck says. "Some people are for a fair trial, some people want *no* trial, some people think the Panthers didn't kill that informer . . . and I guess, in a sense, I can understand how a revolutionary group could torture and kill a police informer. But to me, the real issue is anti-repression. I mean, this notion of institutional neutrality is such garbage. If an important private institution doesn't oppose the state, who will? And hell, the university system has been a prostitute since the Second World War. And it's still filled with these corporate elitist notions about changing things from the top down."

Over at Liggett's, Al, a permanent institution of a clerk, is concerned institutionally.

"We got no image now, no reputation," he says despairingly. "We used to be the best—now we're the worst. It's a terrible thing."

"I don't care," a customer interrupts. "If somebody gets shot down, that's murder."

"That's right," says Al. Just then a middle-aged man, with a suit and tie and a gray mustache, comes up to Al.

"Do you sell anarchist flags?" he asks,

"What?"

"You know, anarchist. Anarchist. Black. Do you sell anarchist flags?"

"Lemme check," says Al.

And a few blocks away, on the border between the campus and the Green, the signboard of the First Methodist Church reads:

"Lord, in this hour of tumult and fears, keep open our eyes, minds, hearts, and ears."

All Tuesday and Wednesday there is a sense of universal, feverish, engagement. At the Law School there are lectures in the history of political trials, questions of pretrial publicity, bail, and the facts in the Panther Case. The Medical School is organizing brigades of medical aides, to take care of any tear-gassed or more seriously injured demonstrators on the weekend. The Russian Chorus is putting on a benefit for the Panther Defense Fund. Across the campus, in the resident colleges, mattresses are being moved into dining rooms, and food committees are planning the work schedules for serving meals to outsiders.

The active participation by the Yale community is a tactical as well as moral imperative for the administration, and for Kingman Brewster. Yale's officialdom is acutely aware of pressures from the outside in response to Brewster's "skepticism" speech to the faculty, and the shutdown of the University. The potential for disaster is clear and present.

Henry Chauncey, an assistant to Brewster, can sit in his office next to Brewster's in Woodbridge Hall and look down at Bienecke Plaza, where small groups of students are arguing, planning, and urging "militant" action this weekend.

"There's been vast preparation for the weekend," he says. "We're lucky in a lot of ways. We don't have a lot of sixty-year-old retired businessmen here; it's a young staff. And our greatest strength is the student body. These guys are motivated in their desire to make this damn thing work."

He shrugs.

"But, hell, if outsiders come in who just want to stir up trouble, there'll be a lot of trouble. The whole thing of opening this place up is that they'll be smothered in affection. It's a calculated risk. If it blows, we'll all be on the next boat to Hong Kong."

This is the key doubt in the minds of everyone at Yale: what kind of people are coming? And how will the different groups participating in May Day behave? Who will they be trying to impress? What will they be trying to prove?

Some of the conflicts are internal, among Panther supporters. On April 22 the New Haven Black Coalition issues a statement, charging that "radical whites, the so-called allies of the oppressed . . . are working out their own agenda in the political atmosphere that surrounds this trial. From their sometimes contradictory rhetoric and frantic posturing blacks can see that the white radicals are only different in method from their daddies and granddaddies in the callous manipulation of the lives of black people. The movement toward black self-determination abruptly removed the pacifier from the lips of the white social reformer. His task was suddenly to deal with the greed and paranoia of his own people. Black lives were no longer his to play messiah with . . . They cry 'right on' and 'all power to the people' but their purpose is not our purpose and their goals are not our goals . . . The truth in New Haven, as in most of the country, is that the white radical, by frantically and selfishly seeking his personal psychological release is sharing in the total white conspiracy of denial against black people."

The message of this and other declarations, by both Panthers and other blacks, is clear: don't start trouble that *we* will have to pay for. The slogan of "Panther discipline" for the weekend is going to grow over the next few days; a slogan which will greatly help keep Yale together, since it puts white radicals in the inescapable position of committing violence not simply against Yale, but against the wishes of the *Panthers*; violence to protest black oppression, as the constituencies are defined this May Day, is itself a racist act since it denies blacks the right to lead a movement in support of blacks.

On Wednesday, April 29, a leaflet issued by SDS members and sympathizers, begins to circulate on the Yale campus, which is preparing for another meeting at Ingall's Rink this night. In a veiled criticism of black student and Panther leadership, the leaflet says, "Be at Ingall's Rink early tonight TO DEMAND AN OPEN MEETING WITH OPEN DISCUSSION *FIRST* ON THE AGENDA." This meeting is the last occasion on which the Yale community will be able to meet together before May Day begins.

Wednesday night in the belly of the whale: Ingall's Rink, a poured-concrete hockey arena, looming up on Prospect Avenue like a beached Moby Dick. Inside, bleachers surround the arena along all four walls. Students are straggling in, climbing up on the bleachers, throwing blankets and jackets on the floor. The students point out celebrities to each other: philosophy teacher Ken Mills, a powerful orator and strike organizer, wanders through the crowd in suede jacket and jeans; Bill Farley, a student organizer, clad in a dashiki.

By 9 P.M. the rink is more than half empty—a far cry from the packed crowd that heard Doug Miranda's impassioned plea for support a week earlier. This meeting has been billed as a discussion of the Five Demands of the strike; and, between the students who have already left New Haven, those preparing for the weekend, and those just plain sick of the talk, the audience for another few hours of debate and rhetoric is not that large.

As the meeting opens, a petition is read to the crowd, parodying Agnew's demand that Yale fire Brewster.

"We, the undersigned, call for the resignation of Spiro Agnew as Vice-President of the United States . . . we do not feel the citizens of the United States can get a fair impression of their country . . ."

The remainder of the petition is drowned out by cheers. So is the reading of a letter to Agnew by Yale trustee William Horowitz.

"Frankly," it reads, "I do not feel that your experience as a chairman of a local PTA qualifies you to comment on the capability of one of the greatest university presidents in the United States." Many of the students stand and applaud. At this point, at least, Brewster has achieved one crucial victory: he has kept the student community on his side. The Yale administration is *not* being identified as the Enemy.

Bill Farley, the Black Student Alliance spokesman, immediately shuts off the SDS strategy of beginning the meeting with an open discussion.

"In the last few days," he says, "we have had to face reality . . . this is our chance to deal with reality. You can sit for an hour to discuss demands if you're so intent on discussion . . ." By a voice vote, the open discussion is put off until the speeches are finished; the white Yale community is not about to repudiate the black leadership of this event.

John Froines, one of the two noncelebrity Chicago Seven defendants (and, not so incidentally, one of the two acquitted of all charges) is the first speaker. In a work shirt, his stomach a trifle overblown, a prominent mustache bisecting his face, Froines talks with hands on hips, analytically, with no rhetorical tricks.

"I'm not going to talk about what will happen," he begins. "I don't feel tension because of this weekend. I feel tension today because that lunkhead Richard Nixon sent troops into Cambodia today; and *that's* violence."

Cambodia? What is Froines talking about? I lean forward and tap a student on the shoulder.

"What does he mean, Cambodia?"

"Oh," is the casual reply. "South Vietnam sent ten thousand troops with a bunch of American advisors into Cambodia today. Nixon's addressing the nation tomorrow night."

Unbelievable. It is Wednesday night. Thirty-six hours from now, thousands of dissidents will be pouring into New Haven; rumor has it that thousands more young people— federal troops and National Guardsmen—will be stationed near New Haven. Now, when the dissidents meet the armed troops and police, a new passion, a new outrage will hang in the air. Suddenly the prospect of violence seems more likely than at any other time; almost as if Nixon & Co. welcomed the picture of violent, fiery outrage as a symbol of the fearful irrationality residing in all who challenged the Indochina death machine.

Froines is still speaking.

"Today's Yippies are really the true descendants of the Sons of Liberty in the first days of the American Revolution. We're not at that stage of revolution . . . but if America doesn't listen, there will be revolution. And we have to see this *doesn't* happen." In his own way, Froines is making the argument of mainstream liberals: change to avoid cataclysmic change. He is speaking straightforwardly; and through his lack of passion, Froines is losing his audience.

"I want to say to you from the Conspiracy that on Friday and Saturday we want a peaceful demonstration [applause] for *one* reason: it helps free Bobby . . . You are the people who freed Doug Hilliard [one of the Panthers cited for contempt by Judge Mulvey] . . . you have to understand that. And you have to understand that the strike can't end here until Bobby Seale is free. All power to the people! Thank you."

The chairman:

"We will now hear from Doug Miranda."

Loud applause and anticipatory buzzing. Miranda, a leader of the Connecticut Panthers, is a star speaker. It was he who fired up Yale a week ago. He mounts the podium, wearing a gray shirt, black jacket. As he begins to speak, his high-pitched voice rising and falling musically, his arm flying out from his chest to point at the audience, electricity starts crackling through the air.

"*Sure*-ly . . . we have not put troop carrier in the *ar*-mo-ry . . . *sure*-ly . . . we did not . . . do that. *Sure*-ly . . .

the Black *Pan*-thers . . . have not man-u-*fac*-tured *na*-palm . . . *Sure*-ly . . . we did not do that.

"*Sure*-ly . . . we have to under-*stand* . . . who *is* . . . the chief ag-*gres*-sor . . . in the world . . . *sure*-ly [he is building now] there are some of us . . . who have said 'no' . . . there are some of us . . . who will re-*sist* . . . you see . . . op-*pres*-sion. Look what hap-pened . . . to the Red Man . . . to Ja-*pan*. We must un-der-*stand* . . . that the pri-mary ques-tion . . . for the black com-*mun*-i-ty and the Third World . . . is: to be or not to be . . . and black people *choose to exist*.

"You ask your-selves . . . who is walking around with the gas . . . who is walking around with the helmets . . . who has the clubs . . . and you will see . . . who *is* . . . the ma-jor ag-gres-sor . . . in the world—all power to the people!" If Ingall's Rink had rafters, they would have shaken from the roar of applause.

Oddly, the emotional release provided by Miranda's ap-pearance does not build; a demagogue, a troublemaker with intentions of violence, could take this crowd and begin to do dangerous things with it. Instead, a different atmosphere emerges, reflecting that desperate urge for participation. Stu-dents begin to talk now about what will happen over the weekend; about what to do if you're arrested; how to get medical help; where psychiatric counseling stations will be; how to cooperate with the marshals. Somehow, the sense of revolutionary free play is gone. What takes its place is a sense of desperate, shared, concern.

"If by some chance there are more people than we are planning for," says a speaker quietly, "we will reduce our food portions. We will have familia for breakfast [groans and laughter]—no, it's really good; and brown rice and salad in the afternoon and evenings. We will feed everyone who comes to town on May Day. There will be enough. Help feed your brothers and sisters." Then, almost in a whisper, "All power to the people." In other mouths, "All power to the people" is a demand, an incantation, an angry cry. In this speaker's mouth, it is a simple statement of fact; an acknowledgment of humanity.

In these moments, as locations, telephone numbers, and plans are read to the audience, a recognized spirit emerges; the same spirit at work at the Marches on Washington, or Woodstock: crisis produces community. Whether passing out leaflets telling where to get help, or manning telephones to give legal aid or check out rumors, or mixing the batches of food that are pouring into the colleges, giving up rooms and comforts of normal university life, these people want to touch each other, to stand together. It is this impulse that represents the single biggest break with the impulses of their parents. More than any political statement, more than the hair length, or attitude toward fighting a war, more than the tie-dyed clothes, the repudiation of atomized America is the key to the Generational Fault.

The children of postwar America watched their Elders separating from each other, carving out their slivers of land in suburban America, insulating themselves from their countrymen with automobiles and tracts instead of neighborhoods, retaining shadowy contact with each other through a television set which flattened regional and cultural diversity into mass tastes. And in millions of us, a voice of doubt, small and murmuring in the '50s, shouting boldly in the '60s, asked us,

"Is this how you want to spend your lives? Do you wish to stand apart? Is there not some way to join together?"

So the crowd inside the belly of the whale cheers the planning for help; and as soon as the speakers stop, and the SDS adherents take to the microphones scattered around the floor, to argue their Marxist dialectics, the audience files out. This is not why they have come. Ken Mills, the professor with an Oxford education and a Little Richard hairdo, abruptly cuts off the political harangue—"If you don't like the way this is being run, you can leave; you'll speak to this list of demands or we will cut off your mike"—and fifteen minutes after it begins, the open discussion is over.

As the remnants of the crowd leave, a speaker takes to the mike.

"For God's sake, help police this arena. If we really mean what we say about the people who work at the University, then the least we can do is to help clean up our elitist mess."

Thursday, April 30. Call it a tale of two Presidents.

Kingman Brewster is preparing to meet the press in the President's Room on the second floor of Woolsey Hall, kitty-corner from his office in Woodbridge Hall. Woolsey is a huge hall, with Yale's biggest auditorium on the first floor, and a connecting entry to the enormous Freshman Commons, where the underclassmen eat and whose paneled, chandeliered surroundings host many of the major banquets at the University. Its columned exterior has a cornice engraved with great battles of past wars, and a monument honors the men of Yale who died for country (and also, presumably, God and Yale as well).

The President's Room is circular, with a bright red round carpet, couches rounded to fit the walls of the rotunda, crystal chandeliers, and formal portraits of past Yale presidents: James Rowland Angell, Noah Porter, Timothy Dwight. Mounted on a wall is a gold Yale seal, a book opened to Hebraic script, the "Lux et Veritas" motto emblazoned below. It is a scene totally out of phase with the mounting tension outside: the walls coated with stenciled slogans, "Why be Afraid?", "Human Rights, not Violence," "Repression of One=Repression of All," and "Violence is the tool of fascism," with a scrawled "non" before the word "violence" on some walls. Inside this room, eight camera crews and a dozen tape recorders grouped near a podium signal that the Media Machine has arrived.

Brewster enters: a well-preserved fifty-one, salt-and-pepper hair, distinctive bulging cheeks, a firm suggestion of a smile something like an airline pilot. He is wearing a three-piece pinstripe suit and a ruddy complexion.

"Brewster looks good," says a TV newsman.

"It's the death flush," replies the New York *Times*. "Say," he whispers as Brewster reaches the podium, "you know that Whiffenpoof song? 'To the tables down at Mory's, to the place where Louis dwells'?"

"Yeah."

"Who is Mory's? Who's Louis? Where are they?"

Brewster looks out over the crowd of newsmen, a trace of a sardonic smile on his face. For seven years he has presided over Yale, watching as the death of John Kennedy began to spread a stain of bitterness through a generation of students, confronting anger and bitterness, not simply among the young, but among the alumni, outraged at a chaplain arrested on freedom rides, incensed over the systematic alteration of tradition at Yale, the admittance of large numbers of poor blacks, the eradication of the prep school base and father-son privileges for prospective undergraduates. In his appearance and speaking style, Brewster suggests the model of a Kennedy liberal, the sort of man James Reston perpetually advocates as a candidate for the Republican nomination for President. There are, however, deeper undercurrents here; as in a man who in 1964 could interrupt a Vietnam argument between good friend McGeorge Bundy and author Peter Maas at Hickory Hill to tell Bundy, Maas is right, this Vietnam thing is headed for disaster; a leader himself as skeptical of the reassurances of his friends as of the charges of outsiders.

He is on top of a volcano now. As he prepares to speak, four thousand federal paratroopers and Marines from North Carolina are being airlifted to Chicopee Falls, Massachusetts, and Quonset Point Naval Air Station, Rhode Island, to wait for the conflagration. They have been sent at the urgent request of Connecticut Governor John Dempsey, who has suggested "the strong possibility of violence" over May Day. A Democratic Senate candidate has called Brewster's "skepticism" statement "outrageous," and demanded a student-alumni referendum on Brewster's removal. Judge Herbert MacDonald says Brewster's comments were "an awful letdown to the courts, the police, and the people of the community in which Yale is located." U. S. Senator Tom Dodd has declared: "I have evidence that clearly indicates that the Administration of Yale University and some of its students

have been led into the position of helping a national conspiracy that seeks to wreck the legal process in the United
States and to threaten the very existence of an American city
and indeed of our whole American society."

If Yale comes apart, Brewster cannot survive as President.
And it is the press that has helped put him there. The New
York *Times*, a blood brother of the liberal establishment of
which Brewster is a part, has not only condemned Yale's
moratorium editorially. It has peppered its news pages with
sensational stories about impending violence ("the campus
police reported the theft of 140 pounds of mercury. The mercury could be used to make explosive devices . . ." "400 rifles and shotguns were stolen in 3 incidents in the area,
touching off a wave of new fears as the news spread over the
tense campus.") Now the press and Brewster face each other.

"I am," he begins, "intensely proud of the energy, common
sense, and good will of the community. This is a question of
social justice and legal justice. The Yale community does not
feel it can turn its back on the rally."

A well-groomed, slick local TV newsman recites.

"What is your sense of the developing situation now?"

"Things could be very good or things could be very bad,"
Brewster says firmly. ("Or it could go either way," whispers
the *Yale Daily News*.)

"How do you summarize the situation? What do you see
coming . . . ?"

"Look," Brewster says, "this is no Woodstock. This is no
picnic. There's always the possibility of violence, but there's
no such group in New Haven. But if it's there, innocence is
no protection."

"You have to understand," reflects his assistant, Henry Chauncey, after the press conference ends, "that Brewster is very calm in moments of crisis. He keeps cracking jokes. For instance, when many of the old guard administrators were fired, we'd give them a testimonial dinner. Well, the other day he said to me, 'Chauncey, are you ready for your testimonal dinner now?'"

Peter Almond ponders whether the Brewster statement of "skepticism" on a black revolutionary's ability to get a fair trial was a political device to unite the students behind him.

"I don't accept that it was. Politically, he didn't want all this shit he's getting now. The key is that Brewster is a man who often *must* say what he means. There was no speechwriter. He determined that Yale *had* to do this."

Nine hours later, as the cars pour into New Haven, as the residential colleges fill with the Community of the Disaffected, another President appears; on the television screen. It is Richard Nixon, announcing that several thousand U.S. troops have invaded Cambodia.

"This is not an invasion of Cambodia," he says, the beads of sweat dancing over his upper lip, and among the knots of students at Yale watching the screens the reaction is beyond contempt, beyond the hissing and booing.

". . . I have rejected all political considerations in making this decision . . . I would rather be a one-term President and do what is right than to be a two-term President at the cost of seeing America become a second-rate power and see this nation accept the first defeat in its proud 190-year history."

He will not, he says, watch America reduced to the role of

a "pitiful, helpless giant." And then he turns directly to New Haven.

"We live in an age of anarchy at home and abroad . . . As I speak, great institutions of learning are under siege . . ." And as the derisive applause wells up in the room, you have to wonder whether, somewhere in the bowels of the White House, someone has calculated the political impact of a real explosion at Yale, turning debate away from Cambodia and Vietnam, to the deadly frolics of radicals, dissidents, and dope-smokers. This Thursday night, once again, the smell of violence hangs in the air. One President has spent the better part of two weeks fighting to hold his institution together; tonight, another President seems to be toying with the consequences of pulling it asunder.

Friday. May Day.

A month ago, this was to be Spring Weekend. Last night should have been Tap Night, with the secret societies, Skull and Bones, Elihu, and the others sending out emissaries to initiate the fortunate few into a hidden world of lifetime friendships, merciless encounter sessions, and automatic connections with the privileges (one Justice of the United States Supreme Court spent hours on the telephone every year persuading high-class juniors to accept the "tap" of his society). Tonight and Saturday should have seen tuxedos and gowns cutting through the Yale campus, and the sound of band music drifting out of colleges. Instead, Yale is flooded with representatives of the Community of the Disaffected. Bush jackets, stenciled with slogans and Viet Cong flags; backpacks, jeans and chinos; motorcycle jackets and (for some) gas masks, suggesting experience with police-youth confrontations of the past; "Either/or" buttons, reflecting Panther co-founder Eldridge Cleaver's teaching that America must choose *either* class struggle *or* race war.

The colleges of Yale are decked with banners. Branford College has renamed itself the "Branford Liberation Front." "Welcome to the communiversity," a bedsheet reads. SDS is heard from: "End Yale's expansion in New Haven! Smash U.S. imperialism around the world! Dare to struggle! Dare to win!"

New stencils line the library exterior: a smoking rifle, with the phrase "Practice makes perfect." "Burn, Babylon." "Amerikkka, burn."

At the Center Church on the Green, a living remnant of a Currier and Ives print, where General Benedict Arnold demanded and got the keys to the arsenal from the town selectmen in the early days of the American Revolution, a press conference with the Chicago Seven members is in place. Around the pulpit, young men in work shirts, leather jackets, and jeans carry the Yippie flag: They cheer every speaker: Tom Hayden, sober, low-keyed, utterly without the borscht circuit antics of Hoffman and Rubin, talking of a "summer of solidarity, or organizing. We will be back with a quarter of a million, or a half a million. And the prisoners will be liberated by any means necessary." Elbert Howard, a local Panther leader known as "Big Man," intimidating with shades, a full beard, and a perpetual scowling, warning that "breaking windows and snatching pocket books will never lay a foundation for the long, hard struggle ahead . . . a pig is a pig—no matter what shape, size or color he may be."

Here again, the sanctity of "Panther discipline" is being invoked: we will not burn, riot, and destroy, *not* because such tactics are immoral, but because it is tactically incorrect, it will not free Bobby Seale, and because such tactics are white elitist joy rides at the expense of elitist blacks.

Over at the Green, on this sunny day, a rock band is playing; picnic lunches, wine bottles, and marijuana cigarettes are being passed around. Along the walkways, middle-aged men are selling the papers of the Old Left: the *Daily World* (Communist); the *Weekly People* (DeLeon Socialist). Across the Green, at city hall, a phalanx of New Haven police group together; quietly, unobtrusively. May Day is under way.

Friday, late morning. Just before the Rally at the Green begins, an open meeting is held in Woolsey Hall. It has the appearance of a prosperous church, an enormous pipe organ surrounding the stage, seats built like pews. As the audience drifts in, Vern Countryman is talking about two months he spent in Cuba. He is low-keyed, thoughtful; but it is not he that this audience is coming to see. Behind him, pacing the stage, flashing eyes sweeping the audience as if counting the house, is Jerry Rubin—the media's arch-fiend of the revolution. On a hundred newsreels, in a thousand columns, it is Jerry Rubin that has come to stand for everything our Elders fear: bearded, tie-dyed shirt, flaming red pants, clenched fist, haranguing, inciting, it is Rubin—over thirty and half a decade past his student years—that stands for the firebomb and the dope, the dissolute commune and the obscene marches. Day after day he is strung up in the pages of the Congressional Record. At this moment, on a dozen radio phone-in talk shows, agitated beauticians and gruff cab drivers are spinning their fantasies of taking that guy Rubin and . . .

Now he is impatiently awaiting his introduction. Vern Countryman speaks of the "sense of community among faculty and students in Cuba . . . they broke down the sense of authoritarianism in which faculty see themselves as experts." He talks of the time spent harvesting sugar cane.

"It's kind of frustrating being here," he says, "because this has not happened. Students in America have not had a sense of struggling for their real needs . . . a sense of revolutionary joy. And we cannot really work for the struggles of more obviously oppressed people without coming to grips with our own oppression."

In the first rows of Woolsey, the claque has come, sporting banners with the Yippie flag—a black field (for anarchy) on which a red star (for revolution) is superimposed on a green cannabis leaf (for marijuana). They have chosen well: the three most-feared possibilities of upheaval are embraced and flaunted. It is a clue to what will follow.

Vern Countryman is finishing now.

"And so we must say to the academics: 'There is no reason why you should have control of their lives . . .' we must really open Yale to the people of New Haven." And then he introduces Rubin.

From the front-row claque comes the salute: "Yip-yip-yip-yip-YIPPIEEE!" The rest of the audience applauds briefly, and Rubin comes to the podium, takes two steps right, two steps left, and throws a clenched fist into the air.

"I'm Johnny Cash and I'm glad to be at Yale Penitentiary!" His voice is guttural, a suppressed shout except when he is shouting for real. For the next hour and fifteen minutes there follows an extraordinary performance. The speech is delivered in a state of hysteria, at full volume until Rubin's voice starts to give. It is a monologue offered by a comic on speed, a boxing match, a battle between lucidity and madness. There is no logic, no argument—it is instead a patchwork quilt of gags, incitements, outright lies, and painful truth.

"I hope people will keep this university closed forever . . . yeah . . . we gotta close it for*ever!*

"The first thing we have to understand is that no white person has the right to judge any black person in America today, dig it? Julius Adolf Hitler Hoffman, that anal menopausal motherfucker, Julius Hoffman is *every* judge. We gotta break down the prisons, free the political prisoners, and put the judges in jail!

"At Santa Barbara, they said I couldn't speak! So I didn't show up! And they had the biggest riot in history!"

"Yip-yip-yip-yip-yippiee!" the claque shouts and up goes Rubin's fist.

"Yeah, what the hell's a riot in the first place? It's a marijuana party! I have a good time at riots! State lines . . . I don't *believe* in state lines, state lines is bullshit. The only reason they have state lines is to give FBI agents something to do. Any FBI agents here? Stand up! We pay their fucking salary! They don't know shit!"

Rubin moves into educational theory.

"The most oppressed people in the world are white middle-class youth, 'cause they're forced to defend all this shit. Don't go saying you got to free Bobby Seale, you got to free yourself. And don't worry about diplomas; the Yippies print free diplomas. See me later, I'll give you a diploma!

"'Cause you know what? School is nothing but an advanced form of toilet training." Here the rest of the audience, by now filling the hall, breaks into its first real applause. "Yeah, it's toilet training! And the first point in the Yippie platform is kill your parents!" Gasps and boos. "Bullshit," a voice yells out.

"'Cause they're our dictators . . . school is a concentration camp. The Panthers got a breakfast for children program. And America's got a children for breakfast program! Yeah, the only reason old people are against the war is 'cause we're getting our ass kicked in!"

Jerry Rubin is moving far afield from the political and cultural attacks of other radicals in this tirade. He is tapping something far more volatile and subtle; the continuing identification of young adults with childhood as a time of ease and purity. This is no revolution; this is the revolt of the Peanut Gallery, cutting the ties that bind Howdy Doody, burning Buffalo Bob at the stake. Listen:

"Spiro Agnew wouldn't let his daughter go on a peace march. And he said when she grows up, she can boss her kids around. That's what freedom means in America! Well, we're gonna get stoned with our kids! We're gonna take acid with our kids! Our kids are gonna tell *us* what to do!"

Listening to this tirade, watching the claque wave the Yippie flag, I begin to understand something important about this sheer outburst of fury and energy. Rubin is not interested in making an argument, defending a point of view. He is proclaiming his own wickedness; inviting his audience to taste the joy of outlawry.

"We are a new race of people . . . we don't want degrees, we don't want careers. We're gonna burn money, because we're anarchistic communists. Everything's gonna be free!

"In the 1950s it was like Pavlov's dog. All they had to do was say 'communism' and every single fucking person salivated like a fucking dog. We don't salivate anymore. We hear 'communism' and we say 'right on!' We are everything— *everything*—they say we are! I haven't had a bath for six months! My brother is a Chinese peasant and my enemy is Richard Nixon! [applause] We're even guilty of child molesting, *child molesting*, we've infiltrated their sperm, they're afraid to have kids! We ain't never, never gonna grow up! We're gonna be adolescents *forever!*" And there is laughter and applause; Rubin moves into some gags.

"You know what's going on in America today? The alcoholics are putting the potheads in jail! Arresting us for smoking dope is like arresting Jews for eating matzoh. We're a conspiracy! A worldwide conspiracy!"

Rubin's next joke, however, produces a different reaction —one which points to so much of why this weekend is happening at Yale. He tells the sick joke involving Senator Edward Kennedy and Mary Jo Kopechne.

". . . So Mary Jo says, 'But Teddy, what if I get pregnant?' . . . and Teddy says: 'Don't worry, we'll cross that bridge when we come to it.' "

A few yips from the claque cannot hide the gasps and the booing that begins. And now Rubin wheels, pounds a fist on the podium, and points an accusing finger.

"All right, you motherfuckers, I brought you out! If it had been Bobby Seale who was in that car with Mary Jo, he'd be hanging from a tree now!" And for the first time, there is real sustained applause. Like the audience, Kennedy is one of the privileged. We are all here because there are black revolutionaries on trial, because the students at Yale will go on to money and power and ease, and because three blocks from them are thousands of black children who will suffer and this audience doesn't know what to do about it. But they know enough to feel bad. Rubin has struck dead center.

"It wasn't Richard Nixon who started the War in Vietnam, it was Jack Kennedy. [applause] If Bobby Seale had to wait on Teddy Kennedy to get free, Bobby Seale would be in jail for the rest of his life! [applause] We can only count on each other!"

A CBS camera crew is pushing its way toward the stage now, sound microphone extended, hand-held lights blazing. From the Yippie claque come hisses, curses, and angry gestures. Rubin intercedes.

"Look," he says, "let me rap about CBS. There're gonna be three-year-olds and four-year-olds watching this; and they're gonna see this—and they're gonna say, 'We wanna be there too.' Spiro Agnew is right about TV—we are using it for our own subversive purposes. I tell you, we're gonna announce the revolution on TV. I was in Nashville, Tennessee, and there were thousands of long-haired, dope-smoking Yippies with southern accents!"

And then, as the camera whirls, Rubin leads the hall in a chant, "Fuck Richard Nixon! Fuck Richard Nixon!" The crew swiftly departs, throwing nervous looks over their shoulder. A twin triumph for Rubin. He had made sure he will get on the evening news—and he has stopped violence.

And suddenly I remember the fervent accusations from some of Rubin's non-admirers: the charge that he must be a paid agent of one federal agency or another. It is nonsense, of course—the federal government does not indict its own. But on another level, it is not true because it is an idea too clever by half for the men who run our country to embrace. Rubin is the perfect symbol for them, the absolute blending of everything that terrorizes mainstream America. He does not debate the terms of horror—he embraces them: anarchism, communism, dope-smoker, outside agitator, foul-mouthed. It is as if a labor organizer could hire a fat man in a silk hat with a dollar sign on it to light cigars with hundred-dollar bills during a collective bargaining vote.

One could fantasize a briefing in some glass-and-concrete office building a few days earlier.

"O.K., Jerry, get your ass up to Yale and stir 'em up. Really lay it on them—the whole shtick. But listen, if anybody tries to beat up on anybody, you know, turn them off it. We don't want anybody hurt."

Rubin is concluding now, with an attack on nonviolence.

"Don't preach nonviolence to the peasants—Mao said it—don't preach nonviolence to oppressed people. See Richard Nixon and Spiro Agnew and preach nonviolence to them! And we don't want sympathy—I've got more sympathy . . . I've got fifteen million Jewish mothers. But I don't want Jewish mothers—I want brothers and sisters!" And he is done, holding both fists high overhead, as the Yippies cavort, the flags wave, and most of the audience stands and cheers.

In his cluttered study on the third floor of the Law School, Professor Thomas Emerson leans back and talks about the movements on campus. Into every space of the shelves are crowded books and law journals, briefs and magazines. Emerson, a white-haired man with an open gentle face, has been in the "Movement" years before it adopted this name. He has been a member of the National Lawyers' Guild all through the McCarthy period; his passion for civil liberties has led him not simply to edit a major casebook on political and civil rights, but to join in the defense of accused subversives when much of the academic and legal community was running for cover. His stands led some law students to nickname him "Tommy the Commie"; now, he talks of the upheaval and the changes it has brought.

"In the '50s," he says, "there was no real attack on us. The only radicals were the Communist Party and their affiliates. They weren't after us—although they viewed the university as a reflection of the business world. But in a sense, they were defending those of us who were under fire. The whole thought was to stand behind us . . . like Marcuse, a radical who argues for the protection of the university.

"Today," Emerson continues, "they are amused by the 1950s. They look at the '50s the way we looked at the Palmer Raids. It was so outrageous, they can't understand pleading the Fifth, instead of standing up and telling the committees where to get off. There's no real sense of history. Still, I find their value system close to mine, except for the whole drug-rock culture—that's not for me.

"Also," says Emerson, "I haven't reached the point where I'm ready to man the barricades . . . and that's a rather sharp division. I'm still a reformist, in a reformist school . . . although the university is tied in with the establishment, it's still an area of free operation. I haven't changed that much."

Emerson's sense of this weekend is clouded by an element of concern.

"I'm concerned because a small group can polarize things. They can destroy the open system so easily . . . the people on the extreme edge have such control over everyone else. And if they push it, the open society may suffer or disappear. That's the thing about the Weathermen: they're not only individually crazy, but socially crazy. The blacks are much more intelligent, much more creative."

The Green at 3 P.M., start of the Rally. The notion of politics as Theatre is being given its most strenuous test of proof here. Each group, it seems, parades onto the Green, now three-fourths filled with people, unveiling its banners and slogans like skits for Sing Night of Color War. Here the Yippies come, waving their flags, barking their chant, "Yip-yip-yip-yip-yippieee!!!", reciting a cheer:

"The only solution is revolution,
The only direction is insurrection."

Singing a parody of the John Lennon, "Give Peace a Chance" theme:

"All we are sayyyyying,
Is sma-ash the state."

And, their smash hit of the afternoon, a new lyric to the 1950s rock tune, "Remember When":

"Machine guns, bombs and—insurrection,
We will make a—new direction,
Don't get into—evolution,
We will make a—revolution,"

replete with the "bomb-bomp-a-bomp-bomp-bomp-a-bomp bomps" and high falsetto "oo-ee-oo-ees" of a 1950s song.

The Women's Liberation contingent enters, chanting, "Free Erica! Smash America!" (a reference to defendant Erica Huggins, a special concern of the radical women's groups). They chant, with agonizing reminders of junior high school girls in the back of a bus on a school outing, singing and cheering for five hours straight:

"Power to the people,
(Power to the people!)
What kind of power?
(Our kind of power!)"

Shuffle to the left, shuffle to the right, come on Lakeside, fight, fight, fight!

Yet summer camp it definitely is not. Along York Street, two long blocks of National Guardsmen stand at the ready, in full battle dress, gas masks on their belts, rifles standing idly by. They look more frightened than the passers-by, on their way to the rally, who mostly stare, and occasionally taunt or mock their presence with salutes. One Yippie named David, in his own private ecstacy, begins to lay a rap on a Guardsman.

"Man," he says, dancing and twisting, "*you* know we're gettin' our asses kicked, and *I* know we're gettin' our asses kicked, an' you know *why?* Man, because they got the world's greatest shit over there, man, an' our guys are so fuckin' *stoned* they can't *see* the V.C., man, I'm gettin' drafted an' I can't *wait* to get over there, man, I'm gonna smoke so much goddamn dope I'm gonna *fly* back, man . . ."

As David cavorts, the Guardsmen turn away, some laughing, some grim-faced. A minister walks by, wearing a medallion in which a cross is held within the peace symbol. He looks at the Guardsmen, smiles, waves, and is gone.

At the Green, the speeches have begun, in general an amalgam of every dissident rally for the last three years. A speech by Jean Genet is read to the crowd; it is very, very long. David Hilliard, the Panther whose contempt sentence sparked Yale's anger, pledges nonviolence this weekend, but adds, "We will take their lives if they don't stop taking ours. All power to the people!"

"All power to the people!" the crowd shouts back.

It is Robert Scheer, however, who makes the best speech of the day. A former editor of *Ramparts,* early organizer of the antiwar movement in California, he is a hawk-faced intellectual with bitter, honed rhetoric stripped of catch-word appeals. He is particularly bitter about the New York *Times.*

"The *Times* did everything it could to invite a bloodbath here today," he says, recounting its eager printing of every rumor of gun-running. "In the eyes of the *Times,* the Panthers are not entitled to legal rights . . . or bail. And the reason for this is, like most liberals, when the institutions they find comfortable are challenged, they will turn to fascism rather than give up power . . . we would prefer nonviolence to violence, but you are not going to kill Bobby Seale."

The speeches wind on, as the crowd drifts about, meeting friends from college, or other demonstrations, sharing food and wine and dope.

A Panther, who delivers his speech in a scream from start to end:

"Don't gimme the fist if you don' mean it! You got to get a gun! You got to get funky! 'Cause if you can't get funky, get out! You know who the pig is! And you know, he's a super-duper punk!"

A women's contingent, reading a statement in support of imprisoned women Panthers, which might have been ghost-written by Adela Rogers St. John:

"Four revolutionary sisters . . . 344 days . . . no trial yet . . . for Frances Carter, it could have been easy . . . but she stood with her sisters . . . 344 days in confinement . . . no trial yet."

David Dellinger, a father figure of the Movement, a revolutionary pacifist:

"George Washington isn't the father of Bobby Seale's country . . . and he's not the father of the country struggling here to be born . . . the real issue isn't whether it will be a peaceful weekend in New Haven; the issue is whether it will be a peaceful weekend in Cambodia."

And finally, like any good theatrical show which saves its boffo act for last, Abbie Hoffman, clad in a cape with a Yippie emblem, a tie-dyed shirt, and thickly curled hair, strides forward, slams his fist on the podium, and bellows:

"It's good to be back in Chicago!"

He proceeds.

"America lost its face in Vietnam and it's gonna lose its ass

in Cambodia . . . there's one billion Davids with rocks in
their hands . . . we are all outlaws in the eyes of America
. . . and we're gonna live like outlaws, and fuck Julius
'Geritol' Hoffman . . . [when we went to jail] not one liberal Senator spoke out—not Clean for Gene, not McGovern,
not Teddy at the Bridge [evidently he and Rubin steal each
other's lines]. We're gonna picket on Monday, and picket on
Tuesday, and if they find Bobby Seale guilty we're gonna pick
up that courthouse and send it to the MOON!" Slam! goes
his fist on the podium. "Free Bobby Seale!" chants the
crowd. And Friday's rally is over.

Friday evening. In Trumbull College, groups of friends sit
in the courtyard in the warm twilight, eating rice, salad,
bread, peanut butter, and marmalade—the "official" weekend
meal (whatever their other sympathies with the counterculture, Yalemen are not yet willing to adopt its culinary habits;
Hungry Charlie's, an emporium specializing in greasy hamburgers, chilidogs, and beer, is doing a land-office business).
Footballs and frisbees sail through the sky; rock music blares
down from open windows.

As the evening moves on, the energy of the days turns to
exhaustion. At Jonathan Edwards College, kids are sleeping
on the mattresses thrown down on the dining room floor;
like a scene out of *They Shoot Horses, Don't They?* In the
courtyard, Tom Hayden speaks to a crowd, answering questions through a portable bullhorn.

Hayden is a tall figure in the last decade. A student editor
at the University of Michigan; principal author of the Port
Huron statement of SDS in 1962, rejecting ideology and

calling for a society of justice and compassion; embittered by the War in Vietnam, yet longing for somebody to set the country right; angry enough to defend the black uprisings in Newark and Watts; innocent enough to cry over the coffin of Robert Kennedy in St. Patrick's. He has always seemed to me a combatant who keeps hearing a small voice of doubt, drawing him away from total immersion in any rigid political stance, and unwilling to act the poseur for a shot on the evening news. There is a famous joke told by resident Harvard wit Barney Frank: Hayden was late for a speech, Frank once said, because when the cab driver asked Hayden, "Where do you want to go?" Hayden said, "No. Where do *you* want to go?"

Hayden is speaking reflectively now, answering a questioner who asks, "Why was nonviolence the order of the day?" At a time when nonviolence is thought be an outmoded tactic, more suited to Martin Luther King than Bobby Seale, Hayden must answer carefully. He, as much as Kingman Brewster or Spiro Agnew, has a problem of keeping his constituency.

"I don't think it would be accurate to write this off as a nonviolent demonstration. The tactics grew out of a whole program of organization that they didn't want to jeopardize." He contrasts New Haven with Berkeley, where "spontaneous trashing kept breaking out. The police, of course, were much more disciplined, and it's impossible to do anything on a sustained basis with those kinds of conflicts."

"Agnew and Nixon," he says, "have already seen that the University community might become like Cambodia. If Kingman Brewster is like Sihanouk—if he's giving cover to those who want to do something about Bobby—they'll attack Yale."

"Ah, nuts," a kid says behind him. "Attack the University. Bunk."

"I think it's important to find out how you feel," Hayden says. Then a voice cuts him off.

"Stop playing the fucking applause meter shit. How are people ever going to learn how to fight?"

"But if you use violence as your first means," Hayden replies, "you have nothing as a follow-up. Suppose you trash a store. Does that free Bobby Seale?" He begins to talk about other tactics; Bobby Seale Brigades and Erica Huggins Brigades; underground railroads to get political prisoners to sympathetic countries.

But as Hayden continues to talk with the crowd, a chant begins to build up outside, faint at first, then growing louder.

> "Fuck Brewster, fuck Yale,
> Get the Panthers Out of Jail!"

It is not a chant coming from any college. It is coming from the streets. Something is happening. Dozens of kids run into the street, looking for the source of the chant. Electric energy: This May Be It.

Hours later, we will learn what started it. Over at Branford College, in the middle of a speech by Jerry Rubin, a black youth jumps up to announce that the pigs have arrested three Panthers down on the Green. Rubin urges the crowd not to move, but it is too late. From Branford, a disorganized group goes halfway to the Green; then into the huge Old Campus, where by far the biggest crowd is bivouacked. Suddenly, leadership: a Youth Against War and Fascism banner bursts out of Phelps Gate, followed by several hundred people, chanting:

"Fuck Brewster, fuck Yale,
Get the Panthers Out of Jail!"

Down College Street, the east border of the forbidden Green, the crowd marches. Then east on York, right on Elm Street, and the crowd is headed straight for the Green, yelling "Join us! Join us!"

It is night, now, about 9:45 P.M. At Elm and College streets, where the campus and the Green meet, dozens of student marshals meet the crowd, many of whom wear helmets, gas masks, and are carrying batons. This is what they have been waiting for, training for these past days and nights. Halfway between the Green and the Superior Courthouse, police and Guardsmen wait; wait to see if the marshals can do what they say they can do.

"Walk! Walk!" the marshals shout in unison. They try to pick out individuals and talk to them, one on one.

"If you're with the Panthers and not the pigs, you'll get back!"

Panthers, clad in leather jackets and black berets, harangue the young whites surging for the Green.

"The shit is going to go down in our community. If you don't move back, you're a racist, motherfucking pig."

"Man," yells a kid at a marshal, "we're here to smash the state."

"You're playing a racist game, goddamit, you're playing right into the hands of the pigs!"

"You're worse than the pigs!" the radical yells back. "Maybe you're playing the pig game for the pig!"

"Please move back if you want to help free Bobby," the marshals plead. But now there is a new instigator, unintentional yet magnetically powerful: the press. More than 560 credentials have been issued to visiting newsmen, and *this* is the story they have come for. Camera crews, sound men, lumbering down the street with lights and shotgun microphones, break through the string of marshals.

"Just what you want," a marshal bitterly says to a network TV man. "Just so you can get your money."

"You begged for pictures in Chicago," the cameraman shouts back as he rushes toward the Green.

Now begins a half hour of surrealism. Knots of people are stumbling along the Green; occasionally, a helmeted youth runs by, throwing something at a cluster of police standing along Elm Street near the Courthouse, the evident target of the crowds of youths. On the other side of the Green, at Chapel and College streets, a cordon of National Guardsmen, with bayoneted rifles, blocks off the street. The camera crews are prowling the length and breadth of the Green, looking for action. It works like this: a clatter or flash of something (a rock? a cigarette lighter? a bomb? who knows?). Instantly the newsmen and camera crews, with reckless courage, are racing in the direction of the noise. The blinding TV lights go on. The crowd, seeing the lights and presuming action, races over to the cameras. Police lob a tear gas canister. The crowd disperses, running headlong.

"Walk, walk!" the marshals shout, trying to head the

youths back across the Green, inside Phelps Gate and sanctuary in the Old Campus.

"Don't go on the Green! The Panthers don't want it!"

"We're gonna make a revolution, but on our terms, and this is not planning a revolution!"

Floodlights sweep across the Green, occasionally catching the tableau of a shock of hair, khaki jacket, and extended arm hurling a rock at police. In their midst is a handsome, white-haired figure, out of central casting. He is Jim Ahern, chief of New Haven police; and he has done his job well. His policemen are never alone; they are in small squads, each man watching the other for an outburst of anger. The mood among the police is calm, almost jocular.

"Damn, I got hit with three rocks," one says to his companion as they stand, club held with both hands, visored helmets in position. Only once does a policeman show real anger, and not at a student. A TV cameraman has been told he cannot move onto the Green.

"You can't stop me," the cameraman says, bellying up to the policeman.

"I'm a police officer and I'm telling you to stay here."

"Yeah," the cameraman sneers at the cop, attired in helmet, jacket, badge, gun, and club. "Let's see you prove you're a cop, c'mon show me you're a cop." He is taunting, daring the officer.

"I'll show you," the policeman says, moving forward, "I'll show you." He is grabbed by another officer and held back, as the cameraman retreats quickly.

In less than an hour, the Green is clear; students and a small cloud of tear gas drift back to the Old Campus, where

Alan Ginsberg is chanting, "Ommmmm, Ommmmm, Ommmmmm," as an effort to calm the crowd and soothe it. Over at the *Yale Daily News*, a kind of refuge for visiting newsmen is unofficially in progress, as Gary Guernsy, a student with an infinite sense of patience, is taking calls.

"Right. Right. Well, we've had some trouble. Why don't you call back in an hour." He hangs up the phone, shaking his head. "Pierson College has a lost radio and they want to put a lost and found ad in the paper."

Steve Kock, an exhausted photographer, staggers in.

"Say, by the way—are you guys still putting out a paper?" A reporter walks in with a silkscreened poster.

"I found this on a tree at the Green," he says. It reads: "A mob is primarily composed of individuals too frightened to assert their own consciences against the tide of what they believe to be a homogenous mass. —Bertrand Russell."

The Green is clear. The streets and college courtyards of New Haven are not. Every few minutes, the sound of broken glass breaks the quiet. A plywood board is ripped off J. Press, and a young man in a red plaid shirt throws a rock against the window; a spiderweb break appears. White-coated medics with handkerchiefs and water bottles are offering help to the tear-gassed. And in Branford College, a furious argument is under way between a youth holding a Youth Against War and Fascism banner and others.

"What did you go out there for, what the fuck for?" a tall blond is yelling.

"Man, did we shoot tear gas? It was the cops, the pigs."

"Bullshit!"

"What we were doing is building people's spirits. It could

have been successful. We weren't trashing. It was a militant
march *around* the Green. Those marshals . . ."

He is surrounded by angry protests.

"Hilliard said this weekend was a building action for July
19—did you listen? No!"

"When you see people struggle, then you learn, that's how
you build the spirit to free Bobby."

"But you're just gonna leave us with your shit," a black
snaps at him.

"But the shit is everywhere!"

As the argument rages, as Ginsberg chants, "Boola boola,
buddah buddah," hour after hour in a witness for calm, the
sounds of the Band drift through the Branford courtyard,
mournful and weary:

> *I see my life come shining,*
> *From the West down to the East,*
> *Any day now, any day now,*
> *I shall be released.*

"WHAT THE HELL IS GOING ON? The same old shit! Do
you think that last night's spontaneous reaction to a pig
provocateur's rumor-mongering was building a revolution? . . . Anyone who heard Douggie Miranda speak or
heard any of the marshals lay down the wishes of the
Black Panther Party and still went out on the Green
again and again can be nothing but flaming assholes. All
for what? To satisfy our egos? To relieve our guilt? To
show how male chauvinist bravados can dominate? It is
time to get rid of the shit in us, start thinking in a serious

way about how we are going to relate to the revolution—
and put it into practice!"

—A Boston Collective

Saturday morning, and as the bowls of familia are dished out
to the thousands, the arguments rage on. A sense of fun and
celebration is missing this morning; there is instead bitterness
and uncertainty.

"The Panthers made it perfectly clear they didn't want
violence. You have to respect their wishes."

"I didn't see Panthers last night. I saw a lot of Yalies."

A group of blacks, some sporting Panther attire, listen to
the argument in Trumbull College.

"You better get on the job, jack," one says quietly. "It
may be time to stop singing and start swinging."

"That's enough philosophy. Let's rake this shit into the
street."

"Look," says another black, calming his friends. "You people ain't ready, man." He is speaking almost kindly, avuncu-
larly. "I was born in this. I was born fighting. All you doing
is smoking pot. I tell you one thing, I ain't going on the
street with you."

Abbie Hoffman is talking with a younger, earnest acolyte:

"I'm not gonna say go out and burn the town, 'cause if the
town burns down I get two years."

At the Green, the warmth of the day is burning off some
of the discontent, although there is still confusion.

"I can't believe it," a latecomer says to his companion. "He
told us to come here and burn Yale down; now we come here
and he tells us not to do it. Shit!"

The speeches drone on. Jerry Rubin loses his audience with a repeat performance, urging the crowd to chant, "Fuck Kingman Brewer! Fuck Kingman Brewer."

"Aw, jesus, Rubin, don't you even know the guy's name?" a listener shouts, and from way back in the Green comes a distinct chant, "Fuck Jerry Rubin! Fuck Jerry Rubin!"

By the time Tom Hayden takes the speaker's stand, to announce a national student strike to oppose the War in Indochina, the crowd is beginning to stream out of New Haven, looking for rides to Boston and New York. Sunday's program of events has been canceled, a response to the tension of Friday night. There are brave promises to return on July 19, but the applause is uncertain and guilty; summer means half-fares to Europe and camping trips, and political consciousness goes only so far.

The night is ugly again; a fire in a building at the edge of the Green draws a few hundred rock-throwing youths, and this time the police are ready with gas generators. The drone of the machines, a steady, insinuating hum, is startlingly reminiscent of the Z soundtrack by Theodorakis; a pulsating, musical undertone to the clouds of tear gas and pepper fog that begin coating the Green. This time, canisters are fired into the Old Campus and into the streets of Yale. The throat constricts, eyes tear; and as I stagger away, a medic comes over.

"Don't rub, pat your eyes with this," he says, handing me a handkerchief. He waits, retrieves the cloth, and calmly wanders into the midst of the fog and gas to treat the wounded.

By Sunday, New Haven is calm again. The troops are

going home. The Yale top leadership—Brewster, Chauncey, Al Fitt (fittingly enough a former Assistant Secretary of Defense), move out of their secret command post in the Alumni House at 320 Temple Street—just half a block from the Green.

Jonathan Fanton, coordinator of special educational projects for Yale, is out on his feet, but exhilarated, like a crisis manager who has won a big one.

"The reason we got out of this," he says, wandering through the command post, "was the marshals, the kids, and the cops. We were very lucky."

It is too early to think through some of the implications of May Day: the fact, for example, that no constituency could be heard to oppose violence on any but tactical terms; that among thousands of visitors, students, and faculty, no one could be heard to oppose the Panthers as the rightful supervisors of strategy, tactics, and decision-making; that the only appeal to orderly conduct was rooted in revolutionary strategy. The measure of the distance between the Yale of three years ago and the Yale of May Day 1970 is too vast to calculate now. It is still standing and perhaps that is victory enough.

And as the crowds leave, as the Community of the Disaffected drifts back to its separate zones, the 560 members of the Media Machine pack their equipment and head for home, with no pictures of death and destruction. Yale did not burn; no one died; no sniper fire; no gun fights. And of these hundreds, who came for the *Walpurgisnacht*, it is a safe bet that not five will be a thousand miles away forty-eight hours from this Sunday, on the campus of Kent State University.

THE FEVER BREAKS

THE UNIVERSITY OF WISCONSIN
AS A CASUALTY OF WAR

Marcus Singer is a dark-haired, dark-skinned man with a fighter's face and a slight facial tic; his mannerisms and his raspy voice suggest something of Humphrey Bogart. His crowded office, cluttered with books, monographs, stenciled papers and examination blue books, suggests his occupation: Professor of Philosophy at the University of Wisconsin.

Singer is not talking of Ethics or Epistemology now, as he stands up at his desk in the basement of Bascom Hall, the colonial keystone at the top of Bascom Hill, in the center of Wisconsin's campus. He is pointing to a long, thin crack in the wall plaster, and a patch of exposed ceiling.

"That's what happened when it went off," he says, pointing out the window to another building. "It exploded in there; tore out almost every window on this side of Bascom. I heard about it on the radio; couldn't believe it."

On this November day in 1970, three months after it happened, the visible traces of a bomb that exploded in the Army Math Research Center late one August night are still faintly visible. What is far more apparent is the psychic scar, not just of the bomb which blew up a graduate student working late one night on his project, but of the last half decade. The University of Wisconsin is a scarred community; past anger and riots and trashings for the moment, numbed and still. It is living testament to what we have gone through in this country.

In the early 1960s, when I spent my undergraduate days here, Wisconsin was the embodiment of the New Pastoral, exploding with ideas and debates, yet comfortably lodged in the MGM image of what a University was supposed to be. It was laid out as if by a scenic designer. To the north, Lake Mendota, stretching the length of the campus, with secluded walkways and woods, and docks for swimming in the summer and early fall. At the foot of Bascom Hill, the Wisconsin Memorial Union, with an outdoor flagstoned terrace with tables and a lawn leading to boats, canoes, and sailboats on the Lake. In the spring and early fall, before the bitter winter, hundreds of people would sit leisurely, drinking, throwing frisbees, playing guitars and banjos. One visiting European professor called the Union terrace "the most European place I have ever seen in America."

Bascom Hill was the set for the Big Dance number; two concrete walkways led up the green mall, classrooms on either side, up to Bascom Hall, a white-columned, neoclassical building for liberal arts classes, and important administrative offices. In front of the Hall was a statue of Abraham Lincoln, with the inscription, "Let us have faith that right makes might . . ."

Yet the greatest appeal of Wisconsin lay beyond the sound-stage campus, where one expected to see rows of coeds tap-dancing out of Bascom, down the walkway, over to the Union for the big Pep Rally. (Indeed, every year before Homecoming, a "Yell Like Hell" rally was held on the steps of the student union.) It lay in its distinct, sometimes mutually hostile, but always independent life styles.

West of Bascom were the dorms, inhabited largely by small-town Wisconsin boys and girls, many of them who had never been in a city the size of Madison (120,000). They walked around the campus in a daze their first semester, wearing their high school athletic jackets, stiff crewcuts, and sweat-shirts, plunging into the whirlwind of Commerce, Engineering, and Agriculture courses that would win them jobs and a ticket out of the small-town life. They were overwhelmed by the right to drink beer at eighteen; my most vivid memory of dormitory Friday nights is the sound of whoops and shouts and tripping footsteps as half-a-dozen youths stumbled into the men's room for an hour of vomiting and groaning. Yet there was also friendliness and warmth and generosity here; a middle-class community at its best, enduring the confinements of dorm life, the wretched food and half-baked discipline of "quiet hours." One freshman, now a well-known *avant-garde* artist, quietly drew an astonishingly cheerful mural on his wall, replete with cartooned figures, balloons, and good will. The dormitory management made him pay to restore the wall to its original Institutional Green.

East of the campus, stretching along Langdon Street from the Union to the Lake, was Fraternity Row, where in 1960 much of the power among the student body was located. In 1960 the Greeks controlled student government, the student press, and almost every other position of importance. The houses, colonial brick and stucco, were filled with young men who spent their Saturdays in easygoing camaraderie, lounging on the lawn downing Blatz and Miller's, and girls with page-boy haircuts and cardigan sweaters with circle pins. It was an *apartheid* society; no blacks were in any fraternity house, Jews were with Jews and gentiles with gentiles, and in the early '60s this became a point of friction between the Greeks and the predominantly liberal faculty and administration. It also brought me a moment of terror. One night, during my tenure as editor of *The Daily Cardinal*, I had gone to bed after writing a particularly nasty editorial. The telephone rang.

"Greeeeen-field?"

"Yeah—who's this?"

"Let's just say I'm a Greek who doesn't like New York Jews. And this is also somebody who knows where you live. And on those nights when you're going home from that red rag you run . . . well, you understand." Click.

After a week of carrying a bicycle chain around in my pants pockets and wondering (a) what the hell you were supposed to *do* with a bicycle chain and (b) why people were staring at a huge bulge in the hip pocket of my chinos, I decided the caller wasn't for real. And, although it left a bad taste in my mouth, there were times when the attraction of the Fraternity way of life was almost agonizing in its appeal.

Each year, on the Thursday night before Homecoming Weekend, the fraternities and sororities would team up to build floats on their lawns. All night they would stuff crepe paper into chicken wire, mounted on wood supports, hooked up to motors, to present a tableau of Bucky Badger stomping on the Northwestern Wildcat, or lassoing a Wildcat, or committing some other form of mayhem. Lamps were hung out of windows to illuminate the lawns; rock music blared from stereos to keep the workers awake, while beer and brandy were passed around, and couples necked in the shadows.

It seemed so purely the essence of Fellowship: the joint participation in a project combining talents and skills, the fusion of all-night energy and easy relaxation, the laughter and urgent whispers from the darkness. All right, part of me was saying, I *know* it's bigotry and exclusion and pushing a peanut across the floor, but damn it, it's *something*.

My turf at Wisconsin, however, lay elsewhere, south of University Avenue, in the ramshackle rooming houses and apartments with threadbare furniture, flabby mattresses, and roach-infested kitchens. It was a shabby neighborhood, but rich in bars with dark beer, secondhand bookstores in two-story frame buildings, rundown screening rooms where faded prints of Chaplin and Marx Brothers movies were shown for fifty cents.

What Wisconsin provided, then, was a sense of *balance* and *retreat*. It was possible to attend a concert, a football game, an experimental play, a lecture, to sit in the bright sunlight of the Union Terrace or the glass-walled cafeteria, overlooking the bright blue (or, more often, the frozen gray) of Lake Mendota, or the inky blackness of the Rathskeller, where bearded New York Jews and Negroes talked of poetry or revolution ("Yes, but under *your* theory, the telephones and steel companies would still have their wealth, and the farms . . ."). It was also possible, by walking a few blocks, to leave behind the University, and gain a sense of solitude and insulation. This retreat came in handy, because the University in the early '60s was an exciting community.

In this time of emerging student political energy, Wisconsin was a school with a long tradition of activism. Its twin articles of faith, both born in the end of the nineteenth century, expressed the liberal creed encapsulated: freedom for the work of the mind, and confidence that the application of reason and learning could solve the questions of social organization.

On the wall near the entrance of Bascom Hill, a bronzed plaque has stood for the length of the twentieth century. It holds the words of the Board of Regents of 1890, answering community pressures for the firing of a radical economist of the day named Richard T. Ely. It reads:

> We believe that, whatever the limitations which trammel academic inquiry elsewhere, the great State University of Wisconsin should ever encourage that continual and fearless sifting and winnowing by which alone the truth may be found.

Wisconsin's community has always turned those words into reality. As a center of resistance to Senator Joseph

McCarthy, as an open forum for everyone from Communist Party officials to John Birchers, with a student paper financially free of any outside control, Wisconsin at times took on the physical appearance of a Jeffersonian ideal. At times the corridor of the Student Union was packed with tables selling literature for conflicting political and cultural creeds; at one point in 1962 Wisconsin was publishing a conservative magazine, a liberal magazine, and *Studies from the Left,* an independent Marxist publication which had a national readership. In my freshman year, the state legislature held hearings on a resolution to commend the House Un-American Activities Committee. One of the witnesses was William Appelman Williams, a history teacher with a Virginia aristocrat demeanor, an Annapolis degree and haircut, and a reputation as a brilliant radical critic of American history.

"What is your occupation?" asked the committee chairman.

"I teach people to think," Williams answered, to the cheers of the students in the hearing room.

For all of the assaults on the "leftist, out-of-state agitators" by state assemblymen and a retired Army captain, Wisconsin was secure in its academic freedom. Nor was this an ivory tower proposition: for the second great article of faith was the "Wisconsin Idea"—the concept that the University had to serve the outside world, not simply by studying problems, but by helping to solve them. In the neo-sacred words of a late University President, "The boundaries of the campus are the boundaries of the world." Wisconsin professors had established the first state Legislative Reference Bureau; they had served as a braintrust for Woodrow Wilson; agricultural extension centers took laboratory discoveries and put them to work for farmers across the state; economists helped write the social programs of the New Deal and the New Frontier. In its enthusiastic involvement with the world, Wisconsin embodied a vision of the Multiversity as expressed by Berkeley Chancellor Clark Kerr: that in the modern world, the academic community had become "a prime instrument of national policy." And it is that very vision which, in the second half of the 1960s, came to haunt Wisconsin, and shatter the whole network of faith in academic freedom and the Liberal Pastoral.

Walking aimlessly across the campus, in this November afternoon, 1970, I can see that the campus as I knew it has been destroyed, as by a technology gone berserk. A twenty-story administration building dominates Bascom Hill, its steel and glass glowering over the other, older buildings constructed to human scale. It is here, hundreds of feet above the campus, that the administrators now work. All along the shoreline, excavations and beams for new structures have gutted Bascom Woods. The flagstones have been ripped out of the Union Terrace; solid concrete has taken its place.

And, incredibly, the whole community south of University Avenue has been wiped out; the two- and three-story wood frames are gone. My old apartment is a parking lot; the dark bars and cheap restaurants are not here. In their place, stretching for block after block, is a huge, plastic complex of dormitories, each like the other, dotted with geometrically correct lights and a strip of shrubbery. Ogg Hall: how true the name rings, something monstrous and impersonal.

An embittered Old Grad speaking? Here is a dormitory counselor, speaking inside the ten-story towers:

"It's a zoo here. The dorms are all cinderblock tile, so sounds carry all over the place; it's like living in a shower. The ceilings are so low, you think you're in a submarine. At night, sometimes, you can hear the kids bellowing out the window, shouting, 'Fuuuuccck yoooouu!' into the courtyards. There's nothing here to hold on to; we've had suicide attempts already. Hell, I expect to be picking them off the walls soon. The frustration and tension is beyond belief."

George Mosse, a round-faced man with a bulldog pipe, is a professor of European history, one of the most brilliant minds on the campus. He shares the revulsion at Wisconsin's new ambience.

"We've become such a multi-university. The President and the administration live up in their tower. It's all so much less personal now. And it *looks* depersonalized. I was down by Ogg Hall last spring, after Cambodia, and you should have seen them streaming out of those dorms to trash the stores; like they wanted to rip the whole place down."

What is so saddening is not simply the physical rape of the University, throwing a kind of natural balance out of kilter. It is that this eradication of insulation has paralleled a sense of outrage and fury that has built each year since 1965, from the order of a Teach-In to the occupation of student buildings to the call-out of the National Guard to the final, savage, desperate act of four fugitive radicals, who last August loaded a panel truck with chemical explosives and sent it smashing into the Army Math Research Center, a prime target of attack by radicals as a link between the University and the Pentagon-Vietnam combine.

My search into the recent past took place at the only possible place for me: the offices of *The Daily Cardinal*. I had worked there almost every day of the four years I spent at Wisconsin; for two years, I was editor-in-chief, playing out my movie fantasy of a crusading editor attacking racism, selfishness, know-nothingism, and reaction. The taste and smell of the place are the same: a horseshoe city-desk, battered typewriters, broken furniture, ink, dust, and endless stacks of paper, magazines, and copy pencils. But sitting in the empty office, running the flaking pages of the past off my fingers and clothes as I read through the bound volumes of five years, the torment of Wisconsin runs by like a horror movie with the projector jammed on fast-forward:

• *1965:* Bob Hope headlines the Homecoming Show, the *Cardinal* declares its support for the War in Vietnam, arguing "either we fight the Communists in Vietnam now, or we fight them in Australia or Hawaii ten years from now." Teach-ins; professors arguing earnestly before polite halls of students the geo-politics, morality, and cost of the burgeoning war.

• *1966:* Students occupy administration buildings to protest the connection between academic achievement and vulnerability to the draft; committees of demonstrators carefully clean up the buildings and pledge their commitment to nonviolence.

• *1967:* In the spring the revelations break concerning the Central Intelligence Agency's control of the National Student Association. Wisconsin's ex-Dean of Students turns out to be a parttime recruiter for the agency, helping to channel bright young student government types into the NSA, and into cooperation with the CIA. That fall, the presence of a Dow Chemical Company recruiter sparks a massive protest, at which city police—for the first time in living memory—pour onto the campus, beating and clubbing some students.

• *1968:* A counterculture community is born along Mifflin Street; they decide to hold a block party, with songs, dancing, and festivities. The police wade into the "illegal" gathering, and a riot breaks out.

• *1969:* In February, a strike in support of black students turns into a major confrontation; the Governor calls out the National Guard, and thousands of troops, bayonets at the ready, line the campus; eight thousand students march to the Capitol in protest. (The last time this many marched the mile along State Street was in the fall of 1962, when Wisconsin won the Big Ten championship with a last-minute victory over Minnesota. That march was led by the band and a jubilant Bucky Badger; this march is led by black students with clenched fists.)

• *1970:* With Cambodia, a massive outburst of marches, trashing, and tear gas. Fred Harrington, president of the University for eight years and a model of the McNamara administrator, spiced with a lifelong commitment to liberal humanism, throws up his hands and resigns in the face of an increasingly hostile, conservative Board of Regents. And finally, in August, a bomb explosion and death to a graduate student-father of three small children.

This history is more than a chronicle of exhaustion and bitterness. It describes, as well, the alteration of the perceived character of the University of Wisconsin, and the destruction of "The Wisconsin Idea" of connection with the outside world. No, not destruction, really: something worse —a sense of *perversion*. By sending grades to the Selective Service system, Wisconsin was a cog in the machine sending young men to combat and potential death in Vietnam. By calling on the armed might of the state to stop a protest against Dow Chemical Company, Wisconsin was allying itself with the Enemy, with the same forces that were perpetuating murder abroad and repression in the hidden corners of black America. The axiom of engagement—the idea that "the boundaries of the campus are the boundaries of the world"—took on a sinister connotation. Wisconsin was not curing yaws, or writing laws, or healing the sick, or rectifying injustice. Instead, it was perceived by growing numbers of students as part and parcel of the System, a system which was implicated in black and foul deeds.

The vast simplifications inherent in such a vision are apparent. So too, however, are its strands of truth. No longer a benevolent institution, Wisconsin becomes another Army unit, another White House, another sortie of B-52s. And the unraveling of the Liberal Pastoral means, too, a contemptuous dismissal of the worth of the University's commitment to academic freedom. Free speech for whom? For people apologizing for mass murder? For companies using Wisconsin students to manufacture napalm? For professors unwilling to put aside their classrooms and routine to support the demands of black students, seeking a share of the University's privileged status? No. Sifting and winnowing was fine, but not when it permitted the untrammeled exercise of evil power; shout them down, blockade their path, confront this Power the only way possible: with our bodies.

Yet even this desperate tactic has been abandoned. In the autumn of 1970, the radicals are faced with the grim fact that the constant escalation of force has killed an innocent human being, precisely the kind of wanton disregard for life that seems symbolized by Vietnam. Unanswered questions hang in the air. Does it stop the war if you break a window in a State Street clothing store? Can we show any positive effect from what we have done these last few years? There is no answer. In its place has come perhaps the most frightening possible of sounds on a university campus, more frightening even than the shriek of a police siren or the crash of breaking glass: the sound of silence.

"Nobody smiles anymore. There's a deathly silence here." The speaker is Paul Ginsberg, head of the Division of Student Affairs, a man in early middle age who looks tired and resigned. "For the last two or three years I at least had the feeling that I knew where most of the students were. Now, they're much more within themselves. I'm probably more frightened by this cycle than by anything else."

"Sure, it was the War," he says. "That was the precipitator of all this. The sense of hypocrisy, the perversion of the University. People are just so much more ready now to believe evil of us who are at the levers."

Robert Ammerman, a philosophy professor with a placid expression and a dry, casual wit, agrees. He has just finished a class about the philosophy of Marx and Freud, in which the students are alive and responsive.

"Yes," he says, "but every one of the students who's spoken

to me tells me this is an exception. I like to think it's because of the brilliance of the lecturer," he grins, "but it's the material: Marx, Freud, thinkers they care about. The rest, they just wave away."

He lights a pipe and shakes his head.

"In the last year, there was a sense of depression, malaise that was just incredible. In the fall of 1969, four kids came to me to discuss a joint suicide. They wanted to test out the philosophical justifications. I saw them on campus a few months later—three of them—so I guess they talked themselves out of it."

"Why?

"There's no question in my mind it started with Vietnam. When you start to seriously entertain the notion that your country is a killer, you're just drawn into desperation."

Desperation for the course of your country; desperation at the apparent betrayal by the University community of its ideals and professions; desperation within the increasingly atomized, isolated University façade. And another kind of desperation: the lack of a model in which trust, affection, and confidence can be reposed.

"We had an interesting phenomenon during the strike in late 1968 and early 1969 over black student demands," one administrator recalls. "The white kids were almost tearful in their acceptance of black leadership. This was one cause the white kids could go with wholeheartedly because there was no ambiguity. *That* fight was clear-cut, because everyone *knew* that if you were black, you had gotten the shaft all your life." And indeed, among the black students there is a unique sense of purpose at work: founding a black cultural center, tutoring high school students in Madison and Milwaukee, fighting for black studies programs.

There is no such core purpose among the concerned whites, and no heroes, no models for emulation. Any human being who seems to possess a vision related to these students' concerns is all but devoured by their affection.

One such person is Harvey Goldberg, a small, scholarly man with a hawk nose and an expression suggesting an absent-minded professor startled into consciousness. When he steps up to the podium of his French history class to read some official announcements, his voice is a bare mumble.

Then he begins his lecture. The voice slowly picks up steam. The sentences are short, crisp, tight. He is setting the stage for the Paris Commune. The statistics flow; the voice is almost martial. By the end of the lecture, nineteenth-century France has come alive; the class is mesmerized. He finishes to a burst of applause, a tribute unheard of apart from the traditional "last lecture" claps.

As Goldberg ends his class, he is surrounded by students; some of them press him on unanswered points about his lecture; others want him to relate the conflict among French radicals to the Movement in America. After forty minutes, Goldberg is finally, reluctantly let go; and a youth armed with leaflets hesitantly asks him for money to help students attend a Black Panther Constitutional Convention. Goldberg smiles, shrugs, and hands over a dollar.

"This happens about thirty times a day," he sighs.

What makes Harvey Goldberg such a magnet is that he is a scholar-radical in the real sense of that term. He has written the definitive biography of Jean Juares, the nineteenth-cen-

tury democratic revolutionary of France; he is a passionate
spokesman against not just the War in Vietnam, but the
American state as it now exists. But more important, Goldberg is a radical on his own terms. He treasures knowledge;
he has not abandoned his books and his research for the barricades. And because he is a man who has found his own way
of living, fusing his skills with his conscience, he is a rare
figure of admiration at Wisconsin.

"I am very tired," he confesses. "I want the chance to get
away for a while; to think, read, write. But you know, when I
suggested I might have to find some place for refuge, a student wrote me a long letter, saying it would be immoral to
leave my teaching." Goldberg's dilemma is that there are not
enough like him to go around.

Instead, there seems a limited choice of models for a student angered and outraged by the broken promises of America; a political model, from which youth's two 1968 heroes
are both missing (one in a grave in Arlington, the other retired by his own choice from politics), or the model of the
Movement. If the progenitors of Revolution are excessive,
they are excessive against immense evils; if they are irrational,
they have been driven to it by too many lies, too many horrors. As Romain Gary put it:

> Our consciousness and consciences, our inbred belief in the
> existence of some kind of honor among men are mercilessly
> teased, baited, provoked day by day and hour by hour,
> through the instant audio-visual contact with the world we
> live in . . . two generations of mass media and communica-
> tions have exposed both the world to us and us to the world

in such a brutal way that our conscience has become an exposed nerve . . .

In the world of Prague, Biafra, Vietnam and Harlem, can anyone tell me what could possibly be meant by an adjusted man?

In their outbursts and their violence, Gary has written, the Movement young are "merely vomiting the world," signaling each other by instant communication—beads, long hair, tie-dyed shirts, boots, grass, tattoos—their common repudiation of the world of their Elders. If the Movement contains much that is ill-reasoned, half-baked, dangerous, totalitarian, faddish, rigid, cruel, it is perhaps explained by the fact that revolutions are not supposed to be shaped, explained, and powered by post-adolescents; and in the America of the 1950s and 1960s, there was no continuum that was visible to the enraged young. Their Movement often was a scream of rage, triggered by the sense that "the power of the human scream is so great that it will smash all the iron laws decreed against man."

Sadly, the sense among Wisconsin's Movement people reflects less this optimistic note of Kafka's than his bleaker visions, a sense that they are at the end of the road, defeated, weary, uncertain now of what to do.

Rena Steinzor is such a person, someone about whom I have a special curiosity since she is editor of *The Daily Cardinal*. A short, dark-haired girl with wide eyes, a crisp speaking voice, and a powerful will, she is a person of clearly radical convictions—convictions she has made a part of *The Daily Cardinal*, much to the vocal outrage of a minority of the staff, some of whom seem personally resentful of serving under a woman.

It has been a rough year for Steinzor. In the spring, with the Cambodian explosion, the paper ran a headline screaming, "Campus in Flames"—a substantial exaggeration. During the periods of highest tension, the editorial page of *The Daily Cardinal* ran—without attribution—leaflets discussing tactics of street-fighting and trashing. The impression left was that Wisconsin's student paper was promoting window-breaking and direct confrontations with the police. And this fall, after two *Cardinal* staff members were implicated in the bombing of the Army Math Research Center, she wrote editorially: "Our purpose here is not to judge the four accused men guilty or not guilty. We are with Leo and David because they are people we care for deeply and know very well."

The response has been intense: thousands of dollars in lost advertising, a Board of Regents decision to force *The Daily Cardinal* to pay ten thousand dollars a year in rental fees, a massive deficit. For Ms. Steinzor, the cost has been psychological as well, for she is no iron-minded dogmatist. She listens to arguments, thinks about them when she is not sure, recognizes her own ambiguities.

"One of my problems was that there was no one around to teach me to write. When I first came to work here, J. was editor; he would look at what I wrote, sometimes tear it apart. I missed that. And also, people thought we were hysterical last spring because we *were* hysterical last spring. We went through a lot of heavy stuff . . . and remember, our reporters and editors were still kids, still involved, still really angry after Cambodia."

Suddenly, talking with Rena in the Union Cafeteria on this gray November day, it hits me that we are talking about college students, of the same measure of experience I had six years earlier. I am asking a college senior for a coherent, justifiable program for national policy; six years ago, what would I have said? These people are dealing not with airy debates about resolutions supporting James Meredith; they are facing police on a college campus. They are debating how willing they are to go to jail to protest a war, not whether Women's Curfews are defensible. Through some appalling lack of cohesion in the mainstream of America, the battleground has shifted violently, lurchingly, into the campus arena.

At one point in our discussion, Rena suddenly sits bolt upright, eyes flashing, body shaking with anger.

"Look!" she shouts. "This country stinks! It shits! It reeks! What do you want me to say? I'm appalled!" That outburst is less an indictment than a cry of pain, a cry for help.

For what she and a generation of her contemporaries have been robbed of is a sense of optimism, a source of anything but despair. She is twenty years old. At thirteen, just coming into political consciousness, she watched John Kennedy die. At fourteen she watched America's cities start to burn. From the time she bothered to read a newspaper, America was at war in Vietnam.

And what she—and we—have not had was the counterweight, the source of hope. There was a Depression in this country, painful and bitter, and there was Roosevelt, and a sense that somebody cared. There was a Second World War, bloody and debilitating, and a nation pulling together for one of the few times in its history, something very close to an Era of Good Feeling, a certainty in the moral worth and tangible value of daily existence, fighting the tide of world fascism, building for a brave new America.

Erik Erikson has spoken of "that traditional prerogative of American trust in one's own resourcefulness and in Fate's store of good intentions." That is not the hand Fate seems to be dealing out these days.

Just before we part, Rena talks about the music and the new discovery of 1950s rock and roll that has taken over the campus, with "Sock Hop Balls" and furious dancing.

"God," she says, "there's so much energy here. So much joy. I think if you took the music away, everybody would die." Football attendance is up, and people seem to be drinking a little more.

And so it is, more neatly than I would dare to construct, that out of the passions unleashed by the music of fifteen years ago has come, in part, a generation so embittered by its battles, so depressed and exhausted, that it retreats back into the blaring tenor saxophones and raucous rhythms of a music which our parents found subversive, but which suggests to them an Age of Innocence, a time before the war, on the other side of the Generational Fault.